SUCCESSFUL
PERSONAL
MONEY
MANAGEMENT

EDITOR: *Paul H. Gross*

MANAGING EDITOR: *Kiril Sokoloff*

ASSOCIATE EDITORS: *Judith A. Creedy and
Roger B. Harris*

SUCCESSFUL PERSONAL MONEY MANAGEMENT

A practical guide to your financial planning

McGRAW-HILL BOOK COMPANY

New York   St. Louis   San Francisco   Auckland   Bogotá   Düsseldorf
Johannesburg   London   Madrid   Mexico   Montreal   New Delhi   Panama
Paris   São Paulo   Singapore   Sydney   Tokyo   Toronto

BOOK DESIGN: *Betty Binns Graphics*
EDITING: *Janine Parson, Earle Resnick*
PRODUCTION: *Kathy Kopf, Leslie Schobel*
GENERAL MANAGER: *Morrie Helitzer*

COMPOSITION: *Computer Typesetting Services, Inc., Glendale, Ca.*

SUCCESSFUL PERSONAL MONEY MANAGEMENT

1234567890wcwc786543210987

LIBRARY OF CONGRESS CATALOGING IN PUBLICATION DATA

Successful personal money management.

    1. Finance, Personal. I. Gross, Paul H., 1944–
HG179.S847   332'.024   76-57728

ISBN 0-07-044750-0

INTRODUCTION

Personal financial planning is coming into
its own—thanks to economic instability, double-digit inflation, job
insecurity, the soaring cost of education, tales of retirement woes, and
a host of other factors. And that, quite frankly, has created a ready
market for personal financial information and advice. Not so
surprisingly, a steady stream of books on various elements of personal
finance has come out in the past year or so. So why bring out yet
another?

Well, Successful Personal Money Management is not just another
book on the subject. First, it's the only one that we're aware of which
deals with the real world, not theories. Everything herein is geared to
the economic and financial conditions that you face now. Second,
Successful Personal Money Management is the only book that we know
of which was written by a staff of experts, rather than by just one
person. What's more, we quote our sources so that you can contact
them yourself if you need further help. (By the way, the staff has 20
years of cumulative experience in analyzing and writing about
personal finance.) Third, this book is completely up-to-date. Most books
on personal finance have been made obsolete by the Tax Reform Act of
1976. Finally, and probably most important, this is more than a book:
It is a personal financial planning tool.

At the end of most chapters, you will find worksheets that will help
you bring your personal financial situation into clearer focus. After
all, you have to know where you are now before you can map out your
next moves. These worksheets, by themselves, could save you hundreds
and possibly thousands of dollars if you eventually decide to seek
individual assistance from a personal financial consultant, estate
planner, insurance man, real estate consultant, or tax expert. Reason:
Most professionals, who charge by the hour, spend close to half their
time collecting the basic information that you can supply yourself by
filling out our worksheets.

Even though there is an order to the book, you don't have to follow it.
For some of you, the chapter on insurance or the one on estate
planning will be of paramount importance, while for others the
chapters on taxes or on real estate will be of greater interest. That's
okay. This book has been written so that each chapter can stand by

itself—even though this has necessitated some repetitions.

Above all, Successful Personal Money Management *is a tool that is designed to be used by you. We heartily recommend that you fill out the worksheets after reading the relevant chapters. It's the only way that you can gain a clear financial picture of where you are, where you're going, and how to get there. It does take work, planning, and foresight. But the truth of the matter is that nobody can do this as expertly as you.*

PAUL H. GROSS

ACKNOWLEDGEMENTS

We would like to gratefully acknowledge everyone quoted in Successful Personal Money Management for the time and expertise they give us on a regular basis. And we are especially indebted to the following people: Steven Lampert of Katten, Mutchin, Gittles, Zanis, Pearl and Galler; Carl Stinchcomb, Vice President of U.S. Trust Co.; Norb Wall, President of Larry Smith & Co.; Irving Price, President of Hudson Michael; George White of Betancourt Hummel & Co.; Joseph Lobel of Coopers & Lybrand; Herbert M. Paul, N.Y. Director of Tax Services of Touche Ross; Edson Gould, Editor of Findings & Forecasts; Richard Russell, Editor of Dow Theory Letter; and the Research Department of Mitchell, Hutchins.

CONTENTS

Introduction

Acknowledgments

1 THE LONG-RANGE ECONOMIC AND FINANCIAL OUTLOOK   *2*
General overview and a quarter-by-quarter analysis of important factors such as consumer spending, capital spending, inflation, corporate profits, the outlook for durables, and soft goods. Comparative tables.

2 THE STOCK AND BOND MARKETS   *12*
The outlook for the stock and bond markets based on fundamental and technical analysis. Investment strategy for stocks based on an analysis of which stock groups look the strongest in 1977—autos, auto parts, capital goods, defense, distributed data processing, electrical equipments, insurance, and uranium. Investment strategy for fixed-income securities such as utilities, bonds, and preferred stocks. Another way to pick stocks. Worksheets for capital gains and losses.

3 REAL ESTATE   *38*
An overview of what's hot and what's not based on demographics, the cost of money and other factors that affect real estate. How to play future demographic trends; inner-city restorations; minimalls; choosing tenants for a minimall; the play in older buildings, apartments are apt; homing in on houses; and timberland. Worksheets.

4 TAX PLANNING   *64*
A tax planning guide for 1977. How to get the most from your travel and entertainment expenses, medical costs, office-at-home and real estate, and charitable contributions. Basic income shifting tactics. Strategies for investors. How to shift income for retirement. A defensive guide to audits. Tax tables.

5 A PRIMER ON FUNDING YOUR CHILDREN'S EDUCATION   *92*
A discussion of the costs involved and how to finance your children's education. How to set up a short-term trust for college costs; the beauty of education benefit trusts; shaking the loan tree; tuition payment plans; and work-study programs. Worksheets.

6 INSURANCE 108

How to evaluate and update your present life, disability, and homeowner's insurance so that you and your family get all the protection you're paying for. Figuring out how much life insurance you need; the kinds of life insurance; whole-life versus term; special policies; participating versus nonparticipating policies; how to shop for a policy; when switching pays; estate planning tactics; disability insurance; homeowner's insurance. Worksheets.

7 RETIREMENT PLANNING 142

How to calculate the costs; insurance in retirement; your retirement income; pension plans; Individual Retirement Accounts and Keogh plans; how to invest in a retirement nest egg; tax strategies for people about to retire; annuities; variable annuities; estate planning for retirees; how to find a place in the sun. Worksheets.

8 ESTATE PLANNING 170

How to set up and update your estate plan. Starting from scratch with an inventory of assets; the role of life insurance; how to protect insurance proceeds; community property problems; the marital deduction and gifts; wills; the many kinds (and uses) of trusts; how to find a good trustee; how to pay the piper. Worksheets.

9 BASICS OF PERSONAL FINANCIAL PLANNING 192

Taking it all into account; how to protect what you've got; fringe benefits; bonuses, profit-sharing plans, and supplemental retirement plans; leverage; what it takes to invest successfully; the pros you need on your team. Worksheets.

Appendix **A** TABLES AND CHARTS 211

Basic tables and charts to help make calculations on interest rates (for mortgage and loan payments as well as for yields on fixed-income securities), amortization; tables; federal estate and gift tax rates.

Appendix **B** GLOSSARY OF TERMS 217

Appendix **C** FOR THE RECORD 231

Worksheets in which you can list all your important records, deeds, mortgages, debts, insurance certificates, and securities—and where they're located. Also contains a place to note the names and addresses of your lawyers, accountants, brokers, and other personal financial advisors.

SUCCESSFUL
PERSONAL
MONEY
MANAGEMENT

1. THE LONG-RANGE ECONOMIC AND FINANCIAL OUTLOOK

GENERAL
OVERVIEW

QUARTER-BY-
QUARTER ANALYSIS

OUTLOOK FOR
DURABLES

OUTLOOK FOR SOFT
GOODS

COMPARATIVE
TABLES

The U.S. economy has staged a remarkable recovery from its near-depression collapse. The current strong recovery is quickly boosting employment, personal income, production, and profits. Consumer confidence and business expectations have improved considerably from the deep pessimism experienced during 1974 and early 1975, but this is by no means a return to "normalcy." The residue of the turbulent past 10 years—the shocks of embargoes, crop shortages, credit crunches, and price controls—have highly sensitized consumers and businesses to potential troubles and have set back the capital formation process, a development which will result in reduced growth rates in the years ahead.

Clearly, economic forecasting becomes more hazardous the further ahead it tries to look. For one thing, our statistical apparatus leaves much to be desired; and while improvements are being made, our national account figures are still subject to frequent revisions. (Errors in forecasting, by the way, are usually made in productivity estimates.) Thus, very minor mistakes, if projected far enough into the future, can by simple compounding lead to major distortions.

More important, even the best methodology would not have been able to forecast in 1970 where we would be in 1976, in view of the various external shocks that have occurred in the intervening years. Consider some of the events: simultaneous crop failures in various parts of the world in 1972, the quadrupling of international oil prices in 1973, the double devaluations of the dollar, the implementation and subsequent lifting of wage-price controls, the massive wheat sale to Russia, the simultaneous worldwide economic booms and recessions, and the political or social aftershocks of Watergate. Only a prophet could have foretold their coming.

While there's no reason to assume that a similar accumulation of distressing experiences lies ahead in the next decade, we simply do not know what will happen to the Organization of Petroleum Exporting Countries (OPEC), the situation in the Middle East, the Common Market, our relations with the Soviet Union, the Third and Fourth Worlds, the weather, or even the political and economic climate in this country.

It is therefore necessary to start with the existence of capital stock—all the factories, machinery, and office buildings now in existence. The collapse of capital spending in 1975 drove productive investment down to nearly 9% of the gross national product, its

3

Start with the existence of capital stock.

Capital stock, particularly of basic processing capacity, is too small.

lowest share since 1963. And since capital spending figures include productive as well as non-productive investments such as pollution control equipment, the amount that's actually spent on the types of investments that increase capacity is even lower than it seems. This occurred in spite of the 10% investment credit and other tax incentives. Plant and equipment spending is recovering, but the 10%+ shares of GNP characteristic of 1965-1970 will not be regained before the end of this decade. Thus the capital stock of the United States, particularly of basic processing capacity, is too small, thereby constraining economic growth, retarding the decline in unemployment, and keeping the inflation rate high.

Production. Potential output will rise only about 3% per year during the next few years, down from the 3.6% compound growth rate officially estimated for the period 1956 to 1965 and the 3.9% growth estimated for 1966 to 1975.

Employment. The rate of increase in the prime working-age population (18 to 64 years old) peaked in the mid-1960s at 2%; by 1985 it will be expanding by less than 1% per year. Still, the relatively high current rates of entry into the labor force will keep the reported unemployment rate well above what some would consider full employment for most of this period; the unemployment rate never falls below 6% in the forecasting horizon.

Inflation. A concomitant of this is a relatively high rate of inflation. Consumer price inflation will not dip below 5% annually through 1978. While this is a lot better than the inflation rates experienced in 1974 and 1975 (when consumer prices rose at double digit rates), it is higher than economists would prefer in the interest of long-term stability.

The fear of losing real income will help create product price increases and defensive wage agreements.

Besides capacity constraints (which may be a real threat in 1978), the fear of losing real income will help create product price increases and defensive wage agreements, thus further boosting the inflation rate. The ongoing process of energy price decontrol, rising use of imported oil, and our desire to become energy self-reliant will also add a further inflation burden.

At this point, it is necessary to specify the assumptions that will be made on economic policy. In turn, this requires a word about the political climate of the country. Jimmy Carter has won the 1976

An essentially conservative budget policy will be followed.

Presidential election and the Democrats still retain control of Congress. It will be assumed, nevertheless, that the economic climate of the country will continue to shift toward conservatism when it comes to government involvement in our economy. This means a greater emphasis on letting the private sector solve its own problems, meaning reduced rather than increased government regulation. More important, from the point of view of quantifying the economic outlook, the assumption is made that an essentially conservative budget policy will be followed, one which allows the budget to return to balance by the end of this decade and run a small surplus during the first half of the 1980s.

While slowing the economy's ability to grow, a budget policy that reduces the government's borrowing from the money and capital markets would seem to make it easier for business to borrow in order to expand its physical production capacity. The cost of these funds, interest rates, would tend to be lower not only because of greater availability of money and credit, but also because of the associated gradual reduction in the inflation rate that would accompany a budget whose deficit is gradually eliminated. The Federal Reserve plainly will be under less pressure to create money and credit, thus causing a gradual reduction in inflationary pressures.

The remaining years of this decade are likely to be a period of strong capital-goods demand as business tries to alleviate growing capacity pressures, comply with stricter environmental requirement, and modernize where costs allow. In addition, the requirements of energy independence and pollution abatement programs will augment the pent-up need for more capacity produced by current investment weakness. Nearly 10½% of real GNP will be devoted to these needs, and debt finance will necessarily play a major role. By 1980, cash flow will barely meet 80% of the nonfinancial corporate sector's need for funds. Continuing inflation will limit the contribution of depreciation charges, and there is no reason to expect a significant improvement in the profit rate of return. Thus, high-grade corporate bond rates are unlikely to dip significantly below their current levels for the next few years.

Short-term interest rates will also remain high.

Short-term interest rates will also remain high during this period. The commercial bank prime rate will still average better than 7% in 1978. If inflation is dissipated faster and stop-go monetary policy is avoided, the prime could average less than 6% toward the end of this period. However, bad luck and poor judgment would add several percentage points to the cost of short-term funds. Loan demand, now

The present outlook contains even more than the usual number of possibilities for change.

Expect changes in how consumer spending is allocated.

approaching a cyclical bottom, will rise throughout the period, with the bigger increase occurring in 1977, owing to the fact that corporations at present are underpaying taxes compared with their liabilities. Domestic loans should rise better than 10% in 1977 with an annual average of 8 to 10% realistic for 1978-1980.

Within the context of this slower growth period between now and 1980, there will be important changes. The present outlook contains even more than the usual number of possibilities for change. Specifically, the higher prices for energy of all types and for all metals and other materials provide ample likelihood of shifts in consumer spending patterns, dictated by relative price changes. For example, the permanently higher prices for electricity, natural gas, gasoline, heating oil, and related products will make ownership of a single-family home in the more distant suburbs much more costly in relation to a residence in a multifamily home closer to the city center than has been the case in the past. While this will be a long process, it should become visible over the forecasting horizon in the form of more and more building of apartments, duplexes, and the like, either in the central cities or in the close-in suburbs. This development would have important implications for the profit prospects of shopping centers and similar enterprises in the distant suburbs. As part of the shift, it might also be expected that there would be other changes in how consumer spending is allocated.

Not surprisingly, the annual rate of increase in real residential fixed investment drops markedly over the forecasting horizon, and winds up being one of the smallest of the contributors to economic growth. Housing starts are unlikely to average two million units until 1980. Increased competition for funds and the deceleration in population growth will further depress residential construction's share of total final demand over the forecasting horizon, as will extraordinary inflation in building costs.

This sluggishness in housing, as well as increased prices of major materials such as steel, copper, and petrochemical plastics and of energy sources, will have an impact on the automobile industry. The forecast projects a 20 to 25% decline in the secular growth rate of constant dollar motor vehicle and parts demand. The average scrapage rate will fall to 6.5% compared with the 7.2% rate that characterized 1955-1973 and the 5.6% energy-crisis related average during 1974 and 1975. However the fundamental reason for the anticipated slowing of automobile sales growth is a decline in the

The relative advantages would seem to favor smaller automobiles.

growth rate of the driving-age population (16 years and older), as well as the movement away from the far-flung suburbs.

To the extent automobiles are bought, the relative advantages would seem to favor smaller automobiles, as opposed to larger ones. The composition of sales from point of origin inside or outside the United States will thus depend more heavily on comparative rates of exchange, rather than size, as has been the case in the past. With the dollar gradually expected to strengthen over the period, it should be anticipated that imports will grow a bit faster than domestic units. Total retail unit car sales are expected to rise only slowly during the forecasting horizon and average 12½ million units toward the end of this period.

There has been a long-term shift away from cyclical manufacturing-type industries to services. This will be accentuated by the fact that most of the service sectors will not be affected by rising material prices as much as the hard-goods segment. The possible adoption, in the forecast period, of some form of national health insurance which would economize on the delivery cost of medical service suggests that a relatively larger part of consumer income might well be spent for more adequate medical care. As the population mix will contain more and more people living in apartments either in cities or close to them, it should be anticipated that a larger part of the family budget will be spent on dining out, going to theaters, and similar service-type activities.

Real purchases will grow less rapidly than potential output.

In line with the trend toward fiscal conservatism noted above, a declining real government-demand share is to be expected. Spending at the federal, state, and local government levels will be moderate even though Jimmy Carter was elected largely on the basis of his promise of greater government spending. Real purchases will grow less rapidly than potential output, although real transfer-payment growth will exceed output growth.

In conclusion, it is anticipated that growth will be slower over the forecasting period, while inflation will be somewhat more rapid than it has been historically. However, any recessions that may occur will be less severe than the one recently concluded. Shifts will occur from manufacturing to service industries, and within manufacturing, from those that favor the consumer to those that favor business for expansion of capacity. Geographically, the suburbs will lose ground to the cities and their immediate outer rings. The slower birthrate will

The slower birthrate will moderate the growth in demand for houses and automobiles.

moderate the growth in demand for houses and automobiles, as well as for such items as baby foods, elementary schools, school furniture, children's clothing, toys, and other child-related items.

The financial markets will continue to reflect interest rates that, by past standards, would seem to be historically high. However, as part of the gradual unwinding process from the inflationary excesses of the late 1960s and early 1970s, both short- and long-term interest rates are expected to gradually—if slowly—decline.

DETAILED ECONOMIC PROJECTIONS FOR 1977

		1977		
		I	II	III	IV

		I	II	III	IV
GNP AND ITS COMPONENTS (BILLIONS OF DOLLARS, SAAR[a])	Total consumption	1,146.8	1,176.5	1,207.4	1,241.0
	Nonresidential fixed investment	175.3	181.2	187.3	193.1
	Residential fixed investment	74.7	78.2	81.3	83.9
	Inventory investment	15.4	17.5	19.3	21.5
	Net exports	7.9	8.0	7.8	8.3
	Total federal	139.5	141.3	144.1	150.3
	State and local	249.1	255.4	261.7	268.0
	Gross national product	1,808.9	1,858.2	1,909.0	1,966.0
	Real GNP (1972 dollars)	1,305.9	1,324.1	1,342.5	1,361.0
PRICES AND WAGES, ANNUAL RATES OF CHANGE (%)	Implicit price deflator	5.3	5.4	5.4	6.5
	Fixed weight deflator	5.4	5.5	5.5	6.8
	Consumer price index	4.9	4.9	5.1	5.3
	Wholesale price index	5.2	5.4	5.9	6.5
	Adjusted average hourly earnings index	7.2	7.4	7.3	7.0
PRODUCTION AND OTHER KEY MEASURES	Industrial production (67 = 100)	1.285	1.308	1.329	1.350
	Annual rate of change (%)	7.3	7.3	6.6	6.4
	Housing starts (millions of units)	1.635	1.675	1.714	1.715
	Total retail unit car sales	10.9	11.0	11.3	11.5
	Unemployment rate (%)	7.1	6.9	6.7	6.5
	Federal budget surplus (NIA[b])	−50.7	−47.2	−45.9	−45.0
MONEY AND INTEREST RATES	Money supply (M1)	317.7	323.1	328.7	335.4
	Annual rate of change (%)	6.2	6.9	7.2	8.3
	New AA corporate utility rate (%)	8.82	8.88	8.95	9.12
	New high-grade corporate bond rate (%)	8.64	8.68	8.73	8.87
	Federal funds rate (%)	6.25	6.68	7.23	7.66
	Prime rate (%)	7.44	7.71	8.05	8.30
INCOMES (BILLIONS OF DOLLARS, SAAR[a])	Personal income	1,469.8	1,511.2	1,555.9	1,604.3
	Real disposable income	922.7	935.8	950.2	965.1
	Saving rate (%)	7.0	7.0	7.2	7.3
	Profits before tax	157.8	162.4	167.9	174.3
	Profits after tax	88.1	90.6	93.7	97.3
	Four quarter percent change	10.5	11.8	11.5	13.5
DETAILS OF REAL GNP, ANNUAL RATES OF CHANGE (%)	Gross national product	5.9	5.7	5.7	5.6
	Total consumption	5.7	5.5	5.6	6.0
	Nonresidential fixed investment	8.1	7.2	7.3	5.4
	Equipment	8.7	8.8	9.0	6.2
	Nonresidential construction	6.8	4.0	3.8	3.7
	Residential fixed investment	14.9	11.9	9.3	5.9
	Exports	7.7	10.0	9.3	8.0
	Imports	10.9	10.4	11.5	10.1
	Federal government	−0.1	0.2	2.9	2.8
	State and local	3.4	3.7	3.8	3.8

[a]Seasonally adjusted annual rates.
[b]National income accounts.

9

DETAILED ECONOMIC PROJECTIONS FOR 1978

		1978			
		I	II	III	IV
GNP AND ITS COMPONENTS (BILLIONS OF DOLLARS, SAAR[a])	Total consumption	1,270.2	1,294.2	1,316.6	1,341.5
	Nonresidential fixed investment	197.5	201.5	204.7	207.8
	Residential fixed investment	85.5	86.6	87.7	89.2
	Inventory investment	22.7	17.0	12.4	9.5
	Net exports	5.9	7.0	8.8	11.3
	Total federal	152.2	154.0	156.7	162.6
	State and local	274.2	280.7	287.0	292.7
	Gross national product	2,008.2	2,041.0	2,074.0	2,114.6
	Real GNP (1972 dollars)	1,372.9	1,377.4	1,382.1	1,388.4
PRICES AND WAGES, ANNUAL RATES OF CHANGE (%)	Implicit price deflator	5.2	5.3	5.2	6.1
	Fixed weight deflator	5.4	5.4	5.2	6.3
	Consumer price index	5.3	5.1	5.0	5.0
	Wholesale price index	5.9	5.5	5.6	5.7
	Adjusted average hourly earnings index	6.7	6.7	6.7	6.5
PRODUCTION AND OTHER KEY MEASURES	Industrial production (67 = 100)	1.369	1.375	1.374	1.376
	Annual rate of change (%)	5.7	1.8	−0.1	0.7
	Housing starts (millions of units)	1.673	1.641	1.634	1.647
	Total retail unit car sales	11.4	11.2	11.2	11.0
	Unemployment rate (%)	6.4	6.3	6.4	6.5
	Federal budget surplus (NIA[b])	−40.9	−45.5	−51.6	−55.2
MONEY AND INTEREST RATES	Money supply (M1)	340.6	344.0	347.3	351.7
	Annual rate of change	6.4	4.0	3.9	5.2
	New AA corporate utility rate (%)	9.18	9.00	8.84	8.69
	New high-grade corporate bond rate (%)	8.91	8.71	8.54	8.39
	Federal funds rate	7.89	7.52	7.11	6.60
	Prime rate (%)	8.54	8.34	7.96	7.40
INCOMES (BILLIONS OF DOLLARS, SAAR[a])	Personal income	1,642.5	1,674.7	1,706.0	1,741.9
	Real disposable income	974.1	980.8	987.2	994.9
	Saving rate (%)	7.2	7.3	7.4	7.5
	Profits before tax	174.1	172.8	174.9	178.4
	Profits after tax	97.2	96.5	97.6	99.6
	Four quarter percent change	10.3	6.4	4.2	2.4
DETAILS OF REAL GNP, ANNUAL RATES OF CHANGE (%)	Gross national product	3.5	1.3	1.4	1.9
	Total consumption	4.3	2.6	2.1	2.7
	Nonresidential fixed investment	2.3	1.7	0.0	-0.4
	Equipment	4.8	4.6	2.7	1.8
	Nonresidential construction	−2.7	−4.4	−5.7	−5.5
	Residential fixed investment	0.2	−1.5	−0.7	0.8
	Exports	7.2	6.9	5.4	4.0
	Imports	10.8	5.6	1.2	−0.4
	Federal government	0.5	0.2	2.5	1.3
	State and local	3.6	3.8	3.2	2.2

[a]Seasonally adjusted annual rates.
[b]National income accounts.

GNP COMPARISONS 1976 THROUGH 1978

		YEARS		
		1976	1977	1978
GNP AND ITS COMPONENTS (BILLIONS OF DOLLARS, SAAR[a])	*Total consumption*	1,078.6	1,192.9	1,305.6
	Nonresidential fixed investment	160.9	184.2	202.9
	Residential fixed investment	66.2	79.6	87.2
	Inventory investment	14.6	18.4	15.4
	Net exports	8.8	8.0	8.3
	Total federal	132.9	143.8	156.4
	State and local	234.0	258.6	283.7
	Gross national product	1,696.0	1,885.5	2,059.5
	Real GNP (1972 dollars)	1,266.5	1,333.4	1,380.2
PRICES AND WAGES, ANNUAL RATES OF CHANGE (%)	*Implicit price deflator*	5.3	5.6	5.5
	Fixed weight deflator	5.6	5.7	5.7
	Consumer price index	5.7	5.0	5.1
	Wholesale price index	4.3	5.3	5.8
	Adjusted average hourly earnings index	7.2	7.1	6.8
PRODUCTION AND OTHER KEY MEASURES	*Industrial production (67 = 100)*	1.235	1.318	1.373
	Annual rate of change	8.9	6.7	4.2
	Housing starts (millions of units)	1.466	1.685	1.649
	Total retail unit car sales	10.3	11.2	11.2
	Unemployment rate (%)	6.8	6.4	7.5
	Federal budget surplus (NIA[b])	−57.1	−47.2	−48.3
MONEY AND INTEREST RATES	*Money supply (M1)*	304.6	326.2	345.9
	Annual rate of change (%)	5.2	7.1	6.0
	New AA corporate utility rate (%)	8.78	8.94	8.93
	New high-grade corporate bond rate (%)	8.47	8.73	8.64
	Federal funds rate (%)	5.22	6.95	7.28
	Prime rate (%)	6.97	7.87	8.06
INCOMES (BILLIONS OF DOLLARS, SAAR[a])	*Personal income*	1,380.0	1,535.3	1,691.3
	Real disposable income	895.7	943.5	984.2
	Saving rate (%)	7.1	7.1	7.4
	Profits before tax	147.6	165.6	175.1
	Profits after tax	82.6	92.4	97.7
	Four quarter percent change	26.5	11.9	5.7
DETAILS OF REAL GNP, ANNUAL RATES OF CHANGE (%)	*Gross national product*	6.3	5.3	3.5
	Total consumption	5.6	5.3	4.1
	Nonresidential fixed investment	4.3	7.9	3.2
	Equipment	4.5	8.9	5.3
	Nonresidential construction	3.9	5.9	−1.2
	Residential fixed investment	19.6	11.8	2.6
	Exports	5.3	7.6	7.3
	Imports	16.4	9.0	7.7
	Federal government	0.3	0.9	1.5
	State and local	1.9	3.4	3.6

[a]Seasonally adjusted annual rates.
[b]National income accounts.

2. THE STOCK AND BOND MARKETS

OUTLOOK FOR THE
STOCK AND BOND
MARKETS

INVESTMENT
STRATEGY FOR
STOCKS IN 1977

INVESTMENT
STRATEGY FOR
FIXED-INCOME
SECURITIES

ANOTHER WAY TO
PICK STOCKS

WORKSHEETS FOR
CAPITAL GAINS AND
LOSSES

The Dow Jones Industrial Average (DJIA) could reach 1200 sometime in 1977, says Edson Gould, editor of *Findings & Forecasts*. For one thing, all of Gould's long-term indicators are very bullish. Monetary conditions are easy, and earnings and dividends are still rising, he says.

What's more, dividend yields on the Dow Jones Industrial Average, which will probably rise further as more dividends are raised, are far from indicating any kind of market top. Gould points out that no bull market in this century ever ended before dividend yields on the DJIA got down to 3%.

Contrary opinion also supports the view of a sharply rising stock market, says Gould. (The theory behind *contrary opinion* is this: if most investors expect a certain event to take place, they will have taken the necessary action to prevent it from happening.) Since most investors are looking for the DJIA to top out at 1050 early in 1977, many of them have already sold their stocks in anticipation of a market top. But when it becomes apparent that the market is going further than they had originally anticipated, their desire to get back in the market will push the DJIA to 1200, or possibly higher, says Gould.

Once the DJIA moves to 1200, however, there'll be a significant correction, says Gould. He thinks that the market could retrace as much as 50% of its move from 570—the bottom of the 1973-74 bear market. When that correction has run its course, there'll be a new long-term bull market of the kind that we had between 1924-1929 and 1949-1966, says Gould.

Just about everything indicates that there'll be a long bull market, says Bob Farrell of Merrill Lynch. Stocks became more oversold in 1974 than at any time in the last 40 years—which is extremely bullish because the longest bull markets follow the longest and deepest bear markets, he adds.

What's more, the fires of speculation—often an indication of an approaching market top—are almost totally dead, according to Farrell. After nearly two years of rising stock prices, preservation of capital is still the most important goal for the majority of investors. Institutional investors are behaving very conservatively—they're buying bonds, stocks with low price/earnings multiples or high yields, and are emphasizing market timing and indexing. (*Indexing* is an investment strategy which tries to equal the performance of broad-based averages.) Retail investors are fed up with stocks and almost totally out of the market, adds Farrell.

The prospects of a long-term bull market are greatly enhanced by what's shaping up to be a long period of economic expansion, say the analysts. The current economic expansion is unlikely to end until consumers and businesses become so confident about the future that they go on a wild spending spree, says Gary Shilling of White, Weld and one of the few economists who correctly forecast the 1974-75 recession. And considering the current skepticism and caution of both consumers and businesses, that's unlikely to happen for a number of years. Hence, stable business expansion may continue for the rest of the decade, he says.

Some analysts think that the huge numbers of people hitting the job force between now and the end of the decade is certain to keep the economy, and hence the bull market, moving at an unusually strong pace. Besides the normal growth in the male work force and the soaring number of female workers, the mammoth baby boom is coming of age and looking for jobs, say David and Jay Levy, well-known private economic forecasters.

Between now and 1980, the labor force will grow at an average rate of 2½ million persons per year, say David and Jay Levy. In that five-year period, 12½ million persons will be added to the job force. The threat of high unemployment will oblige the government to adopt policies that will encourage growth. We therefore face a period in which economic expansion and the opportunities that may accompany it will be extraordinary. The probability is that the United States is entering one of the most prosperous periods in its history.

The stock market may even get another potential dividend from the economy, says the Bank Credit Analyst. We may be in a period of declining inflation soon to be followed by stable interest rates and commodity prices. In the past, such conditions resulted in a "substantial" bull market in stocks, says the Bank Credit Analyst.

INVESTMENT SCENE: THE BEST AND THE BRIGHTEST

The investment pickings in 1977 are as good as they've been in many a year, say the analysts. The recent recession and the bear market of 1973-74 knocked down many stocks and

Stable business expansion may continue for the rest of the decade.

The stock market may even get another potential dividend from the economy.

The investment pickings in 1977 are as good as they've been in many a year.

industry groups to a fraction of their former value—which has created a great buying opportunity. The stock groups which the analysts think have the most potential in 1977 are the autos, auto parts, capital goods, defense, distributed data processing (which may revolutionize the whole approach to data processing), electrical equipment, insurance, and uranium.

Values also abound in the fixed-income markets.

Values also abound in the fixed-income markets—which still offer the best buying opportunity in 50 years. With long-term interest rates still close to the highest levels since the Civil War, these instruments have an outstanding rate of return and the potential for sizable capital gains.

But let's have the analysts speak for themselves:

AUTO STOCKS: A BULL'S TIME TO BUY

Auto stocks are the most undervalued major group in the stock market.

Auto stocks are the most undervalued major group in the stock market, according to Donaldson, Lufkin & Jenrette—which has given auto stocks its highest investment rating and put them on its "must buy" list. Ronald Glantz of Mitchell, Hutchins is also bullish on the outlook for auto stocks because he thinks the companies will show a much higher level of profitability and raise their dividends significantly.

Auto sales for 1977 should be up sharply, say the analysts. Glantz estimates that auto sales for 1977 will be 11.25 million, up 9.8% from this year. David Eisenberg of Sanford C. Bernstein is even more bullish. He's estimating a record 11.4 million units in 1977 and 11.8 million in 1978.

The auto manufacturers' profit margins will also rise, says Eisenberg. For one thing, the higher prices of this year's models will offset higher labor costs arising from the UAW contract. For another, foreign cars are not so competitive with U.S. makes as they were. Hence, Detroit doesn't have to shave profit margins to retain its share of the market, says Glantz of Mitchell, Hutchins. In fact, the profit per unit has snapped back sharply to a level that hasn't been seen for 10 years or more, he says.

Finally, auto stocks may have some substantial price/earnings expansion when investors regain confidence in the group, say the analysts. As profits continue to expand and industry fundamentals improve, investors are likely to forget about the disaster of the oil embargo and the recession, says Donald DeScenza of Donaldson, Lufkin & Jenrette. As that happens, investors will be willing to pay more for a dollar's worth of earnings, he says.

The upside potential for the big three auto stocks is significant.

The upside potential for the big three auto stocks is significant, says DeScenza. GM's stock topped out at ten times peak earnings for 1973 (the industry's last cyclical high) and Ford and Chrysler both topped out around eight times earnings. Assuming 1977 earnings of $13 a share for both GM and Ford, both stocks have significant upside potential from here. Chrysler with 1977 earnings estimated at $7 a share, may have an even greater appreciation potential, says DeScenza.

GM, Ford, and Chrysler are all good buys.

GM (NYSE, 68), Ford (NYSE, 55), and Chrysler (NYSE, 19) are all good buys, says Glantz of Mitchell, Hutchins. GM and Ford will probably end up selling at the same price—hence Ford has more appreciation potential. However, since GM will likely pay $6.50 in dividends in 1977, its stock has greater downside protection.

Ford will probably earn $11 a share in 1976 and $15.50 in 1977, up from $2.44 in 1975, says Glantz. That means Ford is currently selling at 5.4 times 1976's estimated earnings and 3.8 times those for 1977. GM will likely earn $10 in 1976 and $12 in 1977, and Chrysler $6 in 1976 and $8 in 1977, says Glantz.

AUTO PARTS STOCKS: GROWTH SPARKS ARE FLYING

The stocks of auto parts suppliers—both original equipment manufacturers (OEMs) as well as replacement parts producers—may be star performers in 1977, says Mario Gabelli of William D. Witter. He points out that the fortunes of these companies are tied very closely to those of the automobile industry—which may have its best year ever in 1977.

Original equipment manufacturers (OEMs) as well as replacement parts producers may be star performers.

The sales volume of OEM parts companies is very strong, says Gabelli, who points out that U.S. truck and auto production is running some 40% ahead of last year. The pickup in demand has firmed up prices and widened margins. Furthermore, productivity is up sharply—there have been fewer production interruptions, and unit labor costs are stabilizing. All these factors have given these companies some remarkable earnings leverage, says Gabelli.

The stocks of OEM companies are still very cheaply priced, even though their fundamentals are excellent.

1977 and 1978 should both be good years for the automotive after-market industry.

And the longer-term outlook for the OEM parts companies looks just as good, says Gabelli. The new automobile plant being built by Volkswagen could be operating by late 1978 or early 1979. When this plant is operating, it should substantially boost automobile production —which will increase the demand for domestically manufactured auto parts, he says. What's more, the stocks of OEM companies are still very cheaply priced, even though the fundamentals of these companies are excellent, says Gabelli. Many of the stocks are way down from the highs achieved during 1973—the last record year for automobile sales. What's more, many analysts think that automobile sales in 1977 will exceed the record levels reached in 1973.

Houdaille (NYSE, 15), Fruehauf (NYSE, 25) and Stewart-Warner (NYSE, 31) are Gabelli's favorite stocks in this group. All these companies are selling at reasonable earnings multiples, carry high dividend yields, and will report earnings of at least 15% in 1977.

Analysts also think there may be some investor interest in the stocks of companies that supply the automotive aftermarket—a group which has been languishing for the last 12 months. Interest in this industry generally starts picking up a year or two after the beginning of a new boom cycle in the auto industry. It takes just about that long for the new cars that were sold to start needing repairs and new parts. Hence, 1977 and 1978 should both be good years for the industry, says Fred Abrams of First Manhattan Company.

Genuine Parts (NYSE, 34), Champion Spark Plug (NYSE, 11), and Echlin (NYSE, 23) are Abram's favorites. These stocks are way behind the market even though the companies should have some good earnings gains both this year and next. Genuine Parts, which earned $1.86 in 1975, could earn $2.15 in 1976 and $2.45 in 1977, he says. Champion, which earned $1.24 in 1975, could earn $1.47 in 1976 and $1.60 in 1977. And Echlin, which earned $1.25 in 1975, will probably earn $1.85 in 1976 and $2.35 in 1977.

Genuine Parts, Echlin, and Snap-On-Tools (OTC, 32) are favorites of William D. Witter's Gabelli. Genuine Parts is the dominant distributor in the industry and has had a remarkable record of consistent earnings growth—even during the last down cycle in the industry. Echlin has an excellent marketing organization and will benefit from the increasing use of electronic components in automobiles. Snap-On-Tools dominates an exciting market, says Gabelli. It has 2,100 dealers around the country selling to professional mechanics. These are men who make a lot of money and are willing to spend well for tools, he says.

CAPITAL GOODS STOCKS:
A CAPITAL IDEA

Now that the continuation of the economic recovery is assured, it's time to play the capital goods stocks, say the analysts. The earnings of capital goods companies have held up much better than most investors expected, and prospects for the future are looking very bright, says James Love of Paine, Webber.

Capital spending should really start picking up some time in the first half of 1977 and gain strength throughout the year and into 1978. That's not surprising, considering the outlook for corporate profits and cash flow, says Harold Ehrlich, president of Bernstein-Macaulay. He points out that, historically, capital spending starts rising in direct proportion to increases in corporate profits.

But this isn't just a cyclical recovery in business spending, according to Love of Paine, Webber. He thinks U.S. capital goods companies have improved their worldwide competitive position dramatically. They will be able to gain market share abroad because inflation is lower here, the dollar is still fairly cheap, and exchange rates are favorable, he says.

As sales volume for these companies picks up, so will profits—in spades, say the analysts. In fact, the potential for earnings gains hasn't been this good in over ten years, says Love. Higher volume, better turnover of assets and working capital, plus the operating leverage of a manufacturing company ensures that profits for the group will soar, adds another analyst.

Caterpillar Tractor (NYSE, 54), Deere & Co. (NYSE, 29), Briggs & Stratton (NYSE, 28), and Bucyrus-Erie (NYSE, 25) are the favorites of Sherwood Small of Donaldson, Lufkin and Jenrette. He likes Caterpillar because it's the premier, nonelectrical capital goods company. It has excellent research and development, is assuming a major leadership position in the market for diesel engines, and is very strong in the lucrative Middle Eastern and Latin American markets. Deere & Co., a major agricultural equipment manufacturer, should have substantial sales gains from its overseas operations. What's more, the company is in excellent financial shape.

Bucyrus-Erie, the largest manufacturer of strip-mining coal equipment, is basically a coal play, says Small. Western coal must be developed sooner or later and surface mining is the cheapest and fastest way to get it out, he explains. Briggs & Stratton, a producer of small, consumer-oriented gas engines, should benefit from the

Capital spending should really start picking up in the first half of 1977.

As sales volume for capital goods picks up, so will profits.

continued recovery in consumer spending and will score some big earnings gains as volume increases. This company has a high rate of return and a lot of operating leverage, says Small.

Caterpillar, Clark Equipment, Gardner-Denver Ingersoll Rand, and Bucyrus-Erie are favorites.

Caterpillar, Clark Equipment (NYSE, 37), Gardner-Denver (NYSE, 17), Ingersoll Rand (NYSE, 69), and Bucyrus-Erie are favorites of Jim Love of Paine, Webber. Caterpillar has the most potential of any capital goods company, he says, pointing out that earnings in 1975 of $6.97 a share were 70% above the 1974 level and way above the previous peak of $4.32 in 1973. What's more, the company was able to throw off those earnings in 1975 even though gross margins were at the low end of their historical range. Hence, when volume picks up, margins will expand and the company could really rack up earnings, he says. In fact, when the company's $1.6 billion capital improvement program is finished sometime in 1977 or 1978, Love expects Caterpillar to have earnings power of $8 a share.

Clark Equipment is a very lean company and will be helped by a pickup in demand for industrial trucks and construction equipment. It should earn $7.00 in 1977, up from an estimated $4.00 in 1976, he says. Gardner-Denver and Ingersoll Rand will benefit from a continued strength in the energy markets (coal mining equipment and gas pipelines) as well as a pickup in the industrial machinery markets. Bucyrus-Erie, with a backlog carrying into the late 1970s, should earn $1.95 in 1976, up from $1.53 in 1975.

DEFENSE STOCKS: ON THE MARCH AGAIN

Wall Streeters are setting their sights on defense stocks again. After being bombed out for eight years, the defense industry is starting to stage a long-term cyclical recovery, notes Wolfgang Demisch of Smith Barney, Harris Upham.

Wall Streeters are setting their sights on defense stocks again.

Government military spending is finally on the rise, he says. Military procurement funding, which rose 20% in 1975 from the year before, will have a similar rise in 1976. At the very least, military spending will rise 2 to 4% a year in real terms through 1980, says Demisch. That's quite a jump when you consider that military procurement spending declined in real terms an average of 7% a year between 1968 and 1975, he notes.

The increase in military spending is due to an improving attitude toward the military.

Part of the increase in military spending is due to an improving attitude toward the military, says Wolfgang Demisch. Now that the Vietnam war has been over for a while, the antimilitary mood of the American people is fading, he says. What's more, the continued Soviet Union expansion into places like Angola, along with growing political instability around the world, is making voters—and, by extension, politicians—suspicious of détente, he says.

Furthermore, there's a gnawing fear that we're falling behind the Soviets, says Chris Demisch (Wolfgang's brother) of the National Aviation & Technology Corp. Alan Benasuli of Drexel, Burnham points out that the Soviet Union has been spending some 10% of its GNP on defense, while our own defense spending has fallen from 10% in 1968 to 6% now. In fact, U.S. military procurement spending (excluding inflation) has fallen by more than 50% since 1968, says Wolfgang Demisch of Smith Barney, Harris Upham.

Arms sales to the U.S. government aren't the only ace up the sleeve of the defense industry—foreign sales are really booming, say the analysts. Military exports, which were less than $1 billion in 1972 could be $10 billion in 1976, says Wolfgang Demisch.

The commercial aircraft business (about 15% of industry revenues) has excellent potential over the longer term, says Chris Demisch of the National Aviation & Technology Corp. Air traffic, critical to airline spending on new aircraft, hardly declined in 1975. By contrast, purchases of cars and television sets slumped so badly that massive production cutbacks were necessary. Chris Demisch thinks this marks a major change in consumer spending habits, with air travel getting an increasingly greater share of the consumer dollar. Hence, when the economy really gets going, a rise in traffic could stimulate demand for new planes.

Finally, major production runs are starting to get under way for many new weapons, says Wolfgang Demisch of Smith Barney, Harris Upham. (As a new cycle gets underway, the profits of the companies involved really take off.) The F-15, F-16, and F-18 fighter aircraft, the DD-963 destroyer, and new submarines, radios, and radar systems are all entering the major production phase of their life cycles, he says.

Raytheon (NYSE, 59), United Technologies (NYSE, 34), and Boeing (NYSE, 40) are the picks of Smith Barney, Harris Upham's Demisch. Raytheon has a major position in tactical missiles, particularly air defense and air-to-air missiles. The company's products currently enjoy, and will continue to have, great export demand, he says. Raytheon is also involved in the building of power plants, oil refineries, and petrochemical plants, and is one of the two leaders in

Major production runs are starting to get under way for many new weapons.

microwave ovens. The company should continue its growth rate of close to 15% a year for the foreseeable future.

United Technologies dominates the commercial jet engine market.

United Technologies dominates the commercial jet engine market, with almost a monopoly on narrow-body jet transport engines and more than half the wide-body jet market. United Technologies' military prospects look good because it will supply the jet engines for three out of four of the new major U.S. fighters.

Boeing has more than half the commercial jet transport market.

Boeing has more than half the commercial jet transport market, says Demisch. The company has a strong financial position and a big cash flow. Although Boeing's 747 program has not yet recovered its $1.5 billion start-up costs, the aircraft is expected to become profitable soon. On the military side, the company has either won or is a finalist in government contracts totaling well over $10 billion.

McDonnell Douglas (NYSE, 21) is a good long-term investment, says Chris Demisch of the National Aviation & Technology Corp., who points out that the stock moves when commercial aircraft orders strengthen. Although orders won't pick up right away, he says, the outlook could improve in 1977, and he thinks this stock could double in the next three to four years.

Lockheed Aircraft and Grumman are good speculations.

Lockheed Aircraft (NYSE, 8) and Grumman (NYSE, 16) are good speculations, says Chris Demisch. Lockheed is interesting because it has remarkable earnings power in its military business. If you looked at the company apart from its Trijet program and the related debt, Lockheed would be earning $10 a share, he says. Grumman has several products with great export potential, especially the F-14 fighter. Six countries, including Japan, are looking at F-14s, he says.

DISTRIBUTED DATA PROCESSING: A PROFITABLE PRINT-OUT

The most exciting and fastest growing area in data processing today is probably "distributed data processing" or the "data terminal industry," says Margaret Burke of F. Eberstadt & Co. The market for distributed data processing will continue to grow at 30 to 40% a year—at least for the rest of this decade, says Bob Gutenstein of Kalb, Voorhis.

The market for distributed data processing will continue to grow 30 to 40% a year.

Background. In the late 1960s, most industries were acquiring huge, large-frame computers for the company's headquarters. The problem was that field office operations, such as purchasing, manufacturing, selling, shipping, and invoicing, were left without data processing capabilities.

Distributed data processing solves that problem by providing those field offices with "intelligent" terminals capable of transmitting data to the central computer. With the addition of a print-out and memory capabilities at the local office, people in the field can keep local files and do their own processing and computing without being dependent on the central computer. The net advantages of distributed data processing are: availability of data, better control of business, greater utilization of central computers, reduced transmission and handling costs, and fewer input errors, say the analysts.

Compare distributed data processing companies with the minicomputer industry which has been booming.

Another way to view distributed data processing is to compare it with the minicomputer industry which has been booming because of industry's need to automate manufacturing. Distributed data processing does for business (accounts receivable control, order processing, inventory control) what minicomputers do for manufacturing—it improves efficiency, lowers cost and increases control. Distributed data processing and minicomputers were both made possible by the lower cost and increased capabilities of semiconductors.

While any profitable business brings the threat of new competition, it's unlikely that IBM and the other major computer companies will rapidly move away from their central processor concept of distributed data processing, says George Martin, director of research at Unterberg, Towbin. Martin and other analysts figure that these big companies, which have a huge commitment to computer systems built around a large central installation, will move very slowly toward offering the same type of decentralized computer systems that distributed data processing companies do. Adds another analyst: The key to success in the computer business has always been to design a product which does not compete directly with IBM. Distributed data processing fits in that category perfectly.

It is likely that IBM will make some kind of a move into this business within the next three years.

However, it is likely that IBM will make some kind of a move into this business within the next three years, says Martin. But by that time, the companies operating in the market today may be large enough to weather the competition.

Datapoint's incoming order rate is the strongest in the industry.

Datapoint (OTC, 27) is a favorite of Margaret Burke of F. Eberstadt & Co. The company is well financed, has good management, is in the right markets, and has been reporting the best earnings gains in the industry, according to Burke. What's more, Datapoint's incoming order rate is the strongest in the industry.

Sycor and Datapoint depreciate 80% of their equipment within three years.

Sycor (OTC, 11), Datapoint, and Four Phase (OTC, 13) are the favorites of Gutenstein of Kalb, Voorhis, who expects these companies to grow at 30 to 40% a year. What's more, the accounting of these companies is very conservative and so earnings aren't overstated, says Gutenstein. Sycor and Datapoint depreciate 80% of their equipment within three years, he says.

ELECTRICAL EQUIPMENT STOCKS: GENERATING INTEREST

Electrical equipment stocks are Wall Street's power plays.

Electrical equipment stocks are Wall Street's power plays, says Margaret Neilly of Spencer, Trask, considered one of the best analysts in this field. These stocks begin to move when orders for new electrical equipment start picking up—which should happen soon, she says. Customer inquiries, one of the best leading indicators of incoming orders, have increased substantially in the last few months, Neilly says.

New orders for electrical equipment are bound to pick up because the use of electricity is bouncing back faster than even the bulls expected, says Neilly. After being flat in 1974 and up only 2% in 1975, electricity use has risen 5.3% in 1976. What's so remarkable is that this jump in consumption stems almost entirely from rising industrial demand. Household demand is up only slightly this year and has actually declined in several reporting periods from the peaks reached in 1973.

Electricity use will jump.

When household demand picks up, the increase in electricity use will move up at least to the lower end of its historical range of 6 to 7%, says Neilly. She figures household demand has been held down by cautious consumer spending, abnormal weather patterns all over the country, and the low level of consumer appliance sales. (Appliance sales in 1976 were running 20% below those of the last cyclical peak in 1973—which means less new appliances and hence lower demand for electricity.) Neilly thinks that when the economic recovery gets further along and the consumer starts to spend more, home appliance sales and electricity use will jump.

Westinghouse (NYSE, 15), Babcock & Wilcox (NYSE, 31), and Gilbert Associates (OTC, 17) are Neilly's stock picks. She thinks Westinghouse, which is the number one nuclear power plant manufacturer in the world, is probably the best buy in the Dow Jones Industrial Average. It has fallen the most from its previous high and has rallied back the least. What's more, the company's management has pulled itself together after some hard times, and earnings are coming through better than expected. The company has reported record earnings so far in 1976, a lot of debt has been paid off, and its balance sheet has improved greatly, says Neilly.

The only negative factor on the horizon for Westinghouse is the unresolved problem with its uranium contracts, says Neilly. (Westinghouse has told its customers it will be unable to honor its contracts to deliver 60 million pounds of uranium between 1978 and the late 1980s.) Neilly thinks, however, that the company will eventually work out an arrangement that lets it and the utilities involved split the costs of covering the shortfall. In fact, a settlement may be reached by mid-1977, at the latest, she says, pointing out that Westinghouse recently retained John McCloy, a highly respected lawyer, to handle the problem.

Babcock & Wilcox is a major factor in nuclear power, a large producer of specialty steel tubing and one of the two major manufacturers of fossil fuel boilers. The company has been paying down its debt at a very rapid rate and is cheaply priced, selling at six times 1977 estimated earnings of $5.50, says Neilly.

Gilbert Associates, a major architectural and engineering firm for utilities, is one of the first businesses to benefit from a pickup in electricity demand, she says. The company already has a record backlog and is the sixth most important utility engineering firm in the United States and the fifth most important in the rest of the world, Neilly says. The company's balance sheet is in excellent shape and the stock is currently yielding 5.5%, she notes. What's more, even though the company will likely report record earnings next year, Neilly says, the stock is way down from its 1974 peak of 58 a share.

The only negative factor on the horizon for Westinghouse is the unresolved problem with its uranium contracts.

Property-casualty insurance stocks may be some of the best performers in 1977.

INSURANCE STOCKS: SOON AT A PREMIUM

The property-casualty insurance stocks may be some of the best performers in 1977, say the analysts. And even though these stocks have already had big moves, they still have a great potential for appreciation.

A slackening in the rate of inflation has helped slow the cost of doing business for insurance companies.

The property-casualty insurance industry is in the midst of an explosive cyclical recovery, says Gerald Lewisohn of Faulkner, Dawkins & Sullivan. Total earnings for the property-casualty companies could reach $3.5 billion in 1977—against $1 billion in 1975, says Jay Cushman of White, Weld.

According to Cushman, this remarkable turnaround has happened because: (1) Rate increases in 1974 and 1975 are finally starting to have an effect. (2) Eligibility requirements have been tightened, costs are under better control, and unprofitable lines have been discontinued. (3) A slackening in the rate of inflation has helped slow the cost of doing business for insurance companies and has reduced the size of the claims paid out.

Continental Corp (NYSE, 50), INA (NYSE, 41), and U.S. Fidelity & Guaranty (NYSE, 49) are Lewisohn's first picks. These companies are predominantly in the property-casualty business (which is having the biggest turnaround), are favored by pension funds because of their high yields (5½ to 6%) and have good balance sheets, he says. What's more, these companies will probably be able to increase their dividends earlier than most other property-casualty companies because their financial condition wasn't damaged too much in the 1973-74 shakeout.

Other stocks favored by Lewisohn are Ohio Casualty (OTC, 43), Safeco (OTC, 45), and General Reinsurance (OTC, 183). These companies also have a big property-casualty business and strong balance sheets.

Aetna (NYSE, 33), Travelers (NYSE, 42), Continental Corp., General Reinsurance, Safeco, Ohio Casualty, and Chubb (OTC, 38) are favorites of White, Weld's Cushman. All these companies have strong earnings prospects and a solid financial condition.

Alexander & Alexander (OTC, 37), Fred S. James (NYSE, 18), and Frank B. Hall (NYSE, 19) are three insurance brokers which David Seifer of Merrill Lynch likes. He points out that insurance brokers are benefiting from their ability to place new business with companies not actively seeking business in certain unprofitable or marginally profitable lines.

St. Paul (OTC, 34), Chubb, Connecticut General (OTC, 54), General Reinsurance and Mission Equities (NYSE, 16) should have above-average earnings gains in 1977, says Leandro S. Galban of Wood, Struthers & Winthrop. The stocks are cheap and the companies are well managed with an above-average exposure to property casualty insurance, he says.

URANIUM STOCKS: PORTFOLIO ENRICHMENT

The day of uranium is quickly approaching, according to Bob Detwiler of Fechtor, Detwiler & Co. in Boston. The shares of certain uranium companies could double, and in some cases quadruple, from present levels in the next few years, says David Snow of Mitchell, Hutchins.

Uranium prices will continue to rise and could reach $100 a pound within the next two years, says Snow. Spot uranium prices have risen nearly sixfold in the last two years, and long-term contract prices, which is where the real money is, have nearly doubled since last year, says Detwiler.

According to Snow of Mitchell, Hutchins, the outlook for uranium is bullish because: (1) Domestic mine capacity can't be increased rapidly enough to avert a real supply squeeze by 1980. (2) The balance of supply and demand was really thrown off kilter when Westinghouse voided its long-term contracts to supply uranium to utilities.

Very little is being done to avert the upcoming supply-demand squeeze, according to Alan Edgar of Schneider, Bernet & Hickman. He estimates that current annual uranium exploration expenditures in the U.S. total less than $100 million, compared with the billions now being spent on oil exploration.

A higher price of uranium means good earnings for uranium companies which up until now has only been a promise, says Detwiler. Some companies are already reporting sharply higher earnings—Nuclear, for example, earned 73¢ in fiscal 1976 as against 10¢ in 1975.

Reserve Oil & Minerals (OTC, 34) is the favorite of Detwiler. He thinks the company will start showing profits in fiscal 1977, ending August 30. By 1979, Reserve could earn $13.50 a share and as much as $15 by 1980, says Detwiler. The company should soon start to sell at a premium against other uranium stocks because it has milling capacity—which will continue in short supply, Detwiler says. What's more, the company owns some of the best potential uranium ore-producing land in the country, he says. United Nuclear, which has among the highest amount of uncommitted uranium reserves per share in the industry could earn $10 a share by 1980, he adds.

American Nuclear (OTC, 8) which could triple in the next few years, is the pick of Alan Edgar of Schneider, Bernet and Hickman. The company is developing uranium finds that could substantially increase its reserves. In fact, Edgar thinks American Nuclear may soon sign

---

The day of uranium is quickly approaching.

A higher price of uranium means good earnings for uranium companies.

new contracts worth more than the company's present market capitalization.

United Nuclear, Reserve Oil and Minerals, Kerr-McGee (NYSE, 67), and Gulf Oil (NYSE, 25) are the picks of Snow of Mitchell, Hutchins. Based on uncommitted reserves per share, United Nuclear and Reserve Oil could sell at $100 a share in the next few years, he says. Kerr-McGee's uncommitted uranium reserves alone are worth $60 a share today and $120 a share based on future expectations, says Snow. Gulf Oil, currently yielding close to 7%, is number two after Kerr-McGee in quantity of uranium reserves, and has an upside potential of some 65%, he says.

GOVERNMENT BONDS: A BULL'S TIME TO BUY

Government bonds will continue to rally in 1977, says the head of the government desk at a major New York City bank. He thinks bond prices may jump because long-term interest rates could drop significantly. (When long-term interest rates fall, bond prices rise.) By the end of 1977 or early 1978, long-term bond yields could fall to 6%, says Gary Shilling, an economist with White, Weld. He thinks this will happen because the rate of inflation will drop to around 3½% by the end of 1976 and should average no more than 3% in 1977.

The fundamentals of the bond market are excellent, say the bond analysts. For one thing, inflation appears to be under control and the economic recovery is moving at a sustainable pace. For another, the supply of new issues has tapered off—a lot of the government financing is out of the way and the corporate calendar will likely remain very light. What's more, corporations continue to build liquidity—cash flow is improving, corporate equity offerings are helping to strengthen balance sheets, and the pickup in business borrowing has not materialized.

The demand for government bonds is very strong, says Jack Doyle of Jennison Associates. The response last summer to the issue of U.S. Treasury 8s of 1986 (U.S. Treasury bonds with a coupon yield of 8%, maturing in 1986) was so enthusiastic, Doyle says, that the original offering of $4 billion was increased to $7.6 billion. And the U.S. Treasury 8s of 1996-2001 came at virtually the same price as other comparable issues already outstanding. That's very bullish, Doyle

Government bonds will continue to rally in 1977.

The demand for government bonds is very strong.

says, since most offerings of this kind have come at a lower price (and higher yield) than the existing issues of comparable coupon and maturity.

The best buys in the government market are the 10- and 25-year issues.

The best buys in the government market are the 10- and 25-year issues, says Doyle. He particularly likes the U.S. Treasury 8s of 1986 (102), currently yielding 7.37%, and the U.S. Treasury 7⅞s of 1986 (102), currently yielding 7.38% because they are popular issues that trade well and will outperform most other sectors of the market. Furthermore, they both have very attractive current yields, he says.

Doyle also likes any of the 25-year bonds—such as the U.S. Treasury 7⅞s of 1995-2000 (101), U.S. Treasury 8⅜s of 1995-2000 (103), U.S. Treasury 8¼s of 2000-2005 (103), U.S. Treasury 8½s of 1994-1999 (104) and U.S. Treasury 8s of 1996-2001 (101). Doyle believes these bonds will ultimately sell at a premium to the market because they can't be called in for 20 to 25 years. That means investors who purchase the bonds at current yields will be able to receive that same rate of return for the next 20 to 25 years—even if long-term interest rates drop to, say, 6%. (When interest rates fall, corporations as well as the government like to call back high-yield bonds and replace them by issues with lower coupons.) What's more, these issues have less downside risk than most of the intermediate-term issues, Doyle says. If you compare today's yields with those at the bottom of the market in the autumn of 1974, you'll see that the intermediates have rallied the most—and hence have the most downside risk from here if rates rise again.

UTILITY STOCKS: BULLISH METER READINGS

Utility stocks may rally almost as much in 1977 as they did in 1976.

Utility stocks will continue rallying in 1977, say the analysts. The rally in utility shares will be sparked by a continuing decline in long-term interest rates—perhaps to the 6½% range. When long-term interest rates decline, utility stocks (which act like bonds) will rally, they explain.

What's more, the fundamental outlook for utilities is excellent, says Jay McCabe of Donaldson, Lufkin & Jenrette. Earnings will rise some 6 to 8% in 1977, he says, and the prospects for 1978 are also good, say the analysts. And there's a very good chance that many utility companies will raise their dividends in 1977, says John Attalienti of

A lot of the negatives which were worrying utility investors are now out of the way or substantially reduced.

Utilities will have big earnings gains in 1977.

Argus Research. Furthermore, a decrease in the capital requirements of utilities will take a lot of pressure off utility stocks, says McCabe of Donaldson, Lufkin & Jenrette. Utility companies, which have recently raised a lot of equity capital may stay away from the market for a while, say the analysts.

A lot of the negatives which were worrying utility investors are now out of the way or substantially reduced, says Attalienti of Argus Research. Inflation appears to be under control and the defeat of the nuclear initiative in California (which would have put a moratorium on new nuclear facilities in the state) is a big plus for utilities pushing nuclear power.

Ohio Edison (NYSE, 20), Dayton Power & Light (NYSE, 18), New York State Electric & Gas (NYSE, 28), Commonwealth Edison (NYSE, 31), and General Public Utilities (NYSE, 17) are the picks of Dean Witter's Ken Hollister. All these companies are yielding between 8 and 9% and will probably increase their dividends by at least 4% in 1977, he says.

McCabe of Donaldson, Lufkin & Jenrette prefers utilities in Florida and the Carolinas because the regulatory environment in those states is so favorable. His picks are: Florida Power & Light (NYSE, 25), Florida Power Corp (NYSE, 29), Tampa Electric (NYSE, 18), Carolina Power & Light (NYSE, 21), Duke Power (NYSE, 21), and South Carolina Electric & Gas (NYSE, 21). These utilities will have big earnings gains in 1976 and 1977, McCabe says, thanks to the rate relief they've already received from the regulatory agencies. What's more, Carolina Power, Duke Power, and South Carolina Electric have large nuclear commitments—which will be a big plus for these companies in the near future because nuclear power is the lowest cost energy source.

Duke Power and Northern States Power (NYSE, 28) are two favorites of Attalienti of Argus Research. Both utilities are in exceptionally good regulatory environments and use mainly coal and nuclear power.

Potomac Electric (NYSE, 14), New York State Electric & Gas, Long Island Lighting (NYSE, 17), and Florida Power Corp. are other Attalienti favorites. Potomac Electric will benefit from the significant financial turnaround at present under way. New York State Electric and Long Island Lighting also have improving financial conditions and are likely to have big dividend increases in 1977. Florida Power is in a good regulatory environment and serves one of the more rapidly growing parts of the country.

PREFERRED STOCKS: SOMETHING TO CELEBRATE

It may well be that 1977 will be the year of the preferred stock, say the preferred stock analysts. These issues, which outperformed all other fixed-income securities during the last two years, will likely do so again in 1977—and in spades, says a portfolio manager with a large insurance company.

Background. Preferred stocks generally have yields as high as or higher than those of bonds—and so tend to act more like bonds than like common stocks. If long-term interest rates continue to fall, as many analysts expect, preferred stocks will rally. Note that the preferred issues of utilities generally carry yields 1% higher than those of industrial preferreds—which are considered safer and which have a greater coverage of fixed charges and preferred dividends.

Preferred dividends are rarely reduced or omitted. (If dividends are omitted they are usually carried forward.) Take Consolidated Edison: Although the common stock dividends were omitted for several quarters in 1974 and 1975, Con Ed continued to pay dividends on its preferred issues. If for some reason a preferred dividend is missed for three to six quarters, preferred stockholders will receive voting rights—which they normally do not have. Once back dividends have been paid, of course, these voting rights are withdrawn.

The major plus for preferred stocks right now is the extremely favorable outlook for long-term interest rates, say the analysts. Inflation seems to be abating, short-term rates are at low levels, and the overall calendar of new issues may be smaller in 1977 than it was in 1976—all of which will help push down long-term rates.

Investors are showing a good appetite for preferred issues, says Eddie Burke of White, Weld. Fire and casualty insurance companies, which have been out of the preferred market for the last two years because of heavy underwriting losses, are now coming back, Burke says. What's more, corporations and individuals are also starting to buy preferreds in large quantities. Corporations like these issues because 85% of the preferred dividends are exempt from corporate income taxes.

Flannery of Merrill Lynch advises investors to place a heavy emphasis on utilities operating in the Southwest, especially in Texas and Oklahoma. Institutions like the shares of companies doing business in the Southwest because the area's economy is stronger

---

1977 may well be the year of the preferred stock.

The major plus for preferred stocks right now is the extremely favorable outlook for long-term interest rates.

Investors are showing a dramatically increasing appetite for preferred issues.

than that of any other part of the country, Flannery says. (The Northeast, by contrast, is generally the weakest part of the country.) What's more, many institutions and corporations with an office in Texas or Oklahoma are buying issues of utilities in these states because this gives them some tax benefits and may help them politically.

Investors seeking high quality and liquidity can use as a guide the list of preferred stocks in which New York State savings banks are permitted to invest, says Merrill Lynch's Flannery. (Simply stated, New York State savings banks may invest only in the preferred issues of companies whose after-tax earnings are at least 1½ times the total of all fixed charges and the preferred dividends—for at least the last five years.) These issues are actively traded, so investors who want to sell them can be certain of getting a good price, Flannery says.

Some final tips. When you decide to buy a preferred, you may be able to boost your profits by waiting to purchase it until about three weeks before it is scheduled to go ex-dividend, says Flannery. (The ex-dividend date is the date on which the stock begins to trade without the forthcoming payable dividend.) That's because you don't pay separately for the coming dividend, as you do for accrued interest in bonds. So the price you pay for the preferred stock may not reflect the eight weeks or so worth of dividends.

A small investor should go to his broker's preferred department for help in executing preferred stock orders.

Because certain preferred stocks are at times illiquid, a small investor should go to his broker's preferred department for help in executing the order. According to Wall Streeters, the following brokerage houses have strong preferred departments: White, Weld; Kidder, Peabody; Merrill Lynch; Spencer, Trask; Loeb Rhoades; E.F. Hutton; and Weeden & Co.

If you're thinking of buying lower quality preferreds, you should always compare the yield of the preferred with the yields of the issuing company's common stocks and bonds.

Always check before buying a utility preferred to see if it is "old money" or "new money."

Always check before buying a utility preferred to see if it is "old money" or "new money"—that is, if it was issued before or after October 1, 1942. If it's an old-money preferred, the tax exemption to corporations and institutions will only be 60% as against the 85% exemption of new-money preferreds. Hence, old-money preferreds are bought only by individuals and tax-exempt institutions—who don't get any tax benefits from owning preferreds. That means these issues have less liquidity than new-money preferreds. So you should buy an old-money preferred, the analysts say, only if you're sure you'll get a higher yield for the lesser amount of liquidity.

MUNICIPAL BONDS: AN URBAN RENEWAL PLAY

Municipal bonds still offer exceptional value.

Municipal bonds still offer exceptional value, according to the municipal bond analysts. They think municipals will continue to rally throughout 1977. (As a bond's price rises, its yield falls.)

You can best see the value of munis when you compare them to equivalent taxable bonds, says James Lebenthal of Lebenthal & Co. Simply put, municipal bond yields are still at high levels in relation to taxable bonds. Up until the New York City crisis broke in 1975, municipal bonds generally yielded some 66% of what taxable bonds were yielding. But prices fell so far that in spite of the recent rally, A-rated municipal bond yields are almost 80% those of taxables. That means the prices of munis still have a long way to climb just to catch up with those of taxable bonds, even if taxables don't rally any more. But taxables, as well as all other fixed income investments, will rally because inflationary expectations, the key determinant of bond prices, are still fading.

The credit risks of municipalities will soon improve.

With the economic recovery coming along so well, the credit risks of municipalities will soon improve, says a trader with a major Wall Street firm. Tax receipts will soar and lower relief rolls will trim cash outflows. This improvement in municipal credit is already showing up in the spread between yields on high- and low-quality issues—which is narrowing rapidly, according to Richard Curvin of First Boston Corp.

Confidence in municipals is already greatly improved, says Frank Wendt, chairman of John Nuveen & Co. New York State and its agencies are over the hump and New York City is slowly working its problems out, Wendt says. In fact, confidence in New York has improved to the point where MAC bonds have rallied some seven points, and Westchester County had no trouble selling some notes.

The demand for municipals is firming up.

What's more, the demand for municipals is firming up, says Curvin of First Boston. Insurance companies, flush with funds, are coming back into the market and muni dealers are again carrying large inventories—which adds to the price stability of the market. Banks are also buying again for the first time in years, notes Langdon Cook of Langdon P. Cook & Co. He thinks banks will have higher earnings in 1977 and hence will once again be in the market for tax-free income. And individuals will also be big buyers, says Cook. Many investors have large capital gains taxes on their stock investments this year and will be looking around for tax-exempt income.

The supply side also looks rosy, says a trader with a major Wall Street firm. At present, only the highest quality borrowers can sell bonds—which means a limited supply of new bonds. And the volume would be further reduced if Congress passes a recently introduced bill which would let municipalities issue taxable bonds, says Wendt of John Nuveen & Co. He points out that many municipalities, who might otherwise sell bonds in the tax-exempt market, would then use the taxable markets.

Buy municipal bonds that are rated A or better and that have a maturity of over 20 years, says Wendt. The bond should also be noncallable or have a 5- to 10-year call protection—these bonds will rally the most because investors won't hold back for fear of having the bonds called away from them. Long-term discount bonds (selling below par) are also attractive because they offer the greatest upside potential, says Wendt. But be sure that any discount bond has a current return of better than 5%, he says. Investors shouldn't sacrifice current yield while they wait for maturity.

C TIPS FROM TRADERS

Can you beat the Dow Jones Industrial Average? And should you even try? One recent school of thought on Wall Street holds that you should try to match the DJIA—which, by the way, has risen at only a compound rate of 5.7% since 1959. Even so, most investment managers haven't been able to do as well as the DJIA. Maybe that's because they've been selecting stocks on the basis of growth potential and future earnings. Some investment managers think that picking a stock based on its underlying assets yields far better results.

Take the investment record of Tweedy, Browne Inc.—a firm that selects stocks because of their underlying assets. The firm can boast a 20.4% compounded annual growth rate since 1959 as against the DJIA's 5.7%. What's more, Tweedy, Browne had only two down years during that entire period—in 1970 assets fell 1.3% and in 1962, 1.9%. However, Tweedy, Browne's assets increased in both 1973 and 1974, a time when the DJIA was being devastated.

Picking a stock based on its underlying assets yields far better results.

*Diversification is
extremely important.*

*Knowing when to sell is
also a key.*

Tweedy, Browne principals Chris Browne and Ed Anderson look at a stock as if they were a corporate purchaser interested in buying the entire company. They try to figure out what a company is really worth by calculating its *net current assets per share.* This figure is found by subtracting all liabilities, including long-term lease obligations and unfunded pension liabilities, from the current assets and dividing the difference by the total number of shares outstanding. If the value they work up for a company is 30 to 60% higher than the current price of its stock, it's a good candidate for purchase, according to Browne and Anderson.

Diversification is extremely important, say Browne and Anderson. A typical $50,000 account at Tweedy, Browne might be invested in 30 companies. That way, if anything goes wrong with one company, the loss will have only a minimal effect on the whole portfolio. Furthermore, diversification should enhance investment results. You never know when the stock market will properly value your holdings— it might take three years or more. But the odds are great that one or two of the 30 stocks might be recognized soon, they say.

Knowing when to sell is also a key part of the Tweedy, Browne philosophy. Browne and Anderson usually sell when a stock's price approaches its net assets per share. This strategy has several advantages, they say. For one thing, it enables the firm to get out of the market near to a bull market top. If stocks are overpriced, a common occurrence at market tops, there won't be anything attractive to invest in. This strategy also produces a constant source of new cash which can be invested in other attractive bargains. (The firm never wants to sell an unrealized bargain just because a better bargain comes along.)

A.R. Schmeidler & Co., Inc., another investment firm that uses the asset approach, also has a superb track record. Principals Arnold Schmeidler and Peter Stanley look for companies with assets that have not yet been recognized. Here are the criteria they look for in a company: (1) It should offer a solution to a major economic problem— such as the energy crisis, the world food shortage, or the bankrupt rail system in the Northeast. (2) It should have a high current return to offset inflation during the holding period. (3) Its assets should be relatively impervious to executive fiat or to changes in cultural or social habits. (4) Its assets should be valuable, should offer an economic advantage, and be so difficult to acquire that others cannot duplicate them without tremendous amounts of capital.

Certain investments in energy, agriculture, communications, and mass transportation at present meet these requirements, say Schmeidler and Stanley. They also like the oil service stocks because little domestic exploration has been done in recent years and the energy crisis is still very much with us. Agriculture is another exciting investment area because the United States is the breadbasket of the world, say Schmeidler and Stanley. The United States can produce and transport more food at lower prices than any other country in the world.

Belden Corp. (NYSE, 22), Amsted (NYSE, 45), and Koppers (NYSE, 53) are some companies with unique or valuable assets. Belden is developing an optic fibre with greatly increased capacity for carrying telephone message units. Amsted, the largest builder of rail car wheels, and Koppers, the biggest producer of rail beds, are two beneficiaries of the reorganization of the Northeast's rail system. This reorganization, which is expected to be followed by large-scale rebuilding of old track and ordering of new equipment, is a must— because it is the key to the economic rejuvenation of the northeast.

CAPITAL GAIN AND LOSS WORKSHEET

NAME AND TYPE OF SECURITY	PURCHASED		SOLD		LONG-TERM		SHORT-TERM	
	ON	AT	ON	AT	GAIN	LOSS	GAIN	LOSS
		$		$				

TOTAL _____ _____ _____ _____

NET GAIN OR LOSS $ _____ $ _____ $ _____ $ _____

CAPITAL LOSS CARRY FORWARD _____ _____

NET GAIN OR LOSS FOR YEAR $ _____

POTENTIAL CAPITAL GAIN AND LOSS CALCULATOR

| NAME AND TYPE OF SECURITY | PURCHASED | | IF SOLD | | YOU WOULD REALIZE | | | |
| | | | | | LONG-TERM | | SHORT-TERM | |
	ON	AT	NOW	AT	GAIN	LOSS	GAIN	LOSS
		$		$	$	$	$	$

TOTAL _____

NET SHORT-AND-LONG-TERM POSITION _____

CAPITAL LOSS CARRY FORWARD _____

NET GAIN OR LOSS FOR YEAR $ _____

3. REAL ESTATE

WHAT'S HOT AND
WHAT'S NOT IN
REAL ESTATE

HOW TO PLAY
FUTURE
DEMOGRAPHIC
TRENDS

INNER-CITY
RESTORATIONS

MINIMALLS

CHOOSING TENANTS
FOR A MINIMALL

THE PLAY IN OLDER
BUILDINGS

APARTMENTS ARE
APT

HOMING IN ON
HOUSES

TIMBERLAND

WORKSHEETS

On the whole, this should be a good year for real estate investments. Money is clearly available, interest rates are reasonable, and the cost of construction has simmered down. What's more, foreign investors are playing the U.S. real estate market and hence stimulating it. But what does this mean for you? Simply that conditions are favorable. What you decide to invest in depends on the area you live in. For nothing is as important in real estate as location. What's hot in one city or suburb could be the kiss of death in a place just 30 miles away. It can get that close.

Still, there are some broad demographic trends that you may well be able to cash in on. For example, there's a growing demand for housing. Not much housing has been built over the past three years or so, and the generation of war babies is now starting to settle down and have families of their own. On the other hand, the day of the large regional shopping center may be coming to a close. Instead, you'll see big downtown centers and small "strip" centers spring up around the country. Strip centers are cheaper to put up, don't require as much capital, are easier to control, and aren't quite as risky or complicated as the larger centers. Here are some specific deals that might be of interest to you—providing the location is right.

BUILDING ON THE FUTURE

Play the future, says Anthony Downs, chairman of Real Estate Research Corporation in Chicago. Because real estate is a fairly illiquid, long-term investment, demographic trends play a powerful role in the viability and capital gains potential of this investment.

The pattern of U.S. real estate will change dramatically over the next 20 years or so, says Downs. He notes that according to projections prepared by the U.S. Census Bureau the demand for housing will jump more than 20 million households over the next 2½ decades. Much of the increase will be due to changes in family formations: Single people will account for 22 to 26% of all households, as against 21% at present. Family households will drop correspondingly. What's more, the size of the average family will shrink to 2.4 persons by 1990 as against an average size of 2.7 in 1974.

*Changes
in real estate patterns
are starting to show up.*

*The key to a successful
real estate investment
today is financing.*

These demographic changes mean that there will be less land per household, less space per person, fewer schoolrooms and churches, more fast food establishments and more varied recreational facilities, says Downs. All this will dictate a higher degree of obsolescence in much of the existing property, he adds. Some of these changes in real estate patterns are already starting to show up, according to many of the real estate pros we talked to. Here's a rundown on their thinking about financing and what kind of prospects look good.

Financing. The key to a successful real estate investment today is financing, says Norb Wall, president of Larry Smith & Co. of Northfield, Illinois. Money is available, but the bankers' terms are much tighter now. Lenders have been so shellshocked by loan losses and other problems over the past two years, that they now insist investors put up as much as 25 to 30% of a project's cost as against around 10% or less a few years ago. That may not be all that bad. The higher equity requirement means you will have less debt to service—and hence more leeway with your investment should something go sour.

What's more, lenders want as many guarantees as they can get. Some bankers will only give you a mortgage if you can guarantee 60 to 70% of your eventual cash flow by signing up long-term high credit tenants in advance. Try to avoid terms like these, says Ken McElroy of RLS Real Estate Services Corp. in New Orleans. The tenants you try to sign up will probably realize how much you need them to arrange a mortgage, and they'll use that to bludgeon down the terms of a lease, he says.

General strategy. Because building costs are still higher than they were in the past, the pros think that you'd be wise to buy an older building rather than put up a new one. In fact, now is a prime time to pick up older buildings at bargain prices. Some investors are trying to get out of some of their properties because they're overleveraged, says Phillip Kozloff of Advance Mortgage Corp. in Detroit. So they may be willing to sell some of their property at a fairly low price in order to raise enough cash to meet mortgage payments, says Irving Price of Hudson Michael Realty in Hudson, New York. The trick is to distinguish between owners in financial trouble and properties that are financially troubled. A bad bet, regardless of how much of a bargain it is, is still a bad bet.

Apartments in a good location and well maintained are starting to look like a good investment, say the pros. Many think that there will be a shortage of apartments within the next two years because

relatively few apartment buildings are being built at present.
Moreover, the demand for apartments is beginning to climb as the
number of households being formed rises. What's more, a growing
number of people can no longer afford to buy a home and so will have
to live in apartments.

The demand for apartments is beginning to climb.

The combination of increasing demand and a growing shortage of
apartments should make it easier for landlords to raise their rents.
That means a rising return on your investment as well as a
potentially handsome capital gain, says Anthony Downs of Real
Estate Research Corp. (The net income generated by a building is one
of the major factors used to determine its value.) Based on the way
rents are expected to rise, Price of Hudson Michael Realty thinks
investors could sell for a fat capital gain five to ten years from now.

Commercial real estate should do well.

Commercial real estate—such as personal storage warehouses or
anything else that can capitalize on the needs of apartment dwellers—
should do well, says Norb Wall of Larry Smith & Co. (Personal
storage warehouses rent cubicles to people who don't have enough
storage space of their own.) As more and more people move into
apartments or cheaper houses that don't have basements or attics, the
demand for personal storage warehouses will grow.

Fast food chains, bookstores, and movie houses should also prosper.

Fast food chains, bookstores, and movie houses should also prosper.
The trend toward apartments means an increase in population
density in certain areas. And the more cooped up people become, the
more they tend to want to be entertained. Note, however, that as
rents go up, there will be less disposable income—which means people
will have to turn to cheaper entertainment.

Because retail space has been hit by high interest rates and soaring
construction costs, the action is in rehabilitating older neighborhood
stores. Flexibility is vital—a number of different kinds of tenants
should be able to use the space, says Wall of Larry Smith & Co. If you
invest in a "single use" building such as a gas station or a bank
branch, you'll be stuck if your tenants move out. You'll either have to
search for someone else who can use the space as is, or have to sink
more money in converting the building to other uses.

REAPPRECIATING THE CITY

Ever consider an urban renewal project of your own?

Ever consider an urban renewal project of
your own? Buying and renovating two to five-story houses in rundown
neighborhoods that are starting to turn around can give you a hefty

income, handsome capital gains, and some very sweet tax shelter, say the pros. And the kicker is that the deal doesn't cost very much which means that the money you have at risk won't be great.

The larger the city, the greater the probability that some young professionals are moving into a run-down neighborhood and renovating homes for their own use. However, even smaller cities are reporting some renovation work. Neighborhoods that are now on the way up are fairly easy to spot because the signs of renovation are very visible. Make sure that the neighborhood you pick is fairly small, so that the renovation will have a strong and immediate impact on property values.

Property appreciates fastest in an area where people are trying to save the buildings' original interiors and exteriors. The charm of these buildings, usually put up between 1850 and World War I, makes the area more desirable to potential tenants as well as to buyers. What's more, it's cheaper to save the building interior than it is to gut it. But whatever you do, don't get carried away and attempt a museum-quality restoration. An investment in that kind of craftwork is too expensive—and chances are it won't pay off because most people couldn't afford the rents you'd have to charge to cover restoration costs, says Norbert Wall, president of Larry Smith & Co., Northfield, Illinois.

The best time to buy a building is soon after the neighborhood has started to turn around. The houses will still be fairly cheap—say, between $15,000 and $30,000 and possibly even less. Before you buy, however, line up a contractor either familiar with renovation work or willing to learn about it, says Aaron Amarnick, chairman of the National Remodelers Association, New York City. (Some contractors think it means gutting the building.) The cost of renovating a building will run between $10,000 and about $30,000—depending on how extensive the work is. One of the best ways to find a contractor skilled in renovation work is to ask the people in the neighborhood whom they used.

Once you have a good handle on what renovating the building will cost, you're ready to start looking for a mortgage. Finding financing can be tricky. However, banks and thrift institutions now have some experience with renovations—and hence are becoming somewhat less wary of investing their deposits in local housing.

One of the handiest plays we ran across worked this way: You go to a thrift institution and ask for a permanent mortgage commitment based on the projected value of the house once the renovation has

Don't get carried away and attempt a museum-quality restoration.

The best time to buy a building is soon after the neighborhood has started to turn around.

been completed, says Robert Miller of Building Game Ltd. in Washington, D.C. (In effect, you're prearranging the mortgage for an eventual buyer—which should make it much easier to sell the house.) Once you have a permanent mortgage commitment, you can use it to get a short-term loan (to cover most of the acquisition price plus renovation costs) from a commercial bank.

Try to get the seller to give you a purchase money mortgage.

If you have difficulty getting the bank financing, try to get the seller to give you a purchase money mortgage for a least 80% of the building's price, says Bernd Allen of the Allen & Morris law firm in Brooklyn, N. Y. (A *purchase money mortgage* is a note held by the seller to whom you make your payments.) Once you have a purchase money mortgage, you shouldn't have any trouble getting a home improvement loan from a bank. That will add slightly to your costs of carrying the building. But by the time you renovate, you'll be able to charge much higher rents to cover the additional debt burden. Moreover, when the building has been renovated, its value should have increased significantly—which means you should be able to get a permanent mortgage to cover the building's entire purchase price and renovation costs.

Deciding whether to sell right away or rent the building depends on how you're fixed and what kind of capital gains you're looking for. If you renovate and sell as soon as possible, you stand to make about 15% on each deal based on Washington, D.C., experience, says Thomas Black of the Urban Land Institute. However, if you hold the building for five years or so, you'll probably see much greater appreciation. For instance, in Brooklyn's Park Slope, a house that sold for $30,000 four or five years ago and cost $10,000 to renovate, is now worth at least $75,000, says Everett Ortner, former head of the Brownstone Revival Committee, New York City.

You can figure that you'll get a 15 to 22% cash return on your investment.

If you decide to rent, you can figure that you'll get a 15 to 22% cash return on your investment, says Allen. However, with small buildings such as these, renting is feasible only if you or your partner live nearby and can keep an eye on the property. You may also be able to work out a deal with your contractor to do repairs if you're going to keep working with him on more buildings.

The tax shelter you get from a renovation project can be substantial.

What's more, the tax shelter you get from a renovation project can be substantial. In addition to being able to deduct maintenance and interest expenses, you may be able to write off the entire cost of renovation over five years. Chances are that there'll be enough tax deductions to shelter the building's cash flow—and even some of your income from other sources.

For more information. Check out the excellent monthly *The Old-House Journal*, 199 Berkeley Place, Brooklyn, New York 11217. It costs $12 for a one-year subscription. A new national group, Back to the City, Inc., 12 East 41st St., New York, New York 10017, has been formed to share renovation experiences around the country. The group also acts as a clearinghouse for ideas. And a book called *Buying and Renovating a House in the City*, published by Random House for $4.95, is a good buy.

THE ENTREPRENEURIAL SPIRIT

Converting large stores, warehouses or factories into groups of small stores or minimalls is one of the hottest new real estate investments around.

Converting large stores, warehouses, or factories into groups of small stores or minimalls is one of the hottest new real estate investments around. They're sprouting all over the country. The pros figure that you can make a fat profit—possibly without putting up a cent of your own money.

The market. During the recession, while W. T. Grant went under and other large retail chains floundered, many small boutiques and specialty shops flourished. Much of the success of these smaller shops is due to their charm and the personal service they offer customers. And the pros in retailing and real estate think that the trend toward smaller stores will continue for quite a while.

Look at a building that will attract a lot of people.

What to look for. You'd be wise to look at a building that will attract a lot of people because of its architectural qualities or one that is near a proven draw, say, a big food market, or a department store, says C. Lincoln Jewett of Howard P. Hoffman Associates in New York City. Alternatively, you can provide the draw yourself by putting in a service that will fill a large retail gap in your area. For example, an investor who converted a building in an Atlanta suburb attracted people with a home improvement center.

The key turns on the soundness of the building.

The building itself, as well as the small stores in it, should be very accessible. If you're considering a building in the suburbs or in a small city you may need as many as 20 to 25 parking spaces for each store. An architect can tell you whether the space can be converted into a number of accessible stores, how much work is involved, and what it will cost you, says Harold G. Trimble, Jr., a San Francisco real estate consultant. The key turns on the soundness of the building. If it's in good shape, all you'll have to do is put up some walls, redo the electrical fittings and perhaps add some additional plumbing. If the building's in a sorry state, you may have to gut the interior and start from scratch—which would jack your costs sky-high.

Financing. The pros recommend leasing rather than buying—at least for the time being. For one thing, leasing can cut down your front-end costs considerably. For another, it can be tough and in some cases impossible to get a mortgage on a deal involving small merchants. Most bankers won't touch small retail deals unless you have a substantial track record in this kind of venture. However, if your credit rating is good, the pros think you'll have little problem arranging a loan to pay for the cost of the renovation.

When you negotiate the lease—usually for 10 years or so—get an option to buy. If the deal takes off, you'll probably be able to get a mortgage by using your financial statements from the venture to show a bank how successful it is. The option, which gives you the right to buy the building at an agreed-upon price, will probably come to 5% of the purchase price. Of course, the money you pay for the option can be applied to the price of the building if you should decide to buy it.

Hire a management firm that specializes in retailing.

Marketing and management. Since this deal is a combination of real estate and retailing, you'll be wise to hire a management firm that specializes in retailing. It can lease stores to tenants and run the show for you and its expertise and promotion plans for the minimall will help draw tenants and ensure their success. In fact, a management firm may be able to get some retailers to sign leases and put up some money before you start renovating. That will lower your front-end cash needs. What's more, some retailers may even agree to pay extra for a custom design for their store. However, make sure that your architect retains control of the overall design. Otherwise, you'll wind up with an architectural jumble that will turn shoppers off.

Getting a good mix of tenants is crucial to the deal's survival.

Tenants. Getting a good mix of tenants is crucial to the deal's survival. Some, like opticians, dentists, and semiretired professionals who want smaller spaces (as little as 500 to 750 square feet), help build steady traffic. Others, like arts and crafts boutiques, help establish a unique atmosphere that will attract people to the stores. It also pays to lure in some established businesses that are expanding. Since they have a sound track record, they'll be stable tenants that you can count on to pay their rent on time, says Richard Goodwin of Arlen Realty, nationwide retail development specialists.

Generally, you can figure on charging 25 to 30% more for rents than what you could get from a single tenant. Still you'd be wise to write escalator clauses in your subleases so that you can quickly recover any increases in your maintenance and service costs. If you can't get retailers to agree to escalator clauses, write the leases for a short period of time—say, one or two years. That way you'll have the option of raising rents to cover your increased costs.

Here's how the numbers on a typical minimall project work out (see the chart at left). The deal involves a building with close to 21,000 square feet of usable space inside and parking for 11 stores. The conversion, which cost $75,000, was financed with a 10-year loan at 10.5% interest. Operating costs include maintenance, insurance, outdoor lighting, security, and management fees. To play it on the safe side, we're assuming a vacancy rate of 5%.

Not at all bad, when you consider that not one red cent of your own money is tied up in the deal. Even if you figure that the $75,000 loan represents an equity position in the deal, your cash flow return comes to 15.5%. Now for the kicker, most of these deals have an *overage*—which means that the tenants will pay you a set percentage of sales in excess of an agreed-upon minimum—and that could raise your return considerably.

C MINIMALL TENANT MIX

Choosing the right tenants as well as the right mix can make or break your investment in a minimall. The reason is simple. If the merchants who rent stores from you are successful, you can charge higher rents and enjoy greater financial stability. Too often, however, investors are so desperate to get the place rented up that they'll take in anyone and wind up with a mishmash of tenants who don't help boost each other's sales. In successful minimalls, customers shop in several stores during one visit. Here's how to find the right tenants:

You'd be wise to find out what kind of shoppers can be expected to frequent the location you have in mind. For instance, if you're going to be in the middle of a residential neighborhood the merchants who lease from you will probably need a lot of repeat business, and you should think about a mix of stores that will draw in neighborhood

---

Here's how the numbers on a typical minimall project work out:

Rental revenues	$120,258
Less operating expenses	46,500
Net operating income	73,758
Less lease payment	50,000
	23,758
Less debt service	12,143
CASH FLOW	$ 11,615

In successful minimalls, customers shop in several stores during one visit.

shoppers again and again. Many pros think that a drugstore, a women's boutique or two, a bakery, a gourmet food shop, a liquor shop, shoe stores, and perhaps a hardware store would make a good mix for a neighborhood minimall. If, on the other hand, you figure that tourists will be your mall's major customers, you should consider stores that cater to them—with, say, arts and crafts shops and small, quaint restaurants.

Once you've looked into the market for your location, you're ready to start looking for tenants.

Once you've looked into the market for your location, you're ready to start looking for tenants. You can probably find prospective tenants just by announcing your plans with a press conference or by sending out circulars to merchants in the area. Emphasize the diversification of tenants you're aiming at and spell out the advantages they'll have in a mall—such as greater customer traffic and higher impact advertising. Chances are that your interviews of shoppers in the area will also turn up some neighborhood entrepreneurs who might be interested in renting a store from you, says Douglas M. Kleine of Community Management Corp., Reston, Virginia.

A leasing pro can help you evaluate prospective tenants' probable sales volume.

You should consider hiring a leasing specialist, says Irving Price of Hudson Michael Realty, Hudson, New York. (The real estate brokerage firms in your area will probably have someone who specializes in shopping center leasing.) A leasing pro can help you evaluate prospective tenants' probable sales volume and their expertise in retailing. If you're planning to lease a larger space, say 50,000 square feet and up, an expert in leasing can probably find a large, established store that is thinking of expanding into other locations with a smaller store, say, of 30,000 square feet. That strong a store should give you a bigger draw. However, as good as a leasing pro may be, most mall developers strongly recommend that you spend time interviewing all prospective retailers before signing the leases. After all, you're the one who will have to live with them.

Ideally, the first tenants you sign up should be merchants who can be expected to attract a large number of people. Your best bet is to give them more space—preferably in the center of the mall. That will create a traffic pattern that will benefit the other shops, says Elliot Ravech of Peter Elliot & Co., Dedham, Massachusetts. Also try to sign up a restaurant as soon as possible. Mall developers say that neglecting restaurants at the beginning is one of the most common and most serious mistakes investors make.

Since you won't be able to divide the rest of the mall's space until you know what these tenants need, you should resist the temptation to sign up the first merchants who come through the door. Eager beavers like that are probably just starting out with an arts and crafts shop. While they add spice to a mall, they're not the meat and potatoes you're going after at the start.

The established merchants who will act as the nucleus of your shopping center are more likely to succeed and will give you some stability. However, take nothing on faith. Visit the stores they already have and check them out for such things as a good sense of display, adequate inventories, and aggressive market strategies. Also, confirm your hunches. Find out what kind of track record they have had with their previous operations and run a credit check on the store and the retailer. Finally, get some character references.

Take nothing on faith.

Get some character references.

With any prospective tenants that are first-timers, find out how much they know about the business they're planning to go into. With people starting up an arts or craft boutique you should evaluate what they want to produce—say, leather goods or pottery—how big a stock they can manage to make, how long they're willing to work each week, and if other family members will help out. Also, check how they've figured out the capital they'll need, where they expect to get supplies, what their inventory requirements are, what their personal credit rating is, and what their bank thinks of them. Most important, you should make sure they can afford to fix up their stores, stock them, and be able to hang on for at least six months before making a living. If you lease a few stores to professionals, you'll need credit and character references from them.

S OLDIES BUT GOODIES

Savvy investors, especially the Europeans who are crowding into the U.S. real estate market, are scrounging around for sound older buildings. What strikes most people as odd is that these investors are going after buildings that don't necessarily throw off much of an annual return. But there is a method to their madness. The investors are willing to give up some up-front return on their investment because they think they'll eventually make a killing. Here's how they're playing it:

They're going after buildings that will give them a current return of as little as 6 to 8% because these properties can be picked up quite cheaply. Chances are, they'd sell for some 40% or so less than what a new building would fetch. That's because most U.S. real estate is sold at a price that's based on the annual income generated by the property. How well the building might do in the future or how much it might cost to replace it is seldom, if ever, taken into consideration. And that's the point. The pros think older buildings in good or improving locations have a rosy future.

Capitalize on some favorable long-term trends.

Investors who put their money into cheap older buildings can capitalize on some favorable long-term trends, says John White, president of Landauer Associates in New York City. As he sees it, demand for older buildings will soon start to rise. As a result, owners of older buildings will be able to charge steadily higher rents (to boost their return on investment) and are in line for a handsome gain.

Owners of older buildings will benefit.

According to White, owners of older buildings will benefit as the cost of new construction continues to rise and a building shortage develops. As the cost of construction rises, it will boost the replacement cost—and hence the value of existing buildings. Behind the rise in construction costs, of course, are steadily rising labor, material, and mortgage costs.

White thinks that construction loans and mortgages will be more costly as bankers and other financial institutions tighten up their lending requirements. The banks, he notes, are still reacting to the losses they incurred as a result of their easy money policies. By contrast, a mortgage on an existing building is usually cheaper than what a developer would have to pay because it's usually a safer bet for a banker. Finally, White thinks that it will take longer to develop new projects because of environmental restrictions. That will slow the pace of new construction and raise the carrying cost of new projects considerably.

Older buildings tend to rent up faster than new buildings.

The pros suggest that you look for the kind of real estate where new buildings have an excessive vacancy rate. (With normal demand, office space should have no more than a 7 to 8% vacancy rate, shopping centers should have no more than 5% of their small stores empty, and residential property should have no more than a 4 to 5% vacancy rate, says Landauer's White.) Older buildings tend to rent up faster than new buildings because their rents are generally lower. As vacancy rates fall, the older buildings will become fully rented and you can raise the amount you charge tenants. Finally, you'll know an area is ripe for an investment in older buildings if new buildings aren't doing very well because of resistance to high rents. Reason: Developers will not put up more new ones if they can't expect to make a reasonable rate of return. The old days of building just because a developer had the money are over.

Any older building you look at should be competitive with new ones.

Make sure that you can install conveniences.

Any older building you look at should be competitive with new ones, says White. They'll show the most dramatic increases in income and appreciation. Your best bet is a building that's about five to ten years old—since it will already have most modern improvements. Even older buildings are a good bet as long as the total cost of buying and renovating the building to make it competitive is lower than what it would cost to put up a new one. In fact, much older buildings, with larger rooms decorated with moldings, wood paneling, and artistic effects, offer the greatest potential appreciation. People are becoming so tired of the sterility of new buildings that they'll pay extra for the charms of an older building—which now costs too much to replace.

Make sure any building you look at is (1) energy efficient—since fuel bills will continue to rise; (2) easy to secure—an increasingly important consideration in these days of rising crime; a garden apartment complex with one gateway is obviously better than six scattered entrances that have to be manned; (3) safe—features such as sprinklers, elevator controls, and any other legally required safety devices should be easy to install if the building doesn't already have them; (4) low in maintenance requirements—because labor costs are rising rapidly; a building in which you can easily install an automated monitoring system for elevators, heating, and so on will help reduce labor costs.

With a much older building, make sure that you can install fairly easily and cheaply conveniences such as elevators, air conditioning, new plumbing, and adequate wiring for modern appliances and lighting. You should be able to group such systems in a central core. It's the most efficient way to do it. Buildings with a central courtyard are not only more costly to heat but also hard to operate efficiently because the mechanical systems (heating, lighting, plumbing, and so on) are spread out. You must also have enough space—25 to 40 feet from the outer walls to central core—to divide it up into, say, rentable office space.

AN APARTMENT STRATEGY

Investments in apartment buildings—especially existing ones—are looking better every day, say the real estate pros. (New projects are still a little too expensive to make it.) In most areas, vacancy rates are falling because of the rising demand for apartments. Chances are this trend will pick up steam—very few

Very few apartments are being built.

new apartments are being built and most new single-family homes have been priced out of reach of the average family.

What it all means is that investors about to buy an apartment building, as well as those who already own one, will soon be able to boost their income from the deal by raising the rents they charge. But, as with anything else, there are right ways and wrong ways to go about raising your tenants' rents. Here are some tips:

Check the market for apartments in your area.

Since the supply and demand situation for real estate varies from place to place, you'll be wise to check the market for apartments in your area. Focus on the rental levels of buildings comparable with yours in quality and rents charged. That will give you a good handle on what the market is. If vacancy rates are high, you won't be able to raise rents by much, at least for the present. There's too great a risk that your tenants will move out for cheaper digs.

If vacancy rates in your area aren't very high, you can test the actual market for your available apartments by raising the first set of leases, say, 10%. If you don't run into any trouble, you can try raising the next set of leases by 15%, says Norbert Wall, president of Larry Smith & Co., Northfield, Illinois. If all goes well, Wall says, you can safely continue raising rents on renewed leases. But don't go overboard. A huge increase in rents will give your tenants more than enough incentive to move out, says Robert Wilson, an apartment investor in Tulsa, Oklahoma.

Find out what your present return on investment is.

When you raise rents, base the increases on the kind of return on investment you'd like to get. That's what the pros do. Find out what your present return on investment is. If it falls short of what you'd like, you can compare your current rental income with the present value of your building (replacement cost less depreciation), says Wilson. As a rule of thumb, he raises his rents if the net operating income is less than 10% of the building's current value.

There are, by the way, two ways of figuring your return on investment. A *cash flow return* (the actual cash generated by the deal each year) is found by dividing the cash flow by the amount of equity you have invested. A *free and clear return* is found by dividing the deal's net operating income by the purchase price you paid.

In some cases, you'll be wise to raise your rents even if you are already getting a good return on investment. For example, if you have an older building with a relatively low-interest mortgage on it, you may find you're getting 10% on your equity. That's a good return, but you may not be able to sell the building for the kind of price you'd like to get, says Wall of Larry Smith & Co.

Recast your return-on-investment calculations.

Reason: Your present rent roll may not be high enough to cover the annual debt burden of a new mortgage that has an interest rate of 9 or 10%. And even if the rental revenue does cover the mortgage, there may not be much left for profit. That means a prospective buyer will offer you less for the property because of the time and trouble it will take to raise the rents. In some cases, the buyer may not even be able to get a new mortgage because the bank will worry about getting its money back.

Hence, you'll be wise to get your accountant to refigure the building's finances as though it had just been refinanced at a high rate of interest. By using that information to recast your return-on-investment calculations, you can get a good fix on how much you should raise rents. You'll get an even higher return on investment, the building can be sold more profitably, and you'll be in a better position to refinance your mortgage if you need to.

In some cases, you may be able to raise your return on investment without having to raise rents. For example, if utilities are now free to tenants, get them to pick up gas and electric bills for their own apartments. With electricity costs expected to keep on increasing rapidly, that will mean a tremendous saving for you in the future, says Wilson. And chances are that your tenants would rather pay their own utility bills than have you raise their rents. Another way to pass along the items that increase most rapidly, such as property taxes, utilities and labor, is to try writing the new leases with escalator clauses. That way you're not always playing catch-up. A few landlords are not only putting in escalator clauses but also adding an annual increase tied to the consumer price index.

Try writing the new leases with escalator clauses.

HOME, SWEET HOME

We'd be willing to lay you odds that few, if any, of your investments have appreciated in value as much as your house. The average price of a house has jumped some 17% in just the past two years—a trend that's likely to continue because precious little new housing has been built and a shortage is starting to develop. So why not start investing in houses or condominiums?

Some of the real estate pros we talk to think that well-chosen houses or condominiums could give you 20 to 30% return on your investment over the next few years. And while the income from the deal probably won't do more than cover your holding costs, you will benefit from all the tax shelter from depreciation, maintenance, real

Few, if any, of your investments have appreciated in value as much as your house.

estate taxes, interest, and so on. Here's how to find the right kind of deal:

Your first step is to figure out where the action is. Look for areas where people have started flowing in again, says Kenneth McElroy of RLS Real Estate Services Corp., New Orleans. This usually happens either in communities where jobs are good or in towns that lie along the "sunbelt" in the South or Southwest and hence benefit from an influx of retirees. The more demand there is, the sooner housing shortages will be felt—which will send up the prices on housing you buy.

Make sure that land prices in the localities you're looking at are either rising or already high. The combination of rising land prices and construction costs will mean that any buildings that are eventually put up will likely cost more than existing housing. And that will give your property a competitive edge—both in terms of rentals and resale values, says Sanford Goodkin, head of his own real estate research firm in Del Mar, California, and Miami, Florida.

Once you've found a good area, home in on houses or condos that are well built and in a good location in the community, says Goodkin. Well-built, comfortable houses or condos show the best appreciation, says Tom Hornaday of Coldwell Banker in Phoenix. And the better the location, the more desirable the housing is, says Goodkin.

Go for the kinds of houses or units in the greatest demand in your area, says Earle Rader, Jr., head of Rader and Associates in Miami. While this demand varies from area to area, single-family houses are generally your best bet because that's what most families really want. If you're interested in condominiums, the largest demand is usually for two-bedroom units that appeal to empty-nesters—people in their 40s and 50s whose children are grown. On the other hand, two-story townhouse condo units with yards are also growing in demand in areas where there are young families with children.

You'll want to pick housing that's at least a few years old, says Rader. Most of the bugs in older houses will either have been worked out or be readily apparent. Of course, if the developer has a good track record, chances are that any houses you buy that are built by him will be good. Condos in an older building with a track record in a stable or improving neighborhood will probably become more valuable, says Rader. What's more, it's easier to get a handle on maintenance costs with older buildings. Also, look for units in a smaller condominium development, says Irving Price of Hudson Michael Realty, Hudson, New York. They are less likely to have high labor costs and large maintenance increases.

You may well find that you can pick up a bargain from a developer

Home in on houses or condos that are well built and in a good location.

Pick housing that's at least a few years old.

Bargain down the price by 10 to 15% if you buy two or more houses or condo units at the same time.

Be very wary of luxury or recreational condominiums.

Now might be a very good time to buy.

or lender who's been stuck with the houses or condo units he's been holding. In fact, there's a good chance that you can bargain down the price by 10 to 15% if you buy two or more houses or condo units at the same time, says Price. Many units that have been held off the market are now coming up for a quick sale.

In general, you'll be wise to stay under $75,000; a good general figure for condos is around $50,000. If you're looking at an area filled with affluent retirees, look for condos selling for between $65,000 and $80,000. The pros advise that you aim at the lower end of the price range; that way you'll stand a better chance of covering your holding costs. What's more, the less you have to pay for each unit, the more units you can buy to diversify.

When you find a likely prospect, make sure you can carry the expenses (such as interest on your mortgage, taxes, and maintenance) while waiting to sell. You should find out if the rental market in the area is strong enough to cover all or most of the costs. You may well find that you operate at a small loss for a couple of years—it will probably amount to no more than 5 to 10% of your monthly expenses. If that's the case, make sure the tax breaks you get make the deal work out in your favor during your holding period, says McElroy of RLS Real Estate Services Corp.

A word of caution: Be very wary of luxury or recreational condominiums because demand for this type of housing fluctuates wildly—and there'll probably be less appreciation to take advantage of, says Phillip Nutzman of L.B. Nelson Corp. in Menlo Park, California. And unless you fancy living in a large cooperative apartment, you'll be wise to ignore co-ops as an investment. Most co-ops are located in large cities and are beset by rapid maintenance and tax increases. What's more, lenders are more reluctant to make favorable mortgages for co-op buyers. And until the office market in cities picks up, there won't be much of a market for co-ops. However, if you want to live in one, now might be a very good time to buy, says Price of Hudson Michael Realty.

L OH, WOODEN IT BE LOVERLY

Leave it to the pros. They've nailed down another investment possibility that would excite even the most bored investor—timber. The way they see it, demand for wood products will at least double by the turn of the century—and there won't be nearly enough corporate or government timberland to meet the demand. As a result, a long-term investment in timberland could give you as much as a 10% return, a good hedge against inflation, and some sweet tax breaks, says J. Chandler Peterson, a financial planner in Atlanta. (The deal can be set up so that the income produced by timber sales is taxed at capital-gains rates rather than as ordinary income. It's one of the few tax shelters to survive the Tax Reform Act of 1976.) What's more, Peterson says, it's a fairly easy resource to manage—especially since you can count on some free help from government foresters.

Demand for timber will continue to rise.

Demand for timber will continue to rise because its use in home building and paper will pick up as the economy gains strength. Over the longer term, demand is being boosted even higher by the development of new uses for wood, such as in insulation and home foundations. In some cases, wood products are again competitive with plastic—whose price has soared along with the cost of petroleum.

Timberland may be a hedge against inflation.

The pros figure that timberland may be a hedge against inflation in a number of ways. For one thing, the price of timber, as well as that of the land it grows on, will probably increase in value. For another, as the trees grow you'll have more timber to sell. And as the timber matures and goes from one grade of lumber to another your yield, both in timber and dollars, will increase significantly.

A timber investment in the South is your best bet, says Peterson. The pros favor the South and Southeast because timber grows faster there—which means the investment cycle (from planting to harvesting) is shorter. Tip: Pines have a much shorter growth cycle than hardwoods.

What's more, the South gives you a better shot at a nice capital gain on the land. Land values in the South are on the whole still lower than elsewhere. But since the South's economy will probably continue to grow faster than that of the rest of the country, land prices should rise rapidly as demand increases for farmland, recreational facilities, and residential and commercial developments.

Look for land that is still relatively cheap.

Look for land that is still relatively cheap, say around $100 an acre, says John Wilson, who owns timberland in Alabama. Incredible as it may seem, many owners of timberland undervalue their property because they aren't aware of the value of the trees. So you may find that the timber will bring in enough to pay for the land itself. For example, assume that a land owner wants to sell the land for $300 an acre, and that the trees on it are worth $250 an acre. If you buy the land, then sell the trees, you'll in effect be picking up the property for around $50 an acre.

The land should have good access to paved roads and be within the harvesting range of a lumber mill—usually 50 to 100 miles. While most pros think you need at least 500 acres of timberland, smaller properties can sometimes be run productively. Moreover, units of land of less than 500 acres are eligible for a government program that will help you increase your timber yield. In fact, in many areas, the federal government will pay between 50 and 75% (up to $10,000 a year) of the cost of replanting or improving your timber.

Get a consulting forester to look at any timberland you're interested in buying.

You should in any case get a consulting forester to look at any timberland you're interested in buying. The advice, which costs only about $1 an acre, is well worth it. A forester can tell you the per acre value of the timber; how to harvest it; how to prevent damage from fire, insects, and disease; and if there are likely to be any other kind of problems. The Association of Consulting Foresters, Box 6, Wake, Virginia 23176, will help you find a professional forester.

Even if the trees aren't ready to be harvested there are a number of ways to get some income from your property while you're waiting to sell the timber. For instance, you can tap pines for turpentine or selectively cut mature trees. The increase in demand, along with reduced supply as timberland is lost to other uses, may make selective cutting, rather than one-shot clear-cutting, economically preferable. Alternatively, you could lease hunting or fishing rights or set up a small campground. (Make sure, however, that you lease to people who will respect the value of your trees.)

You can lease the timber to a wood products company.

If you don't want to be bothered with the actual timber operation and forestry management, you can lease the timber to a wood products company—which will handle all the details. The lease payments will give you a secure income. At the end of the lease, usually after about 10 years, you get the land back. Leasing the timber may be your best bet if you basically want the land for your retirement or as a vacation retreat. The income you get will hold down your carrying costs, while selective cutting will improve the land.

The worksheets that follow are a handy way of determining whether a prospective real estate venture will generate the kind of income and tax shelter you're looking for—at least on paper. We cannot overemphasize the fact that you will be working with numbers supplied by a real estate developer or broker. How close these numbers may be to actuality should never be taken for granted. As long-time readers of McGraw-Hill's Personal Finance Letter (formerly The Business Week Letter) know, we believe in examining the assumptions behind the numbers. Take nothing at face value.

INVESTMENT CRITERIA CHECKLIST

Here is a handy checklist to help you focus on the kind of real estate you'd like to invest in. Complete the following by placing a check next to the items which are of interest to you and by filling in the blanks as shown.

1. Existing properties primarily ☐
    Proposed properties primarily ☐
    Existing and proposed properties ☐

2. Income cash flow oriented primarily ☐
    Tax shelter oriented primarily ☐
    Income and tax shelter oriented ☐
    Will consider federally assisted apartment projects ☐

3. Garden apartments ☐
    High-rise apartments ☐
    Apartments insured by FHA (nonsubsidized) ☐
    Office buildings ☐
    Shopping centers/malls ☐
    Warehouses ☐
    Hotels/motels ☐
    Other: _____
    _____

4. Net lease properties ☐
    Land: sale-leaseback ☐
    Buildings: sale-leaseback ☐

5. Desire local management agent for property ☐
    Desire to manage property directly ☐
    Flexible on management, depending on deal ☐

6. Minimum percentage equity
   interest acceptable to purchase: _____ %

7. Geographic location restrictions,
   requirements, and preferences: _____

   _____

   _____

8. Prefer acceptable permanent financing to be in place ☐
   Can arrange for permanent financing ☐
   Prefer properties free and clear of financing ☐

9. Will consider work-out distress properties ☐
   Will consider properties only at current full occupancy ☐
   Will consider properties currently operating
   at less than maximum potential ☐
   Will consider properties needing partial or
   substantial rehabilitation ☐
   Flexible on current performance and physical
   condition of property ☐

10. Minimum cash down: $ _____ or _____ %
    of purchase price

    Maximum cash down: $ _____ or _____ %
    of purchase price

11. Minimum acceptable cash flow return on invested equity:

    Apartments _____ %   Commercial buildings _____ %

    Hotels/motels _____ %   Triple net
                            leased properties _____ %

12. Minimum acceptable discounted rate of return (after tax)

    _____ %

13. Other comments or criteria: _____

    _____

CASH FLOW PROJECTION

1. PURCHASE PRICE

   Land allocation $ _____

   Building allocation   _____

   Other allocations   _____

   TOTAL PURCHASE PRICE   _____

   Mortgage loan amount   _____

   Cash equity   _____

2. MORTGAGE TERMS

   Length of loan term   _____ *years*

   Interest rate   _____ %

   Annual payments
   (Principal and Interest)   _____

3. DEPRECIATION

   Estimated economic
   life (building)   _____ *years*

   Estimated economic
   life (others)   _____ *years*

   Depreciation method
   (building)[a]   _____

   Depreciation method (others)[a]   _____

   Is purchaser "first user"?   _____

4. STABILIZED NET
   OPERATING INCOME[b] $ _____

5. PURCHASER'S INCOME
   TAX BRACKET

   (Inclusive of this property)   _____ %

[a]Straight line or accelerated.
[b]From line 18 of the Property Analysis Worksheet that's on page 60.

PROPERTY ANALYSIS WORKSHEET

PURPOSE: _____ DATE: _____   LIST PRICE: $ _____   MARKET VALUE: $ _____

NAME: _____   LOANS: $ _____   LOANS: $ _____

LOCATION: _____   LIST PRICE: MARKET VALUE:

TYPE OF PROPERTY: _____   EQUITY: $ _____   EQUITY: $ _____

_____   EXISTING FINANCING: Annual Payment   Interest

ASSESSED VALUE:

			1st	$ _____	$ _____ _____ %
Land:	$ _____	_____ %	2nd	$ _____	$ _____ _____ %
Improvement	$ _____	_____ %	3rd	$ _____	$ _____ _____ %
Personal Property	$ _____	_____ %	POTENTIAL:		
TOTAL	$ _____	100 %	1st	$ _____	_____ %
ADJUSTED COST BASIS AS OF _____	$ _____		2nd	$ _____	_____ %

	% of gross income			Comments
1. SCHEDULED GROSS INCOME	_____ %		$ _____	_____
2. LESS: *Vacancy and credit losses*	_____		_____	_____
3. GROSS OPERATING INCOME	_____		_____	_____
4. LESS: *Operating expenses*	_____			_____
5. *Taxes*	_____	$ _____		_____
6. *Insurance*	_____	_____		_____
7. *Utilities*	_____	_____		_____
8. *Licenses, permits, advertising*	_____	_____		_____
9. *Management*	_____	_____		_____
10. *Payroll, including payroll taxes*	_____	_____		_____
11. *Supplies*	_____	_____		_____
12. *Services*	_____	_____		_____
13. *Maintenance*	_____	_____		_____
14. *Other (Miscellaneous)*	_____	_____		_____
15. *Lawn care and snow removal*	_____	_____		_____
16. *Accounting*	_____	_____		_____
17. TOTAL EXPENSES	_____	_____		_____
18. NET OPERATING INCOME:		$ _____		

ESTIMATE OF MARKET VALUE

19. INCOME APPROACH: *estimate of market value* _____ % $ _____

20. *Cost Approach:*

21. _____ *sq.ft. @ $* _____ *per sq.ft.* = $ _____

22. _____ *sq.ft. @ $* _____ *per sq.ft.* = $ _____

23. _____ *sq.ft. @ $* _____ *per sq.ft.* = $ _____ $ _____

24. LESS: *Estimate of accumulated depreciation* _____ %   _____

25. *Depreciated value of improvements*   _____

26. PLUS: *Site improvements*   _____

27. PLUS: *Land* _____ *sq.ft. @ $* _____ *per sq.ft.*   _____

28. ESTIMATE OF MARKET VALUE BY COST APPROACH   _____

29. MARKET DATA APPROACH _____ @ $ _____   _____

30. FINAL ESTIMATE OF MARKET VALUE *(correlated)* $ _____

INCOME ADJUSTED TO FINANCING

31. NET OPERATING INCOME (line 18) $ _____

32. LESS: *Loan payments*   *3rd loan*   *2nd loan*   *1st loan*   *total*

33.   Interest   _____ _____ _____ _____

34.   *Principal*   _____ _____ _____ _____

35.   *Total loan payment* _____ _____ _____ _____   _____

36. GROSS SPENDABLE INCOME   Rate: _____ % (line 36 MV equity)   _____

37. PLUS: *Principal payment* Rate: _____ % (line 38 MV equity)   _____

38. GROSS EQUITY INCOME   _____

39. LESS: *Depreciation* $ _____ *Personal property* $ _____ *Improvements* $ _____   _____

40. REAL ESTATE TAXABLE INCOME $ _____

PROPERTY ANALYSIS WORKSHEET

PURPOSE: *Joint Venture* DATE: *1/10/77*
NAME: *Paradise Apartments*
LOCATION: *Urbana, Illinois*
TYPE OF PROPERTY: *216 Unit Complex, New Construction*

ASSESSED VALUE:

Land: 20.88 Acres	$ *61,810*	*7.28* %	
Improvement	$ *786,880*	*92.72* %	
Personal Property	$	%	
TOTAL	$ *848,690*	100 %	

ADJUSTED COST BASIS AS OF _____ $ _____

LIST PRICE: $ *4,500,000*   MARKET VALUE: $ *4,500,000*
LOANS: $ *3,000,000*   LOANS: $ *3,000,000*
LIST PRICE: MARKET VALUE:
EQUITY: $ *1,500,000*   EQUITY: $ *1,500,000*

EXISTING FINANCING: Annual Payment   Interest
1st	$ *3,000,000*	$ *290,100*	*8-½* %
2nd	$	$	%
3rd	$	$	%

POTENTIAL:
1st	$		%
2nd	$		%

		% of gross income[a]		Comments
1.	SCHEDULED GROSS INCOME	100.0 %	$ *574,080*	Includes $24,000 Laundry Income
2.	LESS: *Vacancy and credit losses*	5.0	*28,704*	
3.	GROSS OPERATING INCOME	95.0	*545,376*	
4.	LESS: *Operating expenses*			
5.	Taxes	7.17	$ *41,142*	LOW TAX RATE VERIFIED
6.	Insurance	1.25	*7,200*	
7.	Utilities	4.04	*23,200*	
8.	Licenses, permits, advertising	3.05	*17,520*	
9.	Management	5.00	*28,704*	Includes mgmt. incentive
10.	Payroll, including payroll taxes	3.60	*20,688*	
11.	Supplies	1.40	*8,052*	
12.	Services	.21	*1,200*	
13.	Maintenance	2.49	*14,280*	No reserve for appliance replacement
14.	Other (Miscellaneous)	1.19	*6,840*	
15.	Lawn care and snow removal	.87	*4,968*	
16.	Accounting	1.00	*5,741*	
17.	TOTAL EXPENSES	31.27	*179,535*	
18.	NET OPERATING INCOME:		$ *365,841*	

ESTIMATE OF MARKET VALUE

19.   INCOME APPROACH: *estimate of market value* __8.0__ % $ *4,573,000*

20.   *Cost Approach:*

21.   *201,928* sq. ft. @ $ *21.25* __ per sq. ft. = $ *4,290,970*

22.   _____ sq. ft. @ $ _____ per sq. ft. = $ _____

23.   _____ sq. ft. @ $ _____ per sq. ft. = $ _____ $ *4,290,970*

24.   LESS: *Estimate of accumulated depreciation* _____ %   _____

25.   *Depreciated value of improvements*   _____

26.   PLUS: *Site improvements*   _____

27.   PLUS: *Land* *909,533* sq. ft. @ $ *0.25* per sq. ft.   *227,383*

28.   ESTIMATE OF MARKET VALUE BY COST APPROACH   *4,518,353*

29.   MARKET DATA APPROACH *216 UNITS* @ $ *20,800*   *4,492,800*

30.   FINAL ESTIMATE OF MARKET VALUE *(correlated)*[b] $ *4,492,800*

INCOME ADJUSTED TO FINANCING

31.   NET OPERATING INCOME (line 18) $ *365,841*

32. LESS: *Loan payments*	*3rd loan*	*2nd loan*	*1st loan*	*total*	
33. Interest	_____	_____	*253,600*	_____	
34. *Principal*	_____	_____	*36,500*	_____	
35. *Total loan payment*	_____	_____	*290,100*	_____	*290,100*

36.   GROSS SPENDABLE INCOME   Rate: _____ % (line 36 MV equity)   *75,741*

37.   PLUS: *Principal payment*   Rate: _____ % (line 38 MV equity)   *36,500*

38.   GROSS EQUITY INCOME   *112,241*

39.   LESS: *Depreciation* $ _____ *Personal property* $ _____ *Improvements* $ _____   *351,300*

40.   REAL ESTATE TAXABLE INCOME $ *⟨239,059⟩*

[a]Note that percentages have been rounded off.

[b]Use your judgment as to which approach most accurately reflects the value of the property. In this case it's the Market Data Approach.

Worksheets courtesy of Norbert Wall, president of Larry Smith & Co., Northfield, Illinois.

4. TAX PLANNING

A TAX PLANNING
GUIDE FOR 1977

HOW TO GET THE
MOST FROM
DEDUCTIONS

BASIC INCOME
SHIFTING TACTICS

STRATEGIES FOR
INVESTORS

HOW TO SHIFT
INCOME FOR
RETIREMENT

A DEFENSIVE GUIDE
TO AUDITS

TAX TABLES

Planning pays—especially when it comes to business entertainment and travel deductions. Play within the rules and you can come home with a good time and a fat, legitimate deduction.

Generally, you can deduct the cost of entertainment that is related to the conduct of your business. (Entertaining for the sake of goodwill is not deductible.) Sounds simple enough, except that the Internal Revenue Service (IRS) can get awfully sticky about the details involved in the entertainment.

Entertainment with a direct business benefit is the easiest to deduct. For example, there's absolutely no problem with deducting the cost of having a business meal—say, dinner with a client or business associate at your home or a quiet restaurant. You can even deduct the cost of wining and dining your client's spouse and anyone involved in the business discussion.

Deducting the cost of an "indirectly related" entertainment—say, a night at the theatre or a luau—is trickier to pull off. It's deductible only if the fun and games immediately precede or follow a substantial business meeting. While fun is fun, don't go overboard. The IRS won't go along with a deduction for an entertainment that's too lavish.

Be careful about inviting friends along. According to the IRS, friends are a distraction that could destroy an atmosphere conducive to business. However, there are some quirks in the tax code. For example, while inviting some of your friends to a business dinner you're hosting can put the kibosh on the entire deduction, friends of your business associate are deductible if there's no way of avoiding them. Hence, if you're at a restaurant and a friend of your associate pops by for a drink and sticks you with the tab, it's deductible. You can even bring friends of yours to a bash after a business meeting—without fear of losing the deduction. But, unfortunately, you cannot deduct the cost of entertaining your friends.

Expect the IRS to give you the business if you deduct the cost of your country club dues, upkeep on your yacht or some other type of entertainment facility. You can deduct part of the costs of running a yacht or lodge only if you can prove that you used the facility for business more than 50% of the time. For instance, if 60% of your use of a yacht was to entertain clients, you could deduct 60% of your operating expenses and 60% of the depreciation. You may even be able to get an investment tax credit to boot. However, if you use the

Keep accurate records.

Prove the business purpose of your expenditures.

The rules on foreign travel are a little tougher.

facility for business purposes less than 50% of the time, you can only deduct your out-of-pocket expenses such as meals.

You can lose all your deductions if you don't keep an accurate record of the purpose of the meeting, what you spent, when and where it was spent, and the names and business affiliations of your guests. Your best bet is to jot down this information immediately after the meeting takes place. Silly as it sounds, many business persons fail to keep a simple diary listing these details. For example, one banker who had 1,700 receipts was starved out of deducting any of his entertainment expenses because he didn't keep a diary.

You'd also be smart to keep records of any new clients or business you get from these engagements, says Joseph Lobel of Coopers & Lybrand. That will go a long way to prove the business purpose of your expenditures. Note that if the lunch or entertainment comes to more than $25, you'll also have to have a bill or receipt to show the IRS.

Records are especially important when it comes to deducting the cost of an entertainment facility. The IRS can be a real spoilsport about deducting the cost of, say, a yacht or hunting lodge. You'd be wise to have a log or guest book in which you can list all the details of the entertainment. It will come in handy if you're ever asked to prove that more than 50% of the use was business-related. If at all possible, also list the business benefits you win from the entertainment.

If you make a business trip within the United States, you can deduct all your travel and living costs—as long as they're not more extravagant than your normal life-style. You'll need receipts or bills for major items. Minor expenses can be recorded in a notebook and lumped together later. However, if you combine a business trip with a vacation, you'll have to prorate your living expenses between business and pleasure. (Your travel costs are deductible on the theory that you wouldn't have made the trip had it not been for the convention or business meeting.) And get this: If you're a delegate to a charitable convention or perform a service for it, you can deduct your unreimbursed expenses as a charitable contribution.

The rules on foreign travel are a little tougher. If less than 25% of your time traveling was in pursuit of personal pleasures, you can deduct all your costs. However, if more than 25% of your time overseas was filled with fun, the rules get tighter. For trips of a week or less, you can deduct all your travel costs but will have to prorate all your living costs. And for the trips of more than a week, you'll have to prorate all your costs. Note, however, that the domestic legs of your trip overseas are fully deductible.

The Tax Reform Act of 1976 has made it considerably tougher to get deductions.

Deductions for expenses while abroad will be limited to the government's per diem allowance.

Prevent sickly medical deductions.

If you're attending a convention held abroad, you'll find the Tax Reform Act of 1976 has made it considerably tougher to get deductions. It will be very tough to take these deductions unless your organization has a really compelling reason to go abroad. And even if the overseas convention is valid, you'll generally be able to deduct only the cost of coach or economy fare. You can only deduct the fare if you spend more than half the time you're abroad in business-related activities.

Moreover, deductions for expenses while abroad will be limited to the government's per diem allowance in that location, Two examples: In Paris, you could take up to $90 a day in expenses; in the Canary Islands, you'd be limited to $34 a day. Note also that the tax bill limits deductions for foreign conventions to two a year. Reporting requirements have also been considerably toughened.

Rx FOR HEALTHY MEDICAL DEDUCTIONS

The Internal Revenue Service's rules on medical deductions often give taxpayers a bad case of heartburn. (You can deduct only those medical and dental expenses that exceed 3% of your adjusted gross income; and only those pharmaceutical costs in excess of 1% of your adjusted gross can be considered medical expenses.) But where there's a rule, there's a way. Here's how to prevent sickly medical deductions:

Time regular visits to your doctor and dentist so that you bunch up two years' worth of expenses into a single year. For example, you could make appointments for your annual checkup in January and December of the same year. Or, since medical expenses are deductible only in the year they're paid, you can schedule your payments so that they fall in the same year—even if the actual visits occurred in two different years. Note, however, that you cannot normally deduct prepaid medical expenses.

Make sure you don't overlook anything that can be deducted as a medical expense. Generally you can deduct any expense incurred in the diagnosis, treatment, cure, or prevention of a disease or physical ailment. That covers more than you might imagine. There is practically no area of the tax code where the courts have been so liberal in upholding taxpayers' deductions, says Herb Paul, New York director of tax services at Touche Ross.

Deduct the cost of any special equipment your doctor prescribes.

You can deduct the cost of any special equipment your doctor prescribes for a specific ailment. For instance, crutches, oxygen supplies, prescription shoes, dental aids—even a clarinet and lessons for someone with an orthodontic problem. And, if your doctor prescribes a special diet to supplement your regular one, you can deduct its costs—whether the dietary supplement prescribed is vitamins or whiskey (for a heart condition, of course). However, you can't deduct the cost of special food or drink if it replaces your regular diet.

Get an appraiser to get you a before and after installation report.

You can deduct the cost of a capital improvement to your home if it's installed for medical reasons on your doctor's advice. If the improvement doesn't add to the value of the house—say, a window air conditioner—you can deduct the entire cost. If it does increase the value of the house—say, central air conditioning or an elevator—you can deduct only the cost in excess of the increase in value. Tip: Get an appraiser to get you a before-and-after installation report. You can deduct his cost since he's helping you establish the deduction. You can deduct the maintenance and operating expenses of running the improvement. However, if it's also used for personal reasons, only a portion of these costs is deductible.

Transportation to and from your doctor's office can be deducted as a medical expense. (You can take either 7¢ a mile plus tolls and parking fees or your actual out-of-pocket costs—excluding insurance and depreciation.) Generally you can also deduct round-trip transportation costs to get medical treatment in another city. You can even deduct the cost of meals and lodging en route. However, once you're there you can only deduct the cost of room and board if you stay in a hospital or some other type of medical facility.

The cost of special schooling or a nursing home is deductible.

The cost of special schooling or a nursing home is deductible if the primary care is medical in nature. For example, if the school or home is specially equipped and staffed to handle handicapped children, the full cost of tuition and care is deductible. If your dependents go to a school or home for reasons other than its medical facilities, you can deduct only medical expenses itemized in the school's bill. Note that you can get a current deduction if you prepay the medical costs of a nursing home that will guarantee to take care of a family member in the future.

The cost of hiring someone to take care of a sick family member is deductible.

The cost of hiring someone—trained or not—to take care of a sick family member is deductible. If, however, the employee also does household chores, you can only deduct that part of his or her salary allocable to medical care. When figuring out the costs involved, don't forget to include the cost of room and board you provide, as well as the social security taxes you pay.

You may be able to take a medical expense deduction for a dependent even if you can't claim him or her as a personal exemption. You can deduct any medical costs you pay for a dependent if you provide more than half of his or her support during the year. Hence, if you're recently divorced, you can deduct any medical expenses you incurred or paid for while you were still married. And if your child marries in, say, July and doesn't file a joint tax return with his or her new spouse, you can deduct medical bills you pay that year.

For dependents, have a formal multiple-support agreement.

You'll have to do some planning to get a medical deduction for a dependent if you and several relatives jointly support him or her. Since only one of you can claim him or her as a dependent you'd be wise to have a formal multiple-support agreement that spells out which one of you can claim the deduction. This can be done on a rotating basis from year to year.

You may find it pays to file a separate rather than a joint return.

Because of the 3 and 1% limitations, you may find it pays to file a separate rather than a joint return with your spouse. For example, assume both of you work but only one of you has a large medical bill. By filing separately the spouse that had the large medical bill will be able to get a far bigger medical deduction than you'd both get filing jointly. You'd be smart not to use a joint checking account to pay the medical bills. The IRS will claim that the bills were paid jointly—and you'd have to prove otherwise.

HOMELY DEDUCTIONS

The door has almost been closed on office-at-home deductions—at least, for most of us. Starting last year, you have to meet two tests to be able to deduct an office-at-home. (1) It must be your principal place of business, or the place where you normally meet or deal with patients, clients, or customers. (2) It must be used exclusively and regularly for business purposes. If you work for yourself, and meet these tests, there's no problem. If you work for someone else, the office-at-home must be maintained for the convenience of your employer.

The door has almost been closed on office-at-home deductions.

There are two exceptions to these requirements: (1) You can take an office-at-home deduction if you use a separate structure on your property "regularly and exclusively" as your place of business. (2) You can deduct office-at-home expenses if your home is the "sole, fixed location" of a product-oriented retail or wholesale business and a room is used for inventory storage. However, you can take no more in office-at-home deductions under any circumstances than you earn from your business activities at home.

If you're a part-time freelancer or consultant, you may be plumb out of luck. However, if you do consulting or freelance work at home for someone other than your employer, you would, in effect, have two principal places of business, according to some tax experts. As a result, you would be able to take an office-at-home deduction. However, you would be able to deduct no more than you made from your freelance or consulting business.

The risk of an audit may be worthwhile.

The risk of an audit may be worthwhile so long as you have nothing else to worry about on your return. The worst that can happen is that the deduction will be denied—which will leave you in the same position as before you claimed the deduction, says Herb Paul, New York director of tax services at Touche Ross.

If you qualify for the deduction, you can write off a proportional share of all your household operating expenses—including heating, electricity, gas, air conditioning, homeowner's insurance, cleaning, and maintenance. You can even deduct a portion of the depreciation on your home. Of course, the cost of anything in the room used exclusively for business purposes—such as furniture, file cabinets, typewriter, dictating equipment, and so on—can be depreciated.

Figure out how much you can deduct.

Here's how to figure out how much you can deduct: Compare the number of rooms, or the amount of space used as an office, against the total number of rooms or space in your house. For example, if you use one of, say, eight rooms in your house exclusively as an office, you can deduct 1/8th of the appropriate expenses.

If you own a vacation home, you can deduct only the mortgage interest and property taxes—unless you rent it out. If that's the case you may be able to deduct your maintenance and repair costs, as well as depreciation. However, you should be prepared to show the IRS that you've made a profit in two out of five years. If you meet that test, you'll also have to meet a new test under the Tax Reform Act of 1976. If you use your vacation home personally for more than 14 days or 10% of the rental time and rent to others for more than 15 days, simply allocate the expenses between your personal use and rental use.

Even if you don't make a profit, you may be able to get those deductions by showing that you run the property in a business-like manner and that you are making every effort to rent it profitably.

That means keeping books, advertising, and spending some time and effort on renting. Alternatively, you may be able to establish a profit motive by showing that the property is appreciating in value and will give you a good capital gain when you sell it.

Under the new tax law, you can take deductions only up to the amount of rental income you make. And the expenses have to be deducted in a set order: interest and property taxes first, maintenance next, and depreciation last.

The obvious solution is to stay at your own vacation home for no longer than 13 days. However, if you really can't bear the thought of giving up a long vacation, you can take advantage of a new break in the tax bill. If you rent your vacation home for less than 15 days, you can pocket the entire amount—without reporting it on your tax return. However, you also can't take any deductions for maintenance and depreciation during those two weeks.

Don't overlook a cent of tax deductions.

Don't overlook a cent of tax deductions: While everyone knows one can deduct interest charged on mortgage or home improvement loans, many people neglect to deduct points—fees some lenders charge when mortgage interest rates are held down by usury ceilings. Points are tax deductible if they constitute a mortgage fee.

Deduct any property taxes you pay.

You can also deduct any property taxes you pay—including the personal property taxes imposed by some states on home furnishings, cars, boats, and so on. You can even deduct local and state sales taxes, including that portion of your utility bill labeled taxes—as long as the tax rate on utility bills is the same as the general sales tax levy. However, you can't deduct sewer or water assessments.

THE MANY BENEFITS OF CHARITY

Charity begins at home.

Charity begins at home. Give well and you can reduce your income tax, lower your estate taxes and, in some cases, still get some income from the property you give away.

How much you can deduct depends on the nature of the gift and to whom it's given.

How much you can deduct depends on the nature of the gift and to whom it's given. If you give cash to a public charity recognized by the IRS you can deduct an amount equal to as much as 50% of your adjusted gross income for the year. With gifts of securities or real estate, you can deduct as much as 30% of your adjusted gross or 50% if you give up half the appreciation. Should the value of your contribution be more than the amount allowed for one year, you can carry the remainder over the next five years.

The cost of the appraisal for charitable contributions is also deductible.

If you give to a private foundation, you can deduct up to 20% of your adjusted gross—with no carryover. (If you're thinking of setting up a private foundation, you'll be wise to design it as a conduit that promptly distributes what you give it to public charities. That way you can get all the tax breaks available for gifts to a recognized public charity.) Gifts to charities that aren't recognized by the IRS cannot be deducted at all.

Qualified charities may be found in the IRS master list (Publication No. 78), which is probably available at your public library. If the charity is relatively new, ask your IRS district office what the charity's status is. Note that you'll be wise to get a professional appraisal of the value of art, of stock in a closely held corporation, or of anything else that might be complex—in case the IRS questions the amount you deduct. For hard-to-value property, see your lawyer and get two appraisals, says Conrad Teitell, a New York attorney. The cost of the appraisal, by the way, is also deductible. Here are some of the savviest ways to give to charity:

Fractional contributions of, say, art or your summer property will give you a fat tax deduction and reduce your estate's tax liability—even though you'll still be able to enjoy the use of the property for at least part of the year. (When you make a fractional contribution you give away absolute ownership of a portion of the asset—say, 50% of a Picasso.) With works of art, your deduction will be higher if it serves the main purpose of the institution to which you give it (say coins or a painting to a museum).

A fractional contribution could well give you the biggest possible deduction in the long run. Here's why: Let's say you expect to have an adjusted gross income of about $40,000 a year over the next six years and want to give a painting worth $100,000 to a charity. If you make an outright contribution of the painting, you'll be allowed to deduct 30% of your adjusted gross—or no more than $12,000 each year. Over six years, your deductions will add up to only $72,000—which means you'll lose out on $28,000 in deductions. However, giving only half the painting to the museum, you can fully deduct $50,000 as a charitable contribution over the six years. Later on, you can give the museum the rest of the painting. And if the painting increases in value before you give the rest of it away, you'll get an even bigger deduction. Who gets possession of the painting is subject to negotiation. Many museums want the painting for six months of the year if you've given them half of it. Others will let you keep it all year—providing the museum can take possession of the painting for special exhibits.

A *charitable remainder trust* is probably one of the best ways to give to charity. You'll get an immediate tax deduction when you fund the trust, your estate taxes will be reduced and you'll still get an income from the assets in the trust. Note that you'll have to pay income tax or capital gains tax, depending on how the trust's income is paid out.

The amount you can deduct is figured out in Treasury tables based on your age, the value of the property and the income you'll get. Generally, you can figure the longer your life expectancy, the lower the deduction. Note that if you include, say, your spouse as a second beneficiary of the trust's income, the deduction will be reduced and your estate may have to pay some estate taxes. If you name a second income beneficiary make sure your lawyer puts a clause in the trust agreement retaining the right by your will to revoke that person's interest, says Teitell. That way you can often avoid paying a gift tax, even if you never actually do revoke the beneficiary's interest.

When you die, the charitable remainder trust will be included in your estate. However, that won't increase your estate's tax liability because the trust will be deducted as a charitable contribution. In fact, having the trust included in your estate is actually an advantage because it raises the amount that can pass to your spouse tax free, says Norman Milefsky of Coopers & Lybrand. For example, if your estate (not counting the trust) comes to $500,000, your spouse can get half, or $250,000, tax free under the marital deduction. But if a trust worth, say, $50,000 is included in your estate, you could pass up to $275,000 to your spouse tax free.

A charity's pooled income fund will give you almost all the advantages that you'd get from a charitable remainder trust. (It's just not quite so flexible.) Instead of setting up a separate trust with the charity, you simply put your money into a pool that the charity maintains. The charity then distributes the income earned by the pool on a prorata basis to those who contributed. Any income received is taxed as ordinary income. Check with the charity to find out how well its pooled fund investments have been doing.

A SHIFT IN TIME SAVES MINE

If, after all your savvy tax maneuvers, you find yourself crying uncle because of the taxes you still have to pay, it may be time for you to consider some basic income-shifting tactics—

You'll still get an income from the assets in the trust.

A charity's pooled income fund will give you almost all the advantages that you'd get from a charitable remainder trust.

Consider some basic income-shifting tactics.

providing, of course, you can afford to give up some income. Shifting income to, say, a member of your family who's in a lower tax bracket will lower the tax load on you as well as your estate. Here's how you can lower your taxable income:

Trusts. You can temporarily or permanently shift income to members of your family by putting income-producing assets in a trust set up for them. The beneficiaries of the trust will then be liable for any taxes on the income they receive from it. Or if you don't want, say, a young child to receive the income right away, you can set it up so that the trust accumulates the income and pays taxes on it—probably at a very low rate. When the money is finally distributed, the beneficiary of the trust will have to make up the difference, if any, between the trust's tax rate and his own tax rate. Note that you'll wind up paying the income taxes if the trust's income provides support for your children. That's because you are legally obligated to support your minor children—and that may even include college educations in some states.

If you want to shift income only temporarily, set up a short-term trust.

If you want to shift income only temporarily, set up a short-term trust—which must last for at least 10 years and a day or for the life of the beneficiary. When the term of the trust ends, the income-producing assets in it become yours again. The beauty of a short-term trust is that you can time it so that you get the assets back when you retire and are in a lower tax bracket. If you die while the trust still exists, the assets will be taxed in your estate.

You may have to pay a gift tax.

When you fund a short-term trust, you may have to pay a gift tax that's based on Treasury table computations. However, the gift tax you pay will be lower than what it would have been if you had made an outright gift or set up an irrevocable trust. What's more, you can shelter part of your gift-tax liability by using your $3,000 annual gift-tax exclusion ($6,000 for joint gifts) if you're giving a present interest.

You can permanently shift income to a member of your family by setting up an irrevocable trust—which means that you permanently give up all rights to the assets in the trust. Because of that, the property will not be taxed in your estate. You can use your annual gift-tax exclusion to shelter yourself from the tax liability.

Partnerships and Subchapter S corporations. You can also shift income permanently to a member of your family by making him or her a partner or shareholder in one of your enterprises, even though he or she has no role in it. The beauty of using a partnership or a Sub

S corporation is that any profits and losses will pass directly to you and the other partners or shareholders without being taxed at the corporate level. You'd be wise to make the gift early in the enterprise's life when the shares have little value and are easy to shelter from tax.

Pay yourself a reasonable salary.

When you shift income through a family partnership or a Sub S corporation, you have to make sure that you pay yourself a reasonable salary. If your salary is too low, the IRS may come in and reallocate the profits between you and your partners or shareholders, says Herb Paul, New York director of tax services, Touche Ross. The result: You'll wind up with more income than you want to pay taxes on.

Cheating yourself out of some salary can hurt you in other ways too. Here's how: Let's say your business will throw off $100,000 in gross income this year. Assume further that you pay yourself $20,000 in salary, with the rest of the profits split between you and, say, your two children. So of the $80,000 left, you'll get $40,000 and each child $20,000. Your $40,000 in profits is taxed as unearned income—at a rate of up to 70%. If you pay yourself more in salary, more of your income will fall under the maximum 50% earned income rate.

Avoid the danger of losing a dependency exemption.

If you shift a substantial amount of income to minor children, you should make sure that the profits accrue for your children rather than having them paid out immediately. That way you won't get too much cash into your children's hands and you'll avoid the danger of losing a dependency exemption for them—which would happen if you contributed less than half their support. By having the income accrue instead of having it distributed, the value of your children's partnership share or corporation stock increases until the income eventually is paid out.

A private annuity. You can transfer appreciated property such as stocks, bonds, or even real estate to your children in return for a private annuity that would give you an income for life. Setting up a private annuity may save you a bundle on capital gains taxes—which you would have to pay all at once if you sold the property.

If you set up the annuity carefully you'll probably have to pay only a very low tax on the annual income you receive. Part of the income you get will be considered a tax-free return of capital (what you paid for the property), part is considered capital gains, and part is ordinary income. You only have to pay ordinary income taxes on what you receive when the capital gains portion of the payment has run out. And since you'll probably want a private annuity to start when

Watch out for two fairly common pitfalls that can ruin your tax planning.

Write up a contract with your children.

If you have a stock that looks like a hopeless loser, sell it before you've held it for nine months.

you retire, the odds are that your tax bracket will be a lot lower when you receive the money.

However, you should watch out for two fairly common pitfalls that can ruin your tax planning. (1) If your children's promise to pay is secured, you'll have to pay an immediate capital gains tax—just as you would if you had sold the property to a third party and (2) if the arrangement with your children is too tenuous, the IRS will claim that the transfer of the property was actually a gift and make you pay a gift tax on it. Since you'll probably have to transfer a fair amount of property to get a decent income from the annuity, you won't be able to shelter all of it with your gift-tax exclusion. Hence you'd be wise to write up a contract with your children to head off this possibility, says Paul.

Interest-free loan to a family member. You might consider lending money to your child or parent for investment. Any return on that investment would go into the tax bracket of the child or parent rather than into yours. Caution: Use of the money, which has a value, will be a gift from you to your relative. Your best bet is to come to a reasonable value for the money (say, a 6% interest rate) for gift-tax purposes. Even if you lent your relatives $50,000, you still wouldn't have to worry about a gift-tax liability. That's because 6% interest on $50,000 comes to $3,000 and you can easily shelter that by using your annual gift-tax exclusion. You can increase the amount you can lend tax free to a cool $100,000 if you and your spouse agree to make the gift jointly because your combined gift-tax exclusion comes to $6,000.

SOME TACTICS FOR INVESTORS

Good tax planning can boost the money you get to keep from market winners and take some of the sting out of any losers you've purchased. But whatever you do, don't let tax considerations interfere with your sense of the market.

If you have a stock that looks like a hopeless loser, sell it before you've held it for nine months (one year starting in 1978) so that you can claim it as a short-term loss. At least you'll get the best possible tax break from it. Short-term losses can be deducted dollar-for-dollar from your ordinary income up to a maximum of $2,000 ($1,000 if you're married and filing separately). In 1978, you'll be able to deduct up to $3,000. Long-term losses, while just as painful, give you only half the tax breaks of a short-term loss. It takes $2 of long-term losses to get $1 of tax deduction. Any short- or long-term losses that aren't used this year can be carried over into the future.

If you have any stocks that start to slump later in the year and you see no hope for them, dump them before mid-November if you can. That way, you'll avoid the year end tax-selling spree—which can knock the bottom right out of a slumping stock.

If at all possible, try to balance your long-term capital losses against your long-term gains and your short-term capital losses against your short-term gains. That way, you won't lose the tax benefits of your short-term losses. The way you have to figure it, is that long-term gains already give you a fantastic tax break. The first $50,000 of your long-term gains is taxed at only 25%. Long-term gains above $50,000 are subject to a tax of up to 35%—so why worry about them? Of course, half your gain will now be counted as a preference item which may be subject to the 15% minimum tax. It will also turn part of your earned income into unearned income. Short-term gains, however, are taxed as ordinary income. So using a short-term loss to cover a long-term gain is like wasting a valuable deduction.

Here's how the numbers might work out: Assume you have long-term gains of $8,000 and long-term losses of $4,000—leaving you with a net long-term gain of $4,000 for the year. Assume further that you have short-term gains of $5,000 and short term losses of $7,000—leaving you with a net short-term loss of $2,000. That short-term loss of $2,000 would then reduce your taxable long-term capital gain from $4,000 to $2,000.

Any capital-loss carry-forwards you have from previous years can reduce that further. For example, if you have $5,000 of unused short-term losses, you can wipe out your long-term gain completely, reduce your ordinary income by $1,000, and still have $2,000 of short-term losses to carry over. (Note that capital losses must first be applied against capital gains before they can be used to reduce your ordinary income.) On the other hand, a $5,000 carry-forward of long-term losses will also knock out your gain for this year and reduce your ordinary income by $1,000—but you'll only have $1,000 of long-term loss to carry over.

Capital losses must first be applied against capital gains.

The real rub, however, is a new minimum tax provision.

The real rub, however, is a new minimum tax provision—which took effect in 1976. In fact, if you're a big investor it may no longer pay you to keep holding on to a security just so that you can get the benefits of a long-term capital gains rate, says Herb Paul, New York director of tax services for Touche Ross. (The first $50,000 of long-term gains will still be taxed at no higher than 25%; long-term gains of more than $50,000 will be taxed at up to 35%. Anything held for less than nine months will be taxed as short-term capital gains.)

Some long-term capital gains may, in effect, be slammed with a tax rate as high as 49⅛%—when you take into account the capital gains tax (up to 35%), the new minimum tax (now 15% instead of 10%) and the effect of earned income being treated as unearned or ordinary income, says Joseph Lobel of Coopers & Lybrand. This will sharply reduce the advantage capital gains have over earned income, which is taxed at no more than 50%.

Here's how the minimum tax works: If your preference items exceed $10,000 or one-half the amount of taxes you pay (whichever is greater), you'll be hit with a minimum tax of 15%. In fact, a lot of people will probably face a minimum tax for the first time. Reason: The exemption used to be $30,000 plus all your regular taxes—which was usually more than enough to shield you from the minimum tax.

The list of preference items has been expanded.

Furthermore, the list of preference items has been expanded. Beyond the existing preference items (such as one-half of long-term capital gains, accelerated depreciation, percentage depletion in excess of your cost basis, and the bargain element in stock options), Congress has added some others. The new ones are itemized deductions (other than medical and casualty deductions) in excess of 60% of your adjusted gross income, intangible oil and gas drilling costs that are greater than what could be deducted if they were capitalized and written off over 10 years, and accelerated depreciation on all personal property subject to a lease. What's more, you're no longer allowed to carry over any unused regular taxes to help you in subsequent years.

Tax preference items will convert your earned income into ordinary income.

What's worse, tax preference items will convert your earned income into ordinary income—dollar for dollar. Hence, some of your earned income could be taxed at a rate of up to 70%.

SOME CAPITAL STRATEGIES

As with almost everything else, there's a catch to making a really big killing in the stock market. You can be murdered by taxes. For one thing, long-term capital gains of more than $50,000 are taxed at up to 35%. Only long-term gains of less than $50,000 are taxed at up to 25%.

For another, half your long-term capital gains are treated as preference items. Pile up enough tax preference items and you become liable for the new 15% minimum tax. What's worse, you stand the very real possibility of turning some earned income, which is taxed at up to 50%, into unearned income, which is taxed at up to 70%. And it's not at all hard to pile up a lot of tax preference items when you consider that accelerated depreciation, percentage depletion in excess of your cost basis, amortization of pollution control facilities, and the bargain element of stock options, are preference items. And catch this: Many states (including New York) are rougher on preference items than the IRS.

Tactics for winners. If you have faith in your stocks, you might consider selling up to $50,000 of them this year and the rest at the beginning of 1978. You might even consider using the seller's option rule to shift some of your capital gains into next year. Under this rule, you can sell a stock at today's price but defer delivery and recognition of the sale for as long as 60 days (30 days for odd-lot transactions). Make sure all the dividends up to the delivery date accrue to you. Note also that you may have to sell your stocks at a small discount to attract a buyer.

You may have to sell your stocks at a small discount to attract a buyer.

If you're not too sanguine about the outlook for stocks which would bring you huge long-term gains, consider selling them to a member of your family or a reliable friend on the installment plan. You'll lock in the current price of the stock and spread the capital gains tax over a number of years. You have to pay capital gains tax only on the amount you receive in the year you receive it. And there's no gift-tax liability to worry about.

Lock in the current price of the stock.

However, you have to make sure that you do this according to IRS rules. The IRS will put the kibosh on any prearranged deal where you sell some stocks to, say, your spouse, and he or she turns around and sells them immediately. (Such a resale would mean there would be no capital-gains tax to worry about because there would be no profit over your spouse's cost.)

Most tax specialists think the person who buys stocks from you on the installment basis should hang on to them for at least a year before selling. Even then, there's no guarantee the IRS won't challenge the deal. However, there are some possible exceptions. Your spouse may be able to sell the stocks without worrying about an IRS challenge if he or she does so for a good reason—say, to bail out of a bear market or to raise money for an emergency.

There's no guarantee the IRS won't challenge the deal.

If you're close to retirement you can sell your big winners in return for a private annuity.

As with any kind of installment sale, you cannot receive more than 30% of the total price in the first year. Moreover, since the sale is to a member of your family or a friend, you have to make sure that it's a bona fide deal. You should have a written sales agreement, charge a reasonable interest rate of 6% or so, and spell out the repayment schedule. Note that you can make the repayment schedule as flexible as you like. If you don't need the funds immediately, or if your wife is hard pressed for cash, you can agree to receive the first installment two or three years from now.

Alternatively, if you're close to retirement you can sell your big winners in return for a private annuity. The income you receive from the annuity, either for the rest of your life or for a fixed number of years, is computed on the basis of actuarial tables. The proceeds are taxed according to an IRS formula. Again, the person who buys the stocks from you cannot resell them for a year or so—unless there's a valid business reason for the sale. Whatever you do, don't set up an installment sale or private annuity without consulting your attorney. And since it's a tax matter, the fees are deductible.

Finally, you might consider simply giving the stocks to a member of your family. There's no problem with selling the stocks immediately; there's no capital-gains tax for you to worry about; and the stocks will be out of your estate—where they would be hit by estate taxes.

What's more, you can use your annual $3,000 gift-tax exclusion ($6,000 if you give jointly with your spouse) to shield all or most of the gift-tax liability. Note that it doesn't make sense to give appreciated property to your spouse. If your spouse sells the stocks immediately, you'll still face the capital gains on your joint tax return.

SOME GOLDEN RETIREMENT TACTICS

It's absolutely amazing to us how people don't take full advantage of the various kinds of retirement plans around. All these plans let you shift income from your current high tax bracket to your retirement years, when you'll probably be in a lower tax bracket. What's more, some plans give you a significant tax break when the money is finally paid to you. Here's how to pick the right kind of plan for your needs:

You can make additional voluntary payments to your plan.

Your contributions to an IRA reduce your gross income before taxes.

If you're self-employed or earn extra income as a consultant or a director, a Keogh retirement plan may be your best bet. There is one big drawback with a Keogh, however. If you have employees, those with more than three years service must be included in the plan. You can pay in up to $7,500 or 15% of your annual earned income (whichever is less) to the plan. You can deduct any payments to the plan from your gross adjusted income on your tax return. Moreover, the income earned by assets in a Keogh plan are tax free until the plan's proceeds are paid out when you retire. Even then, you can use a special 10-year forward-averaging formula to reduce this tax bite sharply.

You can make additional, voluntary payments to your plan of up to $2,500 or 10% of your annual earned income (whichever is less). While those voluntary payments are not tax deductible, any earnings on them accumulate tax free. Moreover, you can withdraw your voluntary payment at any time without a penalty or tax liability. If you put in too much money, the Internal Revenue Service may penalize you with a fine or by taking away your right to be in a retirement plan for five years.

If you have a Subchapter S corporation, you can set up a Sub S retirement plan—into which you can contribute up to $7,500 or 15% of your earned income (whichever is less) each year. That amount is tax deductible. With a Sub S plan, you can make a total contribution of up to $25,000 or 25% (whichever is less) of your income without penalty. While those voluntary payments are not tax deductible, any earnings on it accumulate tax free. You also get the special 10-year forward-averaging if the money is paid out to you at retirement in a lump sum.

If you're an employee not covered by a corporate retirement plan, you can set up an individual retirement account (IRA). You can then sock away up to $1,500 or 15% of your annual earned income (whichever is less). The amount you may put in an IRA will probably be increased by Congress during the next few years.

Your contributions to an IRA reduce your gross income before taxes, and the IRA's earnings will accumulate tax free. When the IRA's proceeds are paid out to you at retirement, they will be taxed at ordinary income tax rates. However, you can use the regular five-year income averaging to lessen the tax bite. If you and your spouse are both eligible for an IRA, you can set up separate IRAs to increase the amount of income you defer from taxes. Under the new tax law, you will also be able to set aside money for your spouse—even if your spouse is not employed. That will make your maximum contribution $1,750.

Any money you receive from a corporate retirement plan when you leave the company or because the plan has been terminated can be put into a roll-over IRA. According to the Employee Retirement Income Security Act (ERISA), you have up to 60 days to roll over this kind of pension fund distribution. (Note that about 5,000 corporations have terminated their pension plans since September 1974 when ERISA took effect.)

Don't rush into a rollover IRA.

Don't rush into a rollover IRA before asking your accountant to figure out if you would be better off just taking your pension fund distribution. After all, some of it may be taxed as capital gains. What's more, much of the tax bite can be eased with a special 10-year-averaging provision. On the other hand, IRA distributions are taxed as ordinary income.

The Tax Reform Act of 1976 has made deferred compensation more attractive.

If you usually get a large bonus each year, you should think about deferring it until you retire—when the tax bite will be lower. The Tax Reform Act of 1976 has made deferred compensation more attractive starting January 1, 1977, because the maximum tax rate will be only 50% rather than the 70% of the old law. To qualify for the deferral, you'll have to let your company know your decision before the start of the year in which your bonus will be earned. If you don't, the IRS will assume you've taken the bonus—even if you refuse it and your company holds off giving you the check.

If you're an employee of a corporation with retirement plans, you'll probably be able to salt away some money by voluntarily making contributions to the plans. While you'll have to pay income tax on the money you put in, the interest or capital gains generated by your contributions will accumulate tax free until you retire. At that time (or even earlier) the money you voluntarily contributed can be withdrawn tax free—say, to help fund your children's education. However, don't tap the kitty if you can help it. You can't make up these payments later.

Anything earned by your contributions is taxable.

Of course, anything earned by your contributions is taxable. However, if you get your pension plan's payout as a lump sum, it will be eligible for a special 10-year forward-averaging tax break. If you receive the payout in annual installments, it will be taxed as ordinary income. While ordinary income is normally taxed at up to 70%, under the new law the payout from a pension plan will be liable to no more than a 50% tax rate regardless of the kind of income.

If part of your pension payment is in the form of your company's common stock, you get a special tax break. Here's how it works: Let's say you get a lump-sum payment of $65,000–including $25,000 in your company's securities. Let's also assume that the plan's basis (the cost of that stock) is $10,000. You can then subtract for tax purposes the capital gain of $15,000 (the difference between the stock's basis and its present value) from your total payment. This lets you defer tax on the $15,000 until you sell the stock. So you'll have to pay taxes at retirement on $50,000 instead of $65,000. Moreover, you can use the special 10-year forward-averaging provision to soften the tax bite on that $50,000. But note that if your company offers you stock of another company, you'll have to pay taxes on the full fair market value of the stock.

You can also defer income by purchasing an annuity.

You can also defer income by purchasing an annuity. While you'll have to use after-tax dollars to buy the annuity, the income from the annuity will accumulate tax free. When you retire and the annuity is paid out, some of the money you get each year will be considered a tax-free return of capital and some will be taxed at ordinary income rates. Under the new tax law, the maximum tax rate will be 50%.

You can defer income by putting your money into some U.S. government bonds—bearer and savings bonds. You'll have to buy the bonds with after-tax dollars, but any interest from these securities will accumulate tax free until you sell the bonds or they mature. The beauty of it all is that you can time the maturity date of these bonds to coincide with your retirement, when you'll be in a lower tax bracket, says Herb Paul, New York director of tax services, Touche Ross.

P AUDITS

Part I. Take another look at your tax return. It could be an invitation to an audit if you aren't careful when you fill it out. The Internal Revenue Service is getting a lot better at nailing taxpayers who fudge a bit when they fill out their tax returns. But don't give up hope. There are ways of cutting down the odds of being audited, if you know how the IRS fingers suspicious tax returns.

Know how the IRS fingers suspicious tax returns.

Start by avoiding certain common mistakes and illegal deductions, such as: claiming an exemption for your spouse, if he or she is filing separately; claiming a partial exemption, say, for half a dependent; deducting the interest on the money borrowed to buy tax-exempt bonds. Also pay close attention to the limits set by the tax code. For example, don't claim all your medical and drug expenses as a deduction. You can only write off medical expenses exceeding 3% of your adjusted gross income, and drug costs exceeding 1% of your adjusted gross income. If you're claiming a casualty loss deduction, exclude the first $100 of the loss from your deduction.

True, they're all picky little things, and chances are they probably won't lead to an audit of your tax return. But you never know; they might. At the very least these little errors will kick your return into the IRS's "unallowables program". If you've made just a few simple mistakes, the IRS will call to let you know that you owe additional taxes. If the errors are in your favor, you'll eventually receive a refund or tax credit.

Little errors will kick your return into the IRS's "unallowables program".

Once your return is in the computer, you're at the mercy of what the IRS fondly calls DIF—for discriminant function. Exactly how DIF works is one of the best-kept secrets in Washington. However, tax men have pieced together a fair idea of how it operates. They figure that the IRS uses tax returns from the prior year to create a number of composite taxpayers. Your return is then matched against a model that takes into account your income level, profession, whether your spouse works or not, the number of dependents you're claiming, and even your address. ZIP codes reveal a lot about your income and lifestyle.

The name of the game is to come as close as possible to the computer's norm.

The computer compares your deductions with those listed for its composite taxpayer and grades them accordingly. The name of the game is to come as close as possible to the computer's norm. Since each deduction is graded differently it's not known whether a low deduction will offset one that's very high. Chances are that one outsized deduction probably won't arouse the computer's suspicions. Of course, if you can substantiate a fat deduction and have nothing to hide, take it—even if it will flag an audit. Here are average deductions from 1974 returns filed in 1975:

Adjusted gross income classes	Average deductions for contributions	Average deductions for interest	Average deductions for taxes	Average medical and dental deductions
$ 20,000–25,000	$ 517	$ 1,516	$ 1,722	$409
25,000–30,000	643	1,786	2,123	402
30,000–50,000	921	2,262	2,897	497
50,000–100,000	2,005	3,871	4,952	651
100,000–200,000	5,013	8,341	9,311	933

The returns with the highest scores will be audited.

The computer will also check out your honesty.

In the end, all the deductions are added up for a DIF score. The computer will kick out any returns that score above a certain range for a specified income level. The returns with the highest scores will be audited and those with lower DIF scores will be thrown back into the files on the theory that they have a lower audit potential. Generally, you can figure that the IRS will come after you only if it's worth its while.

The computer is programmed to be suspicious of any deviation from the norm. For example, it would probably cough out your tax return if all your entries were nicely rounded, even numbers. It will check your math for you and double-check the deductions you take. For example, if you take an office-at-home deduction, the computer will scan your return to see whether you had an outside source of income from, say, consulting or investments, to justify the deduction. If you don't have additional income, up goes the DIF score for that deduction.

The computer will also check out your honesty. For example, the W-2 forms filed by your employer are cross-checked against the income you report. If you had three jobs during the year, and only reported the income from two of them, the computer will catch you at it. And it may get even smarter. Banks, brokerage houses, and other financial institutions will have to file reports on the dividends and interest that they pay. That information will be plugged into the computer and checked against your entries.

Despite all your best efforts, there are occasions when you just can't win. The IRS will snoop around your return if it thinks it can find something wrong. Based on past experience, the IRS thinks that returns filed by people who make over $50,000 a year are fertile grounds for an audit. Agents have also had good luck with taxpayers who report a hefty income from a sideline business; those who report a handsome gain on the sale of a capital asset; and the limited partners of a tax-shelter scheme. From time to time, the IRS will also instruct the computer to give an extra careful examination of returns filled out by tax preparers whom the IRS is suspicious of. (That's easy to do since tax preparers are required to put their social security number on your tax return.)

The big problem with an audit is that it's like that spinning wheel: Where it stops nobody knows. The IRS may come after your tax return because a few deductions look suspicious, but that's no guarantee that the agents won't then go on to look at everything you signed your name to. What's worse, an audit makes the returns you filed over the past three years fair game. If an agent shoots down a deduction on this year's return, he'll probably go through your returns for the past three years—to see if you had taken a similar deduction in prior years.

And if that doesn't faze you, catch this: An IRS audit will probably trigger an audit of your state and local income tax returns. Almost all the states have an agreement with the IRS for the exchange of tax information. The agreement gives the IRS the right to check out all types of state tax returns. For their part, the states can examine almost every type of federal tax return.

An IRS audit will probably trigger an audit of your state and local income tax returns.

If the IRS audits you and you have to pay additional taxes, you have to notify your state's Department of Taxation of the additional federal income tax liability—usually within three months. Chances are, the state will ask you for more money. Trying to trick the state generally doesn't pay. The IRS will tip off the state to your new federal tax liability, and the state will come after you for additional taxes as well as the interest on it. Furthermore, the sooner you pay the state, the earlier you start the clock running on the statute of limitations.

Part II. Unlike a regular cop, an Internal Revenue Service agent won't read you your rights when he pays a call on you. What's more, anything you say may be held against you. So, a word to the wise. Hire a good tax lawyer as soon as the IRS notifies you that it's looking into your tax return. A good attorney can be worth his weight in saved taxes and penalties.

Hire a good tax lawyer as soon as the IRS notifies you that it's looking into your tax return.

When you are audited, you can tell what kind of time you'll be in for by the type of audit the IRS throws at you. If it's an office audit, the IRS will probably question just a few items on your tax return. However, if it's a field audit, the IRS is hunting and everything on your tax return is in season. In either event, let your lawyer do all the talking. You might inadvertently blurt out something that could open up a whole new line of questioning. Furthermore, your lawyer probably knows how to concisely answer an agent's question so that an area of examination is closed off as quickly as possible.

Substantiate every deduction you take.

You should be able to substantiate every deduction you take. That shouldn't be difficult if you have a file of cancelled checks, credit card receipts, bills marked paid in full, and a diary. Believe it or not, a little $1 diary—that lists the amount and reason for the expense by date—is one of the best ways of backing up your deductions. Of course, if travel is involved, also record where you went and why.

The IRS has some pretty devious ways of reconstructing your actual income.

If you've fudged on the amount of income you reported, be forewarned that the IRS has some pretty devious ways of reconstructing your actual income. If the IRS suspects that you haven't reported everything, it will examine all your cash transactions listed in your checkbook, ledgers, and diary. The theory is that the cash you have at the beginning of the year plus your actual after-tax income should equal the sum of what you've spent and what you have left at the end of the year. For example, if you started the year with $5,000 in cash, and make $25,000 after taxes, your total expenditures plus what's left over at the end of the year should equal $30,000. If the amount you spent and what you've saved add up to more than $30,000, you'll have to prove that the extra money isn't taxable income.

An agent will also look at your net bank deposits to see if the amount you've deposited over the year plus your expenditures for the year match the taxable income you've reported. For example, if you've made net bank deposits of $6,000 and have expenditures of $22,000, but only listed $25,000 of after-tax income—you'll have some heavy explaining to do.

The IRS might also run a source-and-application-of-funds audit to compare your income against your expenditures. The idea is to find out if your assets and liabilities have stayed the same. If your assets have increased while your liabilities were level, you'll be suspected of failing to report some income.

The IRS will also try to get a picture of your real net worth. An increase in your true net worth that's not accounted for by an increase in your income will tip an agent off to fraud. And getting at your real net worth isn't as difficult as you might think. The IRS can find out how affluent you really are by talking to your neighbors and friends and by looking at your deeds, auto registration, your address, and even the schools your children attend.

The burden of proof is yours.

If something doesn't add up in one of these audits, the burden of proof is yours. Hence, you'll want as many supporting documents as possible. If you've made a loan to a friend or relative, keep a promissory note. Unless you can prove otherwise, the repayment of a loan you've made will show up as unreported income. The same applies to money you borrow. If you don't have a record of the loan, it will show up as unaccounted for income. You should also keep a careful record of your checking and savings accounts. Any transfers between accounts should be carefully documented.

And be certain that you have a record of nontaxable items such as inheritances, gifts, unemployment benefits, tax-exempt interest from municipals, income tax refunds, dividends excluded from federal tax, scholarships, and so on. Otherwise they could be taken as unreported income.

Once an agent has finished auditing you, he or she will tell you how much you owe. If you think the tax assessment's on the high side, you can appeal the decision. You can usually bargain the IRS down—how much usually depends on how good your attorney is. But before you decide to appeal the decision, weigh what you'd have to give up in additional taxes against what you'll save in legal fees, time, and energy. And note this: Agreeing with the agent's assessment will usually end the audit and close off the possibility of new issues being raised. What's more, the interest on the taxes you owe will be frozen 30 days after you file form 870—which usually means waiving your right to additional appeals.

If you think the tax assessment's on the high side, you can appeal the decision.

If you decide to appeal the agent's decision, ask to see his supervisor. If you're still dissatisfied after meeting with the supervisor, ask for a district conference—an informal hearing which can be used to settle disputes. Since district conference personnel can base their decision on what they think might happen if your case actually went to court, your attorney should be able to get a fair compromise. The IRS would rather not take you to court if its case isn't absolutely airtight.

Your attorney should be able to get a fair compromise.

If you're unhappy with the district conference decision, you can take your argument to the IRS appellate division. However, since the appellate division is staffed with the IRS' top agents, you'll probably have a tough time getting any further concessions. Or, you can take your case straight to the tax court without having to pay the tax first. But chances are that the tax court may send the case back to the appellate division (and the IRS regional counsel's office) for further discussion.

If you think your argument might win a jury's sympathy, you can take your case to a district court. Your chances of winning in district court are fairly good because juries composed of your tax-paying peers usually aren't sympathetic to the IRS. If you decide to take it to district court, you'll have to pay your tax deficiency and then sue for a refund. If you win, the government will owe you interest on the excess taxes you paid. Should you lose you can take the decision, in some cases, all the way up to the Supreme Court.

1976 Tax Rate Schedules

If Form 1040, line 47 is more than $20,000, figure your tax on the amount on Form 1040, line 47, by using the appropriate Tax Rate Schedule on this page. Enter tax on Form 1040, line 16.

SCHEDULE X—Single Taxpayers Not Qualifying for Rates in Schedule Y or Z

Use this schedule if you checked the box on Form 1040, line 1—

| If the amount on Form 1040, line 47, is: | | Enter on Form 1040, line 16: | |
Over—	But not over—		of the amount over—
$20,000	$22,000	$5,230+38%	$20,000
$22,000	$26,000	$5,990+40%	$22,000
$26,000	$32,000	$7,590+45%	$26,000
$32,000	$38,000	$10,290+50%	$32,000
$38,000	$44,000	$13,290+55%	$38,000
$44,000	$50,000	$16,590+60%	$44,000
$50,000	$60,000	$20,190+62%	$50,000
$60,000	$70,000	$26,390+64%	$60,000
$70,000	$80,000	$32,790+66%	$70,000
$80,000	$90,000	$39,390+68%	$80,000
$90,000	$100,000	$46,190+69%	$90,000
$100,000	....	$53,090+70%	$100,000

SCHEDULE Y—Married Taxpayers and Qualifying Widows and Widowers

If you are a married person living apart from your spouse, see page 7 of the instructions to see if you can be considered to be "unmarried" for purposes of using Schedule X or Z.

Use this schedule if you checked the box on Form 1040, line 2 or 5—

Married Taxpayers Filing Joint Returns and Qualifying Widows and Widowers (See page 7)

| If the amount on Form 1040, line 47, is: | | Enter on Form 1040, line 16: | |
Over—	But not over—		of the amount over—
$20,000	$24,000	$4,380+32%	$20,000
$24,000	$28,000	$5,660+36%	$24,000
$28,000	$32,000	$7,100+39%	$28,000
$32,000	$36,000	$8,660+42%	$32,000
$36,000	$40,000	$10,340+45%	$36,000
$40,000	$44,000	$12,140+48%	$40,000
$44,000	$52,000	$14,060+50%	$44,000
$52,000	$64,000	$18,060+53%	$52,000
$64,000	$76,000	$24,420+55%	$64,000
$76,000	$88,000	$31,020+58%	$76,000
$88,000	$100,000	$37,980+60%	$88,000
$100,000	$120,000	$45,180+62%	$100,000
$120,000	$140,000	$57,580+64%	$120,000
$140,000	$160,000	$70,380+66%	$140,000
$160,000	$180,000	$83,580+68%	$160,000
$180,000	$200,000	$97,180+69%	$180,000
$200,000	....	$110,980+70%	$200,000

Use this schedule if you checked the box on Form 1040, line 3—

Married Taxpayers Filing Separate Returns

| If the amount on Form 1040, line 47, is: | | Enter on Form 1040, line 16: | |
Over—	But not over—		of the amount over—
$20,000	$22,000	$6,070+48%	$20,000
$22,000	$26,000	$7,030+50%	$22,000
$26,000	$32,000	$9,030+53%	$26,000
$32,000	$38,000	$12,210+55%	$32,000
$38,000	$44,000	$15,510+58%	$38,000
$44,000	$50,000	$18,990+60%	$44,000
$50,000	$60,000	$22,590+62%	$50,000
$60,000	$70,000	$28,790+64%	$60,000
$70,000	$80,000	$35,190+66%	$70,000
$80,000	$90,000	$41,790+68%	$80,000
$90,000	$100,000	$48,590+69%	$90,000
$100,000	....	$55,490+70%	$100,000

SCHEDULE Z—Unmarried (or legally separated) Taxpayers Who Qualify as Heads of Household (See page 7)

Use this schedule if you checked the box on Form 1040, line 4—

| If the amount on Form 1040, line 47, is: | | Enter on Form 1040, line 16: | |
Over—	But not over—		of the amount over—
$20,000	$22,000	$4,800+35%	$20,000
$22,000	$24,000	$5,500+36%	$22,000
$24,000	$26,000	$6,220+38%	$24,000
$26,000	$28,000	$6,980+41%	$26,000
$28,000	$32,000	$7,800+42%	$28,000
$32,000	$36,000	$9,480+45%	$32,000
$36,000	$38,000	$11,280+48%	$36,000
$38,000	$40,000	$12,240+51%	$38,000
$40,000	$44,000	$13,260+52%	$40,000
$44,000	$50,000	$15,340+55%	$44,000
$50,000	$52,000	$18,640+56%	$50,000
$52,000	$64,000	$19,760+58%	$52,000
$64,000	$70,000	$26,720+59%	$64,000
$70,000	$76,000	$30,260+61%	$70,000
$76,000	$80,000	$33,920+62%	$76,000
$80,000	$88,000	$36,400+63%	$80,000
$88,000	$100,000	$41,440+64%	$88,000
$100,000	$120,000	$49,120+66%	$100,000
$120,000	$140,000	$62,320+67%	$120,000
$140,000	$160,000	$75,720+68%	$140,000
$160,000	$180,000	$89,320+69%	$160,000
$180,000	....	$103,120+70%	$180,000

1976 Optional State Sales Tax Tables

If you itemize your deductions on Schedule A, you can use these tables to determine the general sales tax to enter on line 14. If your records show that you paid more than the amount shown you can deduct the larger amount. The sales tax paid on the purchase of an automobile (truck) may be added to the table amount except in the District of Columbia, Vermont and West Virginia where the deduction is limited to the tax paid at the general sales tax rate. **See page 13 for complete list of items on which sales taxes can be added to the table amount.**

If your income was more than $19,999 but less than $100,000, compute your deduction as follows:

Step 1—For the first $19,999, find the amount for your family size in the table for your State.

Step 2—For each $1,000 or fraction of it of income over $19,999, but less than $50,000, add 2 percent of the amount you determined in Step 1, above.

Step 3—For each $1,000 or fraction of it of income over $49,999, but less than $100,000, add 1 percent of the amount you determined in Step 1, above.

If your income was $100,000 or more, your deduction is 210 percent of the amount determined in Step 1, above.

Income[1]	Alabama[2] Family size (persons)					Arizona[3] Family size (persons)						Arkansas[2] Family size (persons)					California[4] Family size (persons)			
	1	2	3&4	5	Over 5	1	2	3	4	5	Over 5	1	2	3&4	5	Over 5	1&2	3&4	5	Over 5
Under $3,000	$45	$53	$66	$71	$72	$51	$67	$70	$84	$84	$85	$38	$45	$54	$58	$59	$51	$61	$68	$68
$3,000–$3,999	55	66	81	89	91	63	82	86	100	101	105	47	56	67	73	74	66	78	87	87
$4,000–$4,999	64	79	95	105	108	73	95	101	114	118	123	54	66	78	86	88	80	93	104	104
$5,000–$5,999	73	90	108	120	124	82	107	115	127	134	140	61	76	88	98	101	93	107	120	120
$6,000–$6,999	81	101	120	134	139	91	118	127	139	149	156	67	85	98	110	114	106	121	135	136
$7,000–$7,999	88	111	131	147	154	99	128	139	150	163	171	73	93	108	121	126	118	134	149	152
$8,000–$8,999	95	121	142	160	168	107	138	151	161	176	185	79	101	117	131	137	130	147	163	167
$9,000–$9,999	102	130	152	172	181	114	147	162	171	189	199	84	109	125	141	148	141	159	176	181
$10,000–$10,999	109	139	162	184	194	121	156	172	180	201	212	89	116	133	151	158	152	171	189	195
$11,000–$11,999	115	148	171	195	207	128	165	182	189	213	225	94	123	141	160	168	163	183	202	209
$12,000–$12,999	121	157	180	206	219	134	174	192	197	224	237	99	130	149	169	178	174	194	214	222
$13,000–$13,999	127	165	189	217	231	140	182	201	205	235	249	104	137	156	178	188	184	205	226	235
$14,000–$14,999	133	173	198	228	243	146	190	210	213	246	261	109	144	163	186	198	194	216	238	248
$15,000–$15,999	139	181	207	238	254	152	197	219	221	256	272	113	151	170	194	207	204	227	249	260
$16,000–$16,999	144	189	215	248	265	158	204	228	229	266	283	117	157	177	202	216	214	238	260	272
$17,000–$17,999	149	197	223	258	276	164	211	237	237	276	294	121	163	184	210	225	224	248	271	284
$18,000–$18,999	154	204	231	268	287	169	218	245	245	286	305	125	169	190	218	234	233	258	282	296
$19,000–$19,999	159	211	238	277	297	174	225	253	253	295	315	129	175	196	226	242	242	268	293	308

Income[1]	Colorado[3] Family size (persons)						Connecticut Family size (persons)				Dist. of Columbia Family size (persons)				
	1	2	3	4	5	Over 5	1&2	3&4	5	Over 5	1	2	3&4	5	Over 5
Under $3,000	$35	$48	$49	$59	$59	$60	$44	$51	$61	$61	$34	$39	$49	$53	$53
$3,000–$3,999	44	58	61	71	73	75	59	68	79	79	41	50	61	66	66
$4,000–$4,999	51	68	72	82	85	88	73	83	96	96	48	60	73	78	78
$5,000–$5,999	58	76	82	91	97	100	87	98	112	112	54	69	83	90	90
$6,000–$6,999	64	84	91	100	107	112	101	113	127	127	60	78	92	101	101
$7,000–$7,999	70	92	100	109	117	123	114	127	142	142	66	87	101	111	112
$8,000–$8,999	76	99	108	117	127	133	127	141	156	156	71	95	110	121	123
$9,000–$9,999	81	106	116	124	136	143	140	154	170	171	76	103	119	130	134
$10,000–$10,999	86	112	124	131	145	153	152	167	183	186	81	111	127	139	144
$11,000–$11,999	91	118	132	138	154	163	164	180	196	201	86	119	135	148	154
$12,000–$12,999	96	124	139	145	162	172	176	193	209	216	90	127	142	157	164
$13,000–$13,999	101	130	146	151	170	181	188	205	222	230	94	135	149	166	174
$14,000–$14,999	106	136	153	157	178	190	200	217	235	244	98	142	156	174	184
$15,000–$15,999	110	141	160	163	186	198	212	229	247	258	102	149	163	182	194
$16,000–$16,999	114	146	167	169	194	206	224	241	259	272	106	156	170	190	203
$17,000–$17,999	118	151	173	175	201	214	236	253	271	286	110	163	177	198	212
$18,000–$18,999	122	156	179	181	208	222	247	265	283	300	114	170	184	206	221
$19,000–$19,999	126	161	185	186	215	230	258	277	294	314	118	176	190	213	230

Income[1]	Florida[2] Family size (persons)				Georgia[2] Family size (persons)					Hawaii Family size (persons)				
	1&2	3&4	5	Over 5	1	2	3&4	5	Over 5	1	2	3&4	5	Over 5
Under $3,000	$30	$40	$44	$44	$40	$49	$59	$65	$65	$69	$87	$91	$101	$101
$3,000–$3,999	40	51	56	56	50	61	72	80	80	85	105	111	123	123
$4,000–$4,999	50	62	68	68	58	72	85	94	94	99	120	129	143	144
$5,000–$5,999	59	72	79	79	65	82	96	106	107	112	135	145	161	163
$6,000–$6,999	68	81	89	89	72	91	106	118	120	123	148	159	178	181
$7,000–$7,999	76	90	99	100	79	100	116	129	133	134	160	173	193	198
$8,000–$8,999	84	99	109	110	85	109	125	140	145	145	172	186	208	215
$9,000–$9,999	92	108	118	120	91	117	134	150	157	155	183	199	222	230
$10,000–$10,999	100	116	127	130	96	125	143	159	168	165	193	211	236	245
$11,000–$11,999	108	124	136	140	102	133	151	169	179	174	203	222	249	260
$12,000–$12,999	116	132	145	150	107	140	159	178	190	183	213	233	261	274
$13,000–$13,999	124	140	154	159	112	147	167	187	200	192	222	244	273	287
$14,000–$14,999	132	148	162	168	117	154	174	196	210	200	231	254	285	300
$15,000–$15,999	140	155	170	177	122	161	181	204	220	208	240	264	296	313
$16,000–$16,999	147	162	178	186	127	168	188	212	230	216	248	274	307	326
$17,000–$17,999	154	169	186	195	132	174	195	220	240	224	256	284	318	338
$18,000–$18,999	161	176	194	204	136	180	202	228	250	232	264	293	329	350
$19,000–$19,999	168	183	201	213	140	186	208	235	259	239	272	302	339	362

Income[1]	Idaho Family size (persons)						Illinois[5] Family size (persons)						Indiana Family size (persons)				
	1	2	3	4	5	Over 5	1	2	3	4	5	Over 5	1	2	3&4	5	Over 5
Under $3,000	$34	$45	$47	$57	$57	$58	$54	$70	$80	$92	$92	$97	$37	$41	$47	$51	$51
$3,000–$3,999	42	55	59	69	69	72	66	86	98	111	113	121	47	53	60	65	65
$4,000–$4,993	49	64	69	79	82	85	77	100	115	128	133	142	56	63	72	78	78
$5,000–$5,999	56	73	79	88	93	97	87	114	131	144	151	162	65	73	83	90	91
$6,000–$6,999	62	81	88	97	104	109	97	126	145	158	168	181	73	83	94	101	103
$7,000–$7,999	68	88	97	105	114	120	106	138	159	171	184	199	81	92	104	112	115
$8,000–$8,999	74	95	105	113	124	130	115	149	172	184	199	216	89	101	114	123	127
$9,000–$9,999	79	102	113	120	133	140	123	160	184	196	214	232	96	110	124	133	138
$10,000–$10,999	84	109	121	127	142	150	131	170	196	208	228	248	103	118	133	143	149
$11,000–$11,999	89	115	129	134	151	159	138	180	207	219	242	263	110	126	142	153	160
$12,000–$12,999	94	121	136	140	159	168	145	190	218	230	255	277	117	134	151	163	171
$13,000–$13,999	99	127	143	146	167	177	152	199	229	240	268	291	124	142	159	172	182
$14,000–$14,999	104	133	150	152	175	186	159	208	240	250	281	305	130	150	167	181	192
$15,000–$15,999	109	139	157	158	183	194	166	217	250	260	293	319	136	157	175	190	202
$16,000–$16,999	113	145	164	164	191	202	173	226	260	269	305	332	142	164	183	199	212
$17,000–$17,999	117	150	170	170	198	210	179	234	270	278	317	345	148	171	191	208	222
$18,000–$18,999	121	155	176	176	205	218	185	242	280	287	328	358	154	178	199	216	232
$19,000–$19,999	125	160	182	182	212	226	191	250	289	295	339	371	160	185	207	224	242

Income[1]	Iowa Family size (persons)			Kansas[2] Family size (persons)					
	1&2	3,4&5	Over 5	1	2	3	4	5	Over 5
Under $3,000	$30	$35	$35	$41	$51	$56	$64	$64	$67
$3,000–$3,999	39	45	46	50	63	69	78	78	84
$4,000–$4,993	47	54	56	58	74	82	90	92	100
$5,000–$5,999	55	63	66	66	84	93	102	106	114
$6,000–$6,999	62	72	76	73	93	104	112	118	127
$7,000–$7,999	69	81	86	80	102	114	122	130	140
$8,000–$8,999	76	89	95	86	110	124	132	142	153
$9,000–$9,999	83	97	104	92	118	133	141	153	165
$10,000–$10,999	89	105	113	98	125	142	150	163	176
$11,000–$11,999	95	113	122	104	132	151	158	173	187
$12,000–$12,999	101	120	131	109	139	159	166	183	198
$13,000–$13,999	107	127	140	114	146	167	174	193	208
$14,000–$14,999	113	134	149	119	153	175	182	203	218
$15,000–$15,999	119	141	157	124	159	183	189	212	228
$16,000–$16,999	125	148	165	129	165	191	196	221	238
$17,000–$17,999	131	155	173	134	171	198	203	230	248
$18,000–$18,999	137	162	181	138	177	205	210	239	258
$19,000–$19,999	142	168	189	142	183	212	216	247	267

Income[1]	Kentucky[2] Family size (persons)				Louisiana[2] Family size (persons)				Maine Family size (persons)				
	1&2	3&4	5	Over 5	1&2	3&4	5	Over 5	1&2	3	4	5	Over 5
Under $3,000	$46	$57	$61	$61	$25	$31	$34	$34	$40	$48	$56	$57	$57
$3,000–$3,999	59	73	78	78	33	40	44	44	52	61	70	72	72
$4,000–$4,999	72	87	93	93	41	49	53	53	64	74	83	87	87
$5,000–$5,999	84	100	107	107	48	57	62	62	75	86	96	101	101
$6,000–$6,999	95	112	121	121	55	64	70	70	86	98	107	114	114
$7,000–$7,999	106	124	134	135	62	71	77	78	97	109	118	126	126
$8,000–$8,999	116	135	146	148	69	78	85	86	107	120	129	138	139
$9,000–$9,999	126	146	158	161	76	85	93	94	117	130	139	150	152
$10,000–$10,999	136	157	170	174	82	92	100	102	127	140	149	161	165
$11,000–$11,999	146	167	182	187	88	98	107	110	136	150	158	172	177
$12,000–$12,999	155	177	193	200	94	104	114	118	145	160	167	183	189
$13,000–$13,999	164	187	204	212	100	110	121	125	154	170	176	194	201
$14,000–$14,999	173	197	215	224	106	116	128	132	163	179	185	204	212
$15,000–$15,999	182	206	225	236	112	122	134	139	172	188	194	214	223
$16,000–$16,999	191	215	235	248	118	128	140	146	181	197	203	224	234
$17,000–$17,999	200	224	245	259	124	134	146	153	190	206	211	234	245
$18,000–$18,999	208	233	255	270	130	140	152	160	199	215	219	244	256
$19,000–$19,999	216	242	264	281	136	145	158	167	207	223	227	253	267

Income[1]	Maryland Family size (persons)				Massachusetts Family size (persons)			Michigan Family size (persons)				Minnesota[2] Family size (persons)		
	1&2	3&4	5	Over 5	1	2,3&4	5 and over	1&2	3&4	5	Over 5	1&2	3,4&5	Over 5
Under $3,000	$33	$42	$46	$46	$13	$17	$24	$35	$43	$45	$45	$27	$30	$30
$3,000–$3,999	43	54	58	58	17	22	30	46	55	58	58	35	38	39
$4,000–$4,999	52	64	70	70	20	27	36	55	66	70	70	42	46	47
$5,000–$5,999	61	74	81	81	24	32	42	64	76	81	82	49	54	55
$6,000–$6,999	69	84	91	92	27	37	47	73	86	92	94	56	61	63
$7,000–$7,999	77	93	101	103	30	42	52	82	96	102	105	62	68	71
$8,000–$8,999	85	101	111	114	33	47	57	90	105	112	116	68	75	79
$9,000–$9,999	93	109	120	124	36	52	62	98	114	122	127	74	82	86
$10,000–$10,999	101	118	129	134	39	57	67	106	123	131	138	80	88	93
$11,000–$11,999	109	126	138	144	42	61	72	113	131	140	149	85	94	100
$12,000–$12,999	116	134	147	154	44	65	76	120	139	149	159	90	100	107
$13,000–$13,999	123	141	156	164	47	69	80	127	147	158	169	95	106	114
$14,000–$14,999	130	148	164	173	50	73	84	134	155	167	179	100	112	121
$15,000–$15,999	137	155	172	182	52	77	88	141	163	176	189	105	118	128
$16,000–$16,999	144	162	180	191	55	81	92	148	171	184	199	110	124	134
$17,000–$17,999	151	169	188	200	57	85	96	155	179	192	209	115	130	140
$18,000–$18,999	157	176	196	209	60	89	100	162	186	200	218	120	135	146
$19,000–$19,999	163	183	203	218	62	93	104	168	193	208	227	125	140	152

[1] Total of adjusted gross income (Form 1040, line 15c) and nontaxable receipts such as social security, veterans', railroad retirement benefits, workmen's compensation, untaxed portion of long-term capital gains, disability income exclusion (sick pay), dividends exclusion, unemployment compensation and public assistance payments.

[2] Local sales taxes are not included. Add an amount based on the ratio between the local and State sales tax rates considering the number of months the taxes have been in effect.

[3] Local sales taxes are not included. Add the amount paid.

[4] The 1¼ percent local sales tax is included. If the ½ cent BART sales tax is paid all year add 8 percent to the table amount. Otherwise add a proportionate amount (see footnote 2).

[5] Local sales taxes are included.

1976 Optional State Sales Tax Tables

If you itemize your deductions on Schedule A, you can use these tables to determine the general sales tax to enter on line 14. If your records show that you paid more than the amount shown, you can deduct the larger amount. The sales tax paid on the purchase of an automobile (truck) may be added to the table amount except in the District of Columbia, Vermont and West Virginia where the deduction is limited to the tax paid at the general sales tax rate. **See page 13 for complete list of items on which sales taxes can be added to the table amount.**

If your income was more than $19,999 but less than $100,000, compute your deduction as follows:

Step 1—For the first $19,999, find the amount for your family size in the table for your State.

Step 2—For each $1,000 or fraction of it of income over $19,999, but less than $50,000, add 2 percent of the amount you determined in Step 1, above.

Step 3—For each $1,000 or fraction of it of income over $49,999, but less than $100,000, add 1 percent of the amount you determined in Step 1, above.

If your income was $100,000 or more, your deduction is 210 percent of the amount determined in Step 1, above.

Income [1]	Mississippi: Family size (persons) 1	2	3&4	5	Over 5	Missouri [2]: Family size (persons) 1	2	3	4	5	Over 5	Nebraska [2]: Family size (persons) 1	2	3	4	5	Over 5	Nevada [3]: Family size (persons) 1	2	3	4	5	Over 5
Under $3,000	$70	$83	$100	$109	$109	$37	$48	$52	$59	$59	$63	$32	$41	$46	$52	$53	$56	$38	$51	$53	$65	$65	$67
$3,000–$3,999	86	104	124	135	135	45	58	65	72	74	79	39	51	57	63	65	70	47	62	66	78	79	82
$4,000–$4,999	100	123	144	159	159	53	68	76	83	87	93	46	59	67	73	77	82	55	72	77	89	92	96
$5,000–$5,999	113	141	163	181	182	59	77	86	94	99	106	52	67	76	83	87	94	62	81	88	99	104	109
$6,000–$6,999	125	158	181	201	204	65	85	95	103	111	118	57	74	84	91	97	105	69	90	98	108	116	121
$7,000–$7,999	136	173	198	220	225	71	93	104	112	122	130	62	81	92	99	107	115	75	98	107	116	127	133
$8,000–$8,999	147	188	214	238	246	77	100	113	121	132	141	67	87	100	107	116	125	81	105	116	124	137	144
$9,000–$9,999	157	203	230	256	266	83	107	121	129	142	152	72	93	107	114	124	135	87	112	125	132	147	154
$10,000–$10,999	167	217	244	273	285	88	114	129	137	151	162	77	99	114	121	132	144	92	119	133	139	156	164
$11,000–$11,999	176	230	258	289	304	93	121	137	145	160	172	81	105	121	127	140	153	97	126	141	146	165	174
$12,000–$12,999	185	243	272	305	322	98	127	144	152	169	182	85	110	127	133	148	162	102	133	149	153	174	183
$13,000–$13,999	194	256	285	320	340	103	133	151	159	178	191	89	115	133	139	156	170	107	139	156	159	182	192
$14,000–$14,999	202	269	298	335	358	107	139	158	166	187	200	93	120	139	145	163	178	112	145	163	165	190	201
$15,000–$15,999	210	281	311	350	375	111	145	165	173	195	209	97	125	145	151	170	186	117	151	170	171	198	210
$16,000–$16,999	218	293	323	364	392	115	151	172	179	203	218	101	130	151	157	177	194	122	157	177	177	206	219
$17,000–$17,999	226	305	335	378	408	119	156	179	185	211	227	105	135	157	163	184	202	126	163	184	184	214	227
$18,000–$18,999	234	316	347	392	424	123	161	185	191	219	235	108	140	162	168	190	209	130	168	191	191	222	235
$19,000–$19,999	241	327	359	405	440	127	166	191	197	226	243	111	144	167	173	196	216	134	173	197	197	229	243

Income [1]	New Jersey: Family size (persons) 4 or under	5 and over	New Mexico [2]: Family size (persons) 1	2	3	4	5	Over 5	New York [4]: Family size (persons) 1&2	3	4	5	Over 5	North Carolina [5]: Family size (persons) 1	2	3&4	5	Over 5	North Dakota: Family size (persons) 1&2	3&4	5	Over 5	Ohio [2]: Family size (persons) 1&2	3&4	5	Over 5	Oklahoma [2]: Family size (persons) 1	2	3&4	5	Over 5
Under $3,000	$28	$37	$58	$77	$78	$92	$92	$92	$37	$44	$53	$56	$56	$46	$53	$66	$72	$72	$34	$41	$42	$42	$27	$33	$33	$34	$25	$29	$35	$38	$38
$3,000–$3,999	38	47	71	94	96	111	111	113	49	57	66	71	71	56	67	81	89	90	44	52	55	55	36	43	44	45	31	37	43	47	48
$4,000–$4,999	47	57	83	109	113	128	128	134	60	69	79	84	84	65	79	95	105	107	54	63	66	67	44	52	54	56	36	44	51	56	58
$5,000–$5,999	56	67	94	123	129	143	146	153	70	81	90	97	97	74	91	108	120	123	63	73	77	78	52	61	64	66	41	50	58	64	66
$6,000–$6,999	65	76	104	135	144	157	163	171	80	92	101	109	109	82	102	120	133	138	71	83	88	89	60	70	74	76	45	56	64	72	74
$7,000–$7,999	74	85	113	147	158	170	179	188	90	102	111	120	120	89	112	131	146	152	79	92	98	100	68	78	83	86	49	61	70	79	82
$8,000–$8,999	82	94	122	158	171	183	194	204	99	112	121	131	131	96	122	141	159	166	87	101	108	111	75	86	92	96	53	66	76	86	89
$9,000–$9,999	90	102	131	169	184	195	209	220	108	122	130	141	142	103	131	151	171	179	95	110	118	121	82	94	101	105	57	71	82	93	96
$10,000–$10,999	98	110	139	179	196	206	223	235	117	132	139	151	154	109	140	161	182	192	103	118	127	131	89	102	110	114	60	76	87	99	103
$11,000–$11,999	106	118	147	189	208	217	237	250	126	142	148	161	165	115	149	171	193	204	110	126	136	141	96	110	119	123	64	81	92	105	110
$12,000–$12,999	114	126	155	199	220	227	250	264	135	151	157	171	176	121	158	180	204	216	117	134	145	151	103	117	128	132	68	86	97	111	117
$13,000–$13,999	122	134	162	208	231	237	263	278	144	160	165	180	187	127	167	189	215	228	124	142	154	161	110	124	136	141	71	91	102	117	123
$14,000–$14,999	130	141	169	217	242	247	276	291	152	169	173	189	198	133	175	197	225	239	131	150	163	171	117	131	144	150	74	96	107	123	129
$15,000–$15,999	138	148	176	226	253	256	289	304	160	178	181	198	209	139	183	205	235	250	138	158	172	180	124	138	152	159	77	100	112	129	135
$16,000–$16,993	146	155	183	235	263	265	301	317	168	187	189	207	220	144	191	213	245	261	145	165	181	189	130	145	160	168	80	104	117	134	141
$17,000–$17,999	154	162	190	243	273	274	313	330	176	196	196	215	230	149	199	221	254	272	152	172	189	198	136	152	168	177	83	108	121	139	147
$18,000–$18,999	161	169	196	251	283	283	324	342	184	204	204	223	240	154	207	229	263	282	158	179	197	207	142	159	176	185	86	112	125	144	153
$19,000–$19,999	168	176	202	259	293	293	335	354	192	212	212	231	250	159	214	237	272	292	164	186	205	216	148	165	184	193	88	116	129	149	159

Income [1]	Pennsylvania: Family size (persons) 4 or under	5 and over	Rhode Island: Family size (persons) 1&2	3	4	5	Over 5	South Carolina: Family size (persons) 1	2	3&4	5	Over 5	South Dakota [6]: Family size (persons) 1	2	3	4	5	Over 5	Tennessee [2]: Family size (persons) 1	2	3&4	5	Over 5	Texas [2]: Family size (persons) 1&2	3&4	5	Over 5
Under $3,000	$24	$31	$39	$47	$56	$57	$57	$52	$61	$73	$80	$80	$52	$66	$71	$81	$81	$83	$52	$60	$74	$81	$81	$32	$41	$44	$44
$3,000–$3,999	33	40	52	61	71	74	74	63	76	90	99	99	64	81	88	99	99	105	64	76	91	101	102	42	52	56	56
$4,000–$4,999	42	49	65	74	84	89	89	73	90	105	116	118	75	95	104	115	117	125	74	90	107	118	121	51	62	67	68
$5,000–$5,999	50	58	77	87	97	103	103	83	102	119	132	135	84	107	118	130	134	144	84	103	121	135	138	59	71	78	79
$6,000–$6,999	58	67	88	99	109	117	117	91	114	132	147	151	93	119	132	144	150	161	93	115	134	150	155	67	80	88	89
$7,000–$7,999	66	75	99	111	120	130	130	99	125	144	161	167	102	130	145	157	165	178	101	127	147	165	171	75	89	98	99
$8,000–$8,999	74	83	110	122	131	142	144	107	136	156	174	182	110	141	157	169	179	194	109	138	159	179	187	83	97	107	109
$9,000–$9,999	82	91	121	133	142	154	157	114	146	167	187	196	118	151	169	181	193	210	117	149	170	192	202	90	105	116	118
$10,000–$10,999	90	99	132	144	152	166	170	121	156	178	200	210	125	161	181	192	207	225	124	159	181	205	216	97	113	125	127
$11,000–$11,999	98	107	143	155	162	178	183	128	166	188	212	224	132	170	192	203	220	240	131	169	192	218	230	104	120	133	136
$12,000–$12,999	106	114	153	165	172	189	196	134	175	198	224	237	139	179	203	213	233	254	138	179	202	230	244	111	127	141	145
$13,000–$13,999	114	121	163	175	182	200	209	140	184	208	235	250	146	188	213	223	245	268	145	188	212	242	257	118	134	149	153
$14,000–$14,999	122	128	173	185	191	211	221	146	193	217	246	262	153	197	223	233	257	281	151	197	222	253	270	125	141	157	161
$15,000–$15,999	130	135	183	195	200	222	233	152	202	226	257	274	159	205	233	242	269	294	157	206	231	264	283	132	148	165	169
$16,000–$16,999	138	142	193	205	209	232	245	158	210	235	267	286	165	213	243	251	280	307	163	215	240	275	295	139	155	173	177
$17,000–$17,999	146	149	203	215	218	242	257	163	218	244	277	298	171	221	253	260	291	320	169	224	249	286	307	145	162	180	185
$18,000–$18,999	153	156	213	225	226	252	269	168	226	252	287	310	177	229	262	269	302	333	175	232	258	296	319	151	168	187	193
$19,000–$19,999	160	163	222	234	235	262	281	173	234	260	297	321	182	236	271	278	313	345	180	240	267	306	330	157	174	194	201

Income [1]	Utah [7]: Family size (persons) 1	2	3	4	5	Over 5	Vermont: Family size (persons) 1	2	3&4	5	Over 5	Virginia [3]: Family size (persons) 1	2	3&4	5	Over 5	Washington [8]: Family size (persons) 1	2	3	4	5	Over 5	West Virginia: Family size (persons) 1	2	3&4	5	Over 5	Wisconsin: Family size 1&2	3&4	5	Over 5	Wyoming [2]: Family size (persons) 1	2	3	4	5	Over 5
Under $3,000	$61	$80	$83	$98	$98	$98	$16	$20	$25	$30	$30	$43	$50	$63	$69	$70	$59	$79	$81	$98	$98	$98	$36	$42	$52	$57	$57	$40	$47	$48	$48	$39	$51	$53	$62	$62	$62
$3,000–$3,999	75	98	103	118	118	122	20	26	32	38	38	52	63	78	86	88	74	97	102	118	119	122	45	53	65	71	71	51	60	62	63	48	63	65	75	76	78
$4,000–$4,999	88	114	121	136	139	145	24	31	38	46	46	61	75	91	101	104	86	114	120	137	141	145	52	63	76	84	85	61	73	75	77	56	73	77	87	89	92
$5,000–$5,999	100	129	138	153	158	165	28	36	44	52	53	69	86	103	115	119	98	129	138	153	161	166	59	73	86	96	97	71	84	88	91	64	82	88	97	101	106
$6,000–$6,999	111	143	154	168	176	185	32	41	49	58	59	76	96	114	128	133	109	143	154	169	179	186	66	82	96	107	109	81	95	100	104	71	91	98	107	113	118
$7,000–$7,999	121	156	169	182	193	203	35	46	54	64	66	83	106	125	141	147	119	156	169	183	197	205	72	90	105	118	121	90	106	112	117	77	99	107	116	124	130
$8,000–$8,999	131	168	183	195	210	221	38	51	59	70	72	90	115	135	153	160	129	168	184	197	214	224	78	98	114	128	132	99	116	123	129	83	107	116	125	134	141
$9,000–$9,999	141	180	197	208	225	238	41	55	64	76	78	96	124	145	164	172	139	180	198	210	230	241	84	106	122	138	143	107	126	134	141	89	115	125	133	144	152
$10,000–$10,999	150	191	210	220	240	255	44	59	69	81	84	102	132	154	175	184	148	191	212	222	246	259	89	113	130	147	153	115	136	145	153	95	122	134	140	154	163
$11,000–$11,999	159	202	223	231	255	271	47	63	74	86	89	108	140	163	186	196	157	202	225	234	261	275	94	121	138	156	163	123	145	155	165	101	129	142	148	163	173
$12,000–$12,999	167	212	235	242	269	287	50	67	78	91	95	114	148	172	196	208	166	213	238	245	276	291	99	128	145	165	173	131	154	165	176	106	136	150	155	172	183
$13,000–$13,999	175	222	247	253	283	302	52	71	83	96	100	119	156	180	206	219	175	224	251	256	291	307	104	135	152	174	183	139	163	175	187	111	142	158	162	181	193
$14,000–$14,999	183	232	259	263	296	317	55	75	87	101	106	124	164	188	216	230	184	234	263	267	305	323	109	142	159	182	192	147	172	185	198	116	148	165	169	190	202
$15,000–$15,999	191	242	270	273	309	331	57	79	91	106	111	129	172	196	225	240	192	244	275	277	319	338	114	148	166	190	201	154	181	195	209	121	154	172	175	199	211
$16,000–$16,999	199	251	281	283	322	345	60	83	96	110	116	134	179	204	234	250	200	254	287	287	332	353	119	154	173	198	210	161	190	205	220	126	160	179	181	207	220
$17,000–$17,999	207	260	292	293	334	359	62	87	100	115	121	139	186	212	243	260	207	263	298	298	345	368	123	160	180	206	219	168	198	215	231	131	166	186	187	215	229
$18,000–$18,999	214	269	303	303	346	373	65	91	104	119	126	144	193	219	252	270	214	272	309	309	358	382	127	166	186	214	228	175	206	224	241	136	172	193	193	223	238
$19,000–$19,999	221	277	313	313	358	386	67	94	108	124	131	149	200	226	261	280	221	281	320	320	370	396	131	172	192	221	236	182	214	233	251	140	177	200	200	231	246

[1] Total of adjusted gross income (Form 1040, line 15c) and nontaxable receipts such as social security, veteran's, railroad retirement benefits, workmen's compensation, untaxed portion of long-term capital gains, disability income exclusion (sick pay), dividends exclusion, unemployment compensation and public assistance payments.

[2] Local sales taxes are not included. Add an amount based on the ratio between the local and State sales tax rates considering the number of months the taxes have been in effect.

[3] Local sales taxes are included.

[4] Local sales taxes are not included. If paid all year add 25 percent of the table amount for each 1 percent of local sales tax rate. Otherwise use a proportionate amount. For New York City add 102 percent of the table amount to include personal services taxed after February 29, 1976.

[5] Local sales taxes are included. Taxpayers not paying local sales tax should use 75 percent of the amount allowed.

[6] Local sales taxes are not included. Add the amount paid.

[7] Local ¾ percent sales taxes are included. Add 5 percent of the table amount if the ¼ percent county sales tax for transportation is paid all year (Davis, Salt Lake and Weber). Otherwise add a proportionate amount (see footnote 2).

[8] Local ½ percent sales taxes are included. If the 3/10's of 1 percent sales tax for public transportation is paid all year (Grays Harbor and King Counties) add 6 percent to the table amount. Otherwise add a proportionate amount (see footnote 2).

5. A PRIMER ON FUNDING YOUR CHILDREN'S EDUCATION

COSTS INVOLVED
FOR YOUR
CHILDREN'S
EDUCATION

HOW TO SET UP A
SHORT-TERM TRUST

THE BEAUTY OF
EDUCATION
BENEFIT TRUSTS

SHAKING THE
LOAN TREE

TUITION PAYMENT
PLANS

WORK-STUDY
PROGRAMS

WORKSHEETS

Many people assume their children will go to college, but few take the time to figure out how they'll pay for their children's education—until it's too late. Then they're forced to scramble for the money to pay the bills. The tab for tuition, room, and board at a state college now comes to around $2,800 a year if your child is a resident of that state and around $3,500 or more if he or she is from another state. And if your child goes to a private college, count on shelling out $4,568 or more a year. What's worse, college costs are still climbing. According to government statistics, the cost of a year at college will rise some 5 to 9% a year for the foreseeable future. The actual cost of attending a state university may climb at a much faster rate because many services that were once subsidized by the government now have to be paid by students.

If you don't plan ahead, you'll probably have to scratch around for the money to pay the bills at the last minute. If that doesn't bother you, think of the interest rate you'd have to pay on a loan taken out today. And then consider this: You'll be going into hock to pay your children's college fees at just about the time that you should be setting aside money for your retirement.

The sooner you start preparing for the cost of sending your children to college, the better shape you'll be in. In fact, you should start planning for your children's college education at least 10 years before they're ready to enter their freshman year, according to personal financial consultants who specialize in educational costs.

For openers, set aside as much money as you can afford each year, say the consultants. It's your best protection against the possibility that your child might not be able to get a scholarship or some other kind of tuition assistance. If you later find that you don't need all you've saved for your children's education, you can always use the extra cash to invest for your retirement.

A savings program can add up faster than you realize. For example, if you put $165 a month into a regular passbook savings account that pays a mere 5¼%, compounded annually, you'd have $27,000 before taxes in 10 years. You can do even better if you put the money into something with a better yield—say, money market funds, bank time deposits, or Treasury bills. But note that while it's tempting to go for the highest yield you can find, you should always keep in mind that your children's education might be at stake if what you invest in goes under.

Your best bet might be to put some of your money into a company savings plan, if one is available. Generally, you can contribute between 6 and 10% of your salary to this type of plan, with the company kicking in, say, half of what you contribute. Most plans give you a choice of having your money invested in either the company's own stock or government bonds. Note: Before you go into a company-sponsored savings plan, make sure there's a provision for periodic distribution. If the plan is set up so that you can withdraw your share of the pot only when you retire or leave the company, the money you'd be able to get would be cut into by penalties.

You may soon see company savings plans designed to help fund your children's education. So far, only Kimberly-Clark Corp. has this kind of plan, but more than 100 other companies have shown interest in it. The Kimberly-Clark plan works this way: Every employee gets an account credited with a certain amount of money, depending on the employee's performance rating and salary, and the company's earnings per share. The employee can add to this base by contributing up to $200 a year to the account. The company then kicks in 20% of the employee's contribution. Kimberly-Clark figures that interest on an account will average 6% or so and estimates that an account could accumulate about $4,600 in 10 years.

If you're still strapped for funds and don't know how you'll meet your child's tuition payments, you should consider tapping your pension plan. According to a recent Internal Revenue Service ruling, you can withdraw money you have contributed voluntarily, along with anything your contributions have earned, whenever you wish.

The sweet part is that you only have to pay an income tax on what your contributions have earned. Reason: Whatever you contribute to a pension plan comes out of your after-tax salary. However, the earnings on your contributions are allowed to accumulate tax-free until you withdraw them from the plan. And chances are that you'll have been in the plan for so long that your initial withdrawals will only amount to what you've contributed—which means you won't have to pay any income tax at all. Of course, you have to figure that any money you pull out of your pension plan will reduce your retirement nest egg. So, you'll have to weigh the consequences carefully: A relatively painless way of digging up the cash needed for your children's education against what it may cost you in retirement.

Consider tapping your pension plan.

Any money you pull out of your pension plan will reduce your retirement nest egg.

TRUST LESSONS AND INSURING THE MARK

It isn't easy to build up an adequate fund to help pay for four years of college—expected to run around $25,000 to $30,000 by 1984. You need every break you can get when saving money for your child's education because it takes a lot to put just a little away. For example, if you're in the 50% tax bracket, it could take $4,000 of income to put just $2,000 a year toward your child's education. What's more, the interest that's earned by that money will also be whittled away by the high taxes you'll have to pay on it.

Hence, you might consider setting up a short-term trust as a tax-wise way of accumulating money for your child's education, says Steven A. Lampert, an attorney with the Chicago law firm of Katten, Muchin, Gitles, Zavis, Pearl and Galler. Short-term trusts are set up for at least 10 years and a day, or for the life of the beneficiary—after which you'll get back what you put into the trust. The beauty of the trust is that its beneficiary, not you, is liable for the income taxes on what it earns.

Chances are that little, if any, of what the trust does earn will be cut into by income taxes. Up to $750 a year of the trust's income can be sheltered from taxes by your child's personal exemption. And even if the trust earns more than that, its tax rate would probably be lower than 14%. By contrast, you'd have to pay up to 70% on unearned income.

Your best bet is to set up the trust for longer than 10 years and a day so that you can make additional contributions to it from time to time—without being hit with a tax penalty, says Lampert. If you make an additional contribution to a short-term trust and the trust ends less than 10 years later, you'll be liable for the income tax on what that contribution earns, he points out. Of course, if you have more than one child, your other children can also use the income from the trust for their college education. Even if there aren't any other children, letting the money ride in the trust for a few extra years shouldn't be a problem—since you'll get it all back when the trust ends.

You cannot normally use the income from a short-term trust set up for your children to pay for any of your legal obligations as a parent. If you do, the IRS will make you pay the income taxes on what the trust earns. However, there are some big exceptions to this rule. For

Consider setting up a short-term trust as a tax-wise way of accumulating money.

Your best bet is to set up the trust for longer than 10 years and a day.

one thing, sending your child to college may not be your legal obligation—it all depends on your income, financial status, and the civil code of the state in which you live. For another, your state may have lowered the age of majority to 18, which means your children won't be minors when they're ready for college. If they're no longer minors, you have no legal obligations toward them.

Another trust possibility: If you're willing to give up the property entirely, you might consider setting up a charitable remainder trust. Your child will get any income generated by the trust property for a set number of years, and you'll be able to take an immediate (and possibly hefty) tax deduction—because a charity will receive whatever is left in the trust when it ends. The amount you can deduct is based on IRS tables. Since he or she receives the income from the trust property, your child, not you, will be liable for income taxes on it.

You might consider setting up a charitable remainder trust.

If you don't like the intricacies of trusts you might think about giving some property (or a bank account) to your children under the Uniform Gifts to Minors Act. The property will then be under the supervision of a custodian until the child reaches majority, when he or she gets the gift outright. Since you no longer own the property you aren't liable for taxes on what it earns—unless the custodian uses income from the gift to meet your legal obligations as parent. The kicker to making the gift, of course, is that it removes the property from your estate. Note, however, that if you name yourself custodian and die before the child reaches majority, the assets will be taxed in your estate.

Regardless of how you accumulate money for your children's education, consider tying in an insurance policy to the savings plan, says Maurice Blond, an insurance consultant who heads his own agency in New York City. That's one of the best ways to ensure there'll be enough to pay the college bills if something happens to you. Many personal finance planners suggest taking out a 10-year decreasing-term policy pegged to your savings plan.

For your children's education tie in an insurance policy to the savings plan.

Here's how it works: If you wanted to save $30,000 for your child's education, you'd take out a policy for that amount. As your savings increase, the amount of term-insurance protection decreases. If you were to die, what you'd saved, along with the insurance proceeds, would total $30,000.

Or you might consider taking out a $20,000, 10-year endowment policy on your life. If you die, the policy pays $20,000 then and there; if you live, it pays the $20,000 at the end of the 10 years. Note, however, that in that case the $20,000 will be taxed as ordinary income.

Don't make the mistake of taking out the endowment policy on your child's life just to save on the premiums.

Don't make the mistake of taking out the endowment policy on your child's life just to save on the premiums. There's not that much of a saving and it doesn't make sense. There won't be any reason for the policy if your child dies, and if you die your family could have trouble coming up with an endowment policy's high premiums.

A TRUST ON THE HONOR ROLL

Here's a handy way of funding your children's college education painlessly: Have your company set up an educational benefit trust to finance their schooling. It's close to the perfect deal. Your children get funds to pay their college costs, your company gets an attractive incentive package for key employees, and everyone concerned may get some handsome tax breaks.

The beauty of the trust is that it's funded by pretax dollars.

The beauty of the trust is that it's funded by pretax dollars—which means that your corporation can afford to contribute more of its earnings to it. And that means more cash working for you. What's more, the money that the company contributes to the trust should be tax-deductible as a business expense as long as it can be shown that the trust helps retain or attract employees. The Internal Revenue Service has issued several private letter rulings stating that it will go along with this kind of deal, according to H. Bradley Jones, a Los Angeles attorney who's set up many of these trusts.

Any corporation, from a small, closely held Subchapter S to a multinational giant, can set up an educational benefit trust as a fringe benefit for key employees. The corporation should hire good lawyers to help set up the trust. That's especially important now, because the IRS is starting to take a serious look at educational benefit trusts. Generally, you can figure that you'll need a legal team consisting of a specialist in federal tax law and a local lawyer who can steer the deal through state statutes.

It should be fairly easy for a publicly held company to show the IRS that the trust is a valid fringe benefit.

Tax experts think it should be fairly easy for a publicly held company to show the IRS that the trust is a valid fringe benefit. If you're in a closely held corporation, you'll have to show the IRS that the corporation will remain in business after the original shareholders retire or die. Note, however, that an educational benefit trust can't be set up for the children of a sole proprietor or of limited partners.

An educational benefit trust can be set up to finance the education of as few or as many children as the company wants to fund. It can even be structured so that the children of higher-level executives get more than those of lower-level executives, so long as it doesn't unduly benefit shareholder-employees. For example, the trust might pay out a maximum of $4,000 a year to each child of the highest-level executives, and $2,000 a year to children of executives on the next rung. Trusts that Educo, Inc., in Chicago has set up for publicly-held corporations have been paying out about $3,500 for each year of college. Professional corporations have been planning for about $4,500 a year for each child.

The company can also tailor the rate of funding.

The company can also tailor the rate of funding. For instance, if your children are set to start college soon, the company might make fat initial contributions so that there's enough in the kitty to cover their expenses. Once they've been taken care of, the company can ease up on the contributions it makes to the trust.

When your children are ready to start college, the trust distributes the money either to them or directly to the school. The trust's money can only be used to cover actual college expenses such as tuition, room and board, books and so on—regardless of how much has been set aside for each child. For example, if your child's expenses come to $3,000 a year, that's all he'll get, even if $4,000 is available from the trust. Note, however, that your child might be able to carry over any funds not used during his undergraduate years to cover some of the cost of graduate school.

The question of who (if anyone) has to ante up the income tax on what the trust distributes to your child is still a sticky issue. According to groups setting up educational benefit trusts, there are three possibilities—you, your child, or the company will be hit with the tax. However, many tax experts think that you yourself will be liable for the income tax because they figure the IRS will treat the deal as a form of compensation.

Even if you wind up being taxed, you'll still come out ahead of the game.

But even if you wind up being taxed, you'll still come out ahead of the game, says James Jetton, president of College Educational Plans in Dallas. Here's what he means: Let's say it will cost you $50,000 to send your children to college. If the trust covers the entire tab, you'll have to pay close to $25,000 if you're in the 50% tax bracket. Note that you have to pay income taxes only on the amount your company contributes to the trust. The trust pays taxes at its own (generally lower) tax rate on anything its assets earn. Painful as that may seem, compare it with what it would cost you to save $50,000 yourself. Since half of what you earn is being raked off by taxes, it would cost you $50,000 to put $50,000 away.

If your child is taxed, very little, if any, of the trust's distribution will be eaten into by taxes.

Other tax experts think your child will probably be liable for the taxes on the distribution. That shouldn't be a problem, since your child will likely be in a very low tax bracket. Hence very little, if any, of the trust's distribution will be eaten into by taxes.

A few people think that the trust's distributions aren't taxable. However, if that is the case, the IRS will probably take the position that the money going into the plan should be taxed as it's put in. On the other hand, the IRS could say that the corporation can only deduct the money as it's distributed to the child or to the school.

CREDIT TO GET THROUGH COLLEGE

The way college costs are soaring, you may find that you haven't been able to salt away enough to pay for your children's education—despite your heroic efforts. Don't despair; you're not alone. In fact, it happens so frequently, that there are special educational loans and tuition payment plans designed for people who run short of college funds.

There are special educational loans and tuition payment plans designed for people who run short of college funds.

Your best bet is to have your child borrow money under the federally insured student loan program—it's about the cheapest money around. Under this program, your child may borrow up to $2,500 a year (less in some states) at 7% interest and have 10 years in which to pay off the loan. Note, however, that your child can borrow no more than $7,500 for undergraduate expenses and $10,000 for both undergraduate and graduate school.

If your child needs more money, consider making up the difference with a commercial tuition plan or loan.

If your child needs more money to cover college costs, you might consider making up the difference with a commercial tuition plan or loan. Basically, all these plans give you a line of credit against which you write checks to cover college costs. You'd be wise to shop around for the best terms you can get. Here's how the plans stack up at present:

□ Tuition Aid Plan, National Shawmut Bank of Boston, 542 Commonwealth Avenue, Boston, Massachusetts 02215. You can establish a line of credit, the amount of which depends on your credit standing, for up to five years of college. You'll be charged 12% interest on the unpaid balance and have up to eight years to pay off what you borrow. Shawmut, whose plan is more generous than most of the others, will let you use part of what you borrow to pay for

You can establish a line of credit, the amount of which depends on your credit standing, for up to five years of college.

transportation and living expenses. You automatically get life insurance with the plan. But the insurance only covers the unpaid balance of what you borrowed, up to $10,000.

□ Edu-Check, Girard Bank, 1 Girard Plaza, Philadelphia, Pennsylvania 19101. You can get a line of credit of up to $30,000. You'll have to pay 12% a year interest on the first $7,000 outstanding and 6% on anything over that, and you'll have up to eight years to pay off the loan. The checkbook you get can only be used to write checks directly to the school your child attends—not for transportation or other incidental expenses. Edu-Check provides insurance that covers the amount outstanding as well as what's left of your line of credit in case you die or are totally and permanently disabled. The insurance costs 52¢ a month for each $1,000 of the loan outstanding, plus the remaining available credit.

□ School-Chex, Irving Trust Co., 1 Wall Street, New York, New York, 10005. You can get a line of credit of up to $20,000 at 12.17% a year on the outstanding monthly balance, and you have up to seven years to pay off the loan. The checks you write must go directly to the college. An optional life insurance policy, which guarantees the continued education of your child if you die, costs 60¢ a month per $1,000 of the loan outstanding plus the remaining available credit.

□ Tuition Plan, Inc., and Tuition Plan of New Hampshire, Inc., Concord, New Hampshire 03301. The two plans differ only in how they're paid out. With the first, the school is paid directly; in the second the money goes to the parent, who can spend it for education-related costs such as transportation. Both plans give you a line of credit of up to $20,000 at an interest rate that varies from 13.62 to 17.94%, depending on the amount borrowed and how long you plan to take paying it back. You have up to six years to pay off the loan.

It pays to figure out what you'll need and to sign up for a four-year line of credit. That way you'll be charged a low interest rate and you'll have four years worth of life insurance coverage on the outstanding balance and the remaining available credit. The insurance costs from around 50¢ to 90¢ a month for each $1,000—depending on the state you live in.

□ Insured tuition plans, offered by Richard C. Knight Insurance Agency, Inc., 53 Beacon Street, Boston, Massachusetts 02108. You have a choice of two kinds of plans. With the extended repayment plan there's no limit on the amount you can borrow. You'll be charged

The checkbook you get can only be used to write checks directly to the school your child attends.

You can get a line of credit of up to $20,000 at 12.17% a year on the outstanding monthly balance.

It pays to figure out what you'll need and to sign up for a four-year line of credit.

at 12% a year on the monthly outstanding balance and have up to six years to pay back the money you borrow. There's a $25 application fee which is returned if the plan cannot be put into effect. The insurance—for life and total permanent disability—costs 60¢ a month for each $1,000 outstanding if you're between 40 and 55. The money goes directly to the college.

The prepayment plan lets you spread out a year's college expenses.

The prepayment plan lets you spread out a year's college expenses so that you don't have to ante up everything at the beginning of a semester. You pay Knight a set sum each month—usually starting a few months before your child begins college. Then Knight will pay the college as bills become due. There's a $25 application fee and a 50¢-a-month bank service charge. If you're between 40 and 60, insurance costs 80¢ a month for each $1,000 of your outstanding balance. Since the plan will pay 5% interest on the money you prepay, Knight estimates that the charges over four years come to less than 4% of the total amount advanced to the college.

IN PURSUIT OF SCHOLARSHIP

Even if you're worth a mint, there's no reason why you should foot all your child's college costs yourself. There's more than $1 billion a year in scholarships and tuition assistance grants waiting to be plucked from federal and state governments, fraternal and professional societies, and other sources. It's even possible your child might get enough scholarship and tuition assistance to bankroll most of his or her education. The trick lies in finding the scholarships and grants your child qualifies for.

The trick lies in finding the scholarships and grants your child qualifies for.

Generally, the higher your salary, the less your child can expect by way of a scholarship. But even though most scholarships are based on need, there's still a chance your child can get some aid, in spite of your high income. If you have extreme circumstances—say, very heavy medical bills or a number of children hitting college at the same time—your child should be able to pick up some college aid, says Alexander Sidar, executive director of the College Entrance Examination Board's Scholarship Service.

If you have extreme circumstances, your child should be able to pick up some college aid.

You can find out how much tuition assistance your child can qualify for by sending a parents' financial statement to the College Scholarship Service, Princeton, New Jersey, or a family financial statement to the American College Testing Program, Iowa City,

Iowa. The statement should describe your entire financial picture so that these organizations can get a fix on what you can realistically contribute to your child's college education. After reviewing your financial statement they will send their recommendations on what you can afford to pay to the colleges your children are interested in.

Your child should also compete for national scholarships by taking nationwide examinations such as the National Merit Scholarship Test or the Westinghouse Science Talent Search. The Merit test is taken during your child's junior year at high school. At the very least, your child could win a nonrenewable scholarship worth $1,000. If your child's score is high enough and if your company or child's college is a merit sponsor, your child could qualify for a four-year scholarship worth from $100 to $1,500 a year, depending on need.

Most states also have tuition assistance programs.

Most states also have tuition assistance programs worth up to $2,500 a year for students entering colleges in that state. While these scholarships are based on need, almost everybody has a chance of getting some sort of financial help. Of course, the more you make, the less financial assistance your child stands to get. In about half the states, students can get additional tuition assistance by doing well in the Merit Scholarship exam.

The college your child wants to attend may also have a lot of scholarship money to dole out. General scholarships offered by the college as a whole are based on academic merit, and are worth between $100 and $1,200 a year. Although they don't like to admit it, many colleges also have an additional general scholarship fund which they use to attract bright students from around the country. A scholarship from one of these funds is usually used as an incentive to attend the college and may be worth about $400 a year. You can find out what kinds of scholarships are available by contacting a college's director of financial aid.

A college's various academic departments may also offer scholarships to incoming freshmen. These can range between $100 to $1,000 a year. You can find out about this type of scholarship from the head of the department your child plans to major in.

Don't overlook scholarships offered by organizations.

Don't overlook scholarships offered by organizations such as the Elks or Lions, college fraternities, or professional organizations you belong to, or even the company you work for. Some of these scholarships are worth as much as $1,500 a year. You'd be surprised how many scholarships go begging because no one knows about them. Contact every group of which you are or have ever been a member to see if there's a scholarship floating around.

You can make the hunt for scholarships easier through Scholarship Search, New York City.

You can make the hunt for scholarships easier by letting Scholarship Search, New York City, do most of the work for you. For a $39 fee this service will find at least five scholarship sources your child qualifies for. Then it's up to you to chase them down. To play it safe, you should make your contacts when your child is about to enter the senior year of high school.

You should also get *Need a Lift?*, a book put out for 50¢ by the American Legion, Indianapolis, Indiana 46206. It gives a good run-down on many of the scholarships available. You might also consider *Student Aid—Annual* published at $7.50 by Chronicle Guidance Publications, Inc., Moravia, New York 13118. Either book gives you the scholarship picture quite clearly.

SHARING THE BURDEN WITH YOUR CHILD

Why not let your child help pay his or her way through school? It will ease some of the strain on your pocketbook as well as give your child a healthy respect for the value of the dollar— while there's still some left.

At the very least, your child can expect to save between $1,000 and $1,200 of what he or she makes from summer employment and part-time jobs during the school year, says Richard Tombaugh, executive secretary of the National Association of Student Financial Aid Administrators. That might be enough to cover tuition in many schools. Your child would be wise to find a job related to the field that he or she plans to enter because earnings will probably be higher. There's also the possibility that your child's employer may offer an employee scholarship. What's more, there's a good chance that your child will get offered a job after graduation, or at least have some good contacts to trade upon.

Your child would be wise to find a job related to the field that he or she plans to enter.

Most colleges have student employment offices, which try to place students in jobs either on or off campus. Generally, the employment office will try to come up with jobs that mesh with a student's schedule. Some schools also have student business organizations that could help your child start a business on campus. A must book on student jobs and student-run firms is *Making It: A Guide to Student Finances*, published by E. P. Dutton & Co. for $4.95.

Two nationwide programs gear work to a student's career goals. The College Work-Study Program provides federally subsidized jobs

The College Work-Study Program provides federally subsidized jobs for students.

The money earned from a work term can be applied in a lump sum to meet the next study term's costs.

Your child can also save you money by squeezing four years of college into three.

for students. Most of the available jobs will be with your child's college, say, in the laboratory. The rest are with public service agencies. For instance, an aspiring accountant might be assigned to a city's budget bureau. Because the program is federally subsidized your child's eligibility depends on your family finances.

A Co-operative Work-Study Program lets a student alternate a term of work with a term of study. Although most of the programs used to take five or six years to complete, many colleges are starting to offer four-year programs. About 800 colleges now have work-study programs—however, some of them are restricted to the students in certain departments. Since the emphasis is on work as a learning experience, these programs are open to any student who's in good standing with the college. Your financial circumstances are immaterial.

The money earned from a work term can be applied in a lump sum to meet the next study term's costs. However, since students are usually required to live off-campus during the work term, your child should try to find a job close to home. Otherwise, all the money he or she earns might be eaten up by living expenses. You can find out about the types of work-study programs, and which colleges offer them, by writing to the National Commission for Co-operative Education, 360 Huntington Avenue, Boston, Massachusetts 02115.

There also are some ways that your child can substantially cut down the cost of his or her room and board. For example, your child can save you a bundle by living in cooperative housing, either on or off campus. Students who live in cooperative housing trade their labor for a cost savings. In one such house at the University of Michigan, students were able to lop $450 to $500 off the normal dormitory bill for the school year by working a mere four hours a week. You can find out which campuses have cooperative housing by sending $1 to the North American Student Co-operative Organization, Box 1301, Ann Arbor, Michigan 48106.

Your child can also save you money by squeezing four years of college into three. However, your child probably won't have the time to work summers if he or she is in one of these programs. You can find out which campuses operate on a trimester system or have summer schools by consulting the College Board Handbook in your high school's guidance library.

Finally, you and your child should consider the dramatic differences in costs between a community college and a four-year institution. If your child spends the first two years of college at a community school,

Consider sending your child to one of the excellent Canadian schools.

you'll pay an average of $300 in tuition each year (nothing for a school in California if you're a resident). Of course, after your child finishes at a community college, he or she will have to go to a more costly four-year school. Still, the total cost will be less than if your child had gone to a four-year school from the beginning.

Or your child might attend a public university in your state for around $578 in tuition a year—which is much lower than the $2,240 average annual tuition charged by private universities. Note that while these costs are expected to go much higher in the future, the difference in costs should stay about the same.

You might also consider sending your child to one of the excellent Canadian schools: They average $600 to $800 in tuition and $1,000 to $1,400 in board and room a year. You can get a list of Canadian colleges by sending $8.25 to the Association of Universities and Colleges of Canada, 151 Slater Street, Ottawa, Ontario. One caveat: It's extremely unlikely that a U.S. citizen would be able to work in Canada or get a scholarship or loan.

EDUCATION WORKSHEET

First, you have to figure out how much one year of college will cost when your child is ready to enter his or her freshman year. For example, if your child were about to enter college this fall, all you'd have to do is to use the total you just worked out in Step 1 and multiply it by the appropriate multiplier in the table in Step 2. If your child wants to attend a private college four years from now, you'd have to make an additional computation to take inflation into account. For example, if an academic year at a private college currently costs $5,000, it will cost around $6,800 a year four years from now ($5,000 × 1.36 = $6,800) according to the table in Step 3. Finally, use this base figure to calculate your total costs by using the appropriate multiplier in the table in Step 2. For example, if the cost of an academic year at a private college will come to $6,800 four years from now, you could safely figure that four years of college will run you $6,800 × 4.5 or $30,600.

Step 1: Current cost of one academic year.

	Commuting student at a public college	Resident student at an in-state public college	Resident student at a private college
Tuition	$ _____	$ _____	$ _____
Books and supplies	_____	_____	_____
Room	_____	_____	_____
Meals	_____	_____	_____
Transportation	_____	_____	_____
Personal expenses	_____	_____	_____
TOTAL:	$ _____	$ _____	$ _____

Step 2: Multiply the total current costs of one academic year by the appropriate multiplier in the table below. For example, if the annual cost of a private college came to $5,000 a year, the tab for four years would amount to $22,500 (4.50 × $5,000).

Number of years	Public	Private
2	2.04	2.08
4	4.25	4.50
6	5.41	5.86

Step 3: Now, you have to figure on inflation. The experts estimate that the cost of a public college will rise by around 4% a year, and that the cost of a private college will rise by some 8% or so a year. The table below will help you calculate how inflation will affect the cost of college.

Years	Public (.04%)	Private (.08%)
1	1.04	1.08
2	1.08	1.17
3	1.12	1.26
4	1.17	1.36
5	1.22	1.47
6	1.27	1.59
7	1.32	1.71
8	1.37	1.85
9	1.42	2.00
10	1.48	2.16

6. INSURANCE

HOW TO EVALUATE
AND UPDATE YOUR
INSURANCE

HOW MUCH LIFE
INSURANCE DO
YOU NEED?

KINDS OF LIFE
INSURANCE

HOW TO SHOP
FOR A POLICY

WHEN SWITCHING
PAYS

ESTATE PLANNING
TACTICS

DISABILITY
INSURANCE

HOMEOWNER'S
INSURANCE

WORKSHEETS

Willing to make a bet? We'll lay you odds that you don't have as much life, health, disability, and homeowners insurance as you should. What's more, we'll wager that you're probably paying too much for the protection you're now getting. The simple truth is that most of us buy insurance haphazardly. Either a salesman calls and we're in the mood to buy, or we hear of some disaster and decide to get more coverage. That's a pity.

Unless you buy insurance according to a rational plan it will cost you and your family dearly. First, take the cost of premiums for health, liability, homeowners, and automobile insurance policies: They're going to go through the roof in 1977—as if they weren't high enough already. To make matters worse, you're probably underinsured as it is. Increasing your coverage could cost you plenty, unless you shop around and buy insurance wisely. Now consider the matter from your family's point of view. The more you pay for premiums, the less insurance you can afford to buy. Sounds dismal? It shouldn't, because there's something you can do about it. Review your insurance needs—how much you now have and how much it's costing you each year. Then shop around for a better policy, or for a better way of carrying insurance—group coverage if possible. And be sure to pay close attention to beneficiary and ownership provisions because they can materially affect the after-tax results of the proceeds.

LIFE INSURANCE

There just aren't any pat answers or ready formulas. Some life insurance agents, for example, bandy a rough rule-of-thumb that says your life insurance protection should equal four or five times your annual income. Sounds good, but what happens if, after five years, your family still needs all the money you make now? The most realistic way of figuring out how much life insurance you should have is to determine the monthly income your family would need if you had died yesterday.

The first step is to figure out what your family's immediate cash needs will be—what it will have to spend on your hospital bills, funeral expenses, paying your debts, and settling your estate. Generally, hospital bills, funeral expenses, and estate settlement costs will amount to around 10 to 20% of the value of your entire estate. You

Figure out what your family's immediate cash needs will be.

can quickly calculate the approximate worth of your estate by adding up the value of all your property, held individually or jointly, and the total proceeds from the life insurance policies you already own. When you add up all your debts, be sure to include the outstanding balances on all your charge accounts, installment loans, short-term notes, as well as your mortgage and other long-term debts.

Most of, if not all, these "final" expenses can probably be paid for with the marketable or liquid assets you leave your family. But just to be certain, take an inventory of all your assets—including money in savings or checking accounts, money-market funds, bonds, and stocks. Don't list any assets not readily marketable such as antiques, coins, art, stamps, or real estate. If they have to be sold in a hurry, your family may take a beating on the price it gets for them, says Joseph Belth, a well-known professor of insurance at Indiana University. He also thinks you should appraise your assets conservatively, just to be on the safe side.

Appraise your assets conservatively, just to be on the safe side.

The next step is to figure out how much a month your family needs to live in the style to which they're accustomed. Start by totaling up your normal monthly expenses: utility bills, food, insurance, transportation, mortgage payments or rent, clothing, health care, even entertainment. (Leafing through your checkbook should give you a ball-park estimate of these costs, as well as some you may have missed.) If you have children still in school, you'll also have to figure out their education costs. The American Council of Life Insurance says you should allocate 65% of your present monthly income for all these expenses.

Now take your family's total monthly income requirements and subtract what they will get in Social Security survivors' benefits. (Your local Social Security office will know what your family can expect to receive.) The difference between your family's income needs and what Social Security will provide is the amount of insurance you need. Note that Social Security payments to your spouse could fall off to almost nothing if he or she works—and stop altogether if your spouse remarries. Normally, your children will continue to receive payments until they are 18 (or 22 if they go to college). However, if a child has health problems, you should consider providing for him or her for the rest of your child's life.

Of course, your spouse and family will also get the proceeds from your group and government life insurance policies as well as the payouts from your profit-sharing and pension plans. This money, plus any liquid assets left after your final expenses have been met, is your family's hedge against inflation. Chances are that it will amount to a handsome sum. And your family will probably wind up needing every cent of it, considering the way the rate of inflation has been soaring over the past few years.

Every five years or so, you should recalculate how much income your family will need. Then check to see if your net worth has increased enough to provide them with the extra money they'll need because of inflation. If it hasn't, or if you've suffered some investment losses, you should buy additional insurance to make up the difference.

A final note. You can use these same calculations to determine how much health and disability insurance protection you should buy. Having adequate health and disability insurance is every bit as important as having enough health or life insurance. After all, if your family needs, say, $1,500 a month if you die, they'll need just as much (and possibly more) if you become ill or disabled.

COMING TO TERMS WITH LIFE INSURANCE

Once you've found out how much life insurance you need, you're left with the difficult task of figuring out what kind of insurance policy to buy. While there seems to be a bewildering array of types of life insurance policies to choose from, the real question boils down to term versus whole life—the two basic forms of life insurance.

Term insurance is usually a better bet than whole life because it gives you more protection for each premium dollar, says G. Scott Reynolds, an agent in Atlanta for several insurance companies. For example, a $100,000, 20-year term policy taken out at the age of 45 costs around $1,400 a year in premiums—$1,000 cheaper than the annual premiums for the same amount of whole life insurance taken out at the same age. That's because term insurance is pure insurance and pays out nothing but death benefits to your beneficiaries. With a whole life policy only part of your premiums goes toward insurance protection; the rest is used to build up a cash value.

There are two basic types of term insurance—level-term and decreasing-term. Both types can be purchased for various lengths of time, from 1 year to as long as 30 years or longer. With level-term insurance, the yearly premiums as well as the face value of the policy

Every five years or so, recalculate how much income your family will need.

The real question boils down to term versus whole life.

There are two basic types of term insurance—level-term and decreasing term.

stay the same throughout the life of the policy. When the policy expires, you can take out another policy for the same length of time, or longer. Of course, the premiums you have to pay for a new term contract will be higher. (Understandably enough, the premiums on new policies rise as you grow older and become a greater insurance risk.) For example, a $100,000, five-year term policy taken out at 45 costs about $800 a year, while the same policy taken out at 50 jumps to about $1,200. But to get that amount of whole-life insurance for $800 you'd have to take it out at 20, and for $1,200 at 30 years of age.

With decreasing term insurance, the premium generally stays level for the life of the policy—but the face value of insurance protection falls off by given amounts each year. At the end of the policy's term, which could be anywhere from 10 to 40 years, the amount of insurance drops to zero. Decreasing-term policies are often used to pay off the amount outstanding on a mortgage, or to make sure there's enough money to send children to college. That's because the proceeds of the policy can be geared to specific financial needs—which will fall as the years progress.

Term insurance may also be "renewable." Usually this is limited to level term insurance. What it means is that the policy can be renewed for a similar period of time—without requiring any new evidence of insurability. For example, assume you have a five-year level-term policy. When it expires, you could take out another five-year policy. The premiums you'll have to pay for each new policy will, however, be higher, because premiums are based on your age at the time each "new" policy is taken out. The rub is that term policies can't be renewed after you reach 60 or 65.

Many personal financial consultants recommend decreasing-term insurance because the premiums are even lower than what you'd pay for a similar term policy. (A $100,000, 10-year decreasing-term policy taken out at 45 is some $400 cheaper than a 10-year renewable term policy for the same face value taken out at the same age.) S. Travis Pritchett, a professor of insurance at the University of South Carolina, figures that you can use what you save on annual premiums with a decreasing term policy to invest in high yielding securities. The "living estate" you create with these investments should more than make up the difference in protection between this kind of policy and renewable term or whole-life, insurance consultants note. However, they also recommend conservative investments—lest you kill your living estate with some risky deal.

If you buy a term policy, make sure it has the following features:

Many personal financial consultants recommend decreasing-term insurance.

□ A *guaranteed renewability clause*—which gives you the right to renew your policy without having to take a new physical exam. You can usually renew term insurance policies until you're 65. (There are some term policies that can be purchased for life, but they're very expensive.) □ A *convertibility clause*—which gives you the right to convert the term policy to a whole-life policy when you reach 65 or 70 years. Of course, when you convert to a whole-life policy, the premiums will be higher—how much depends on your age. □ A *waiver of premium*—which keeps your insurance in force if you become permanently disabled.

Whole-life insurance policies are usually much more costly than term policies—which means you're not getting as much insurance protection for your premiums. The younger you are, the greater the gap will be. What's more, the premiums for whole-life policies remain the same for the rest of your life. That means that you have to start out with high premiums when you're younger and least likely to be able to afford it.

The annual cost of whole-life insurance is higher than term insurance because part of your premiums is used to build up a cash value—which you can borrow against or cash in the policy for. This is the chief argument used by insurance agents to sell whole-life insurance. But the argument doesn't hold up all that well.

The only ways to take advantage of the forced savings in a whole-life policy are: Using it as collateral for a loan, borrowing against it, or cashing it in. If you cash it in, you lose the insurance coverage. If you borrow against the cash value of the policy, the insurance company will deduct the amount outstanding from your loan when it pays your beneficiaries. Furthermore, the company will charge you anywhere from 5 to 8% to borrow the money.

While many insurance analysts are solidly in favor of term insurance, they often recommend buying a small whole-life policy to handle any contingencies that might crop up. If you don't borrow against the cash value of the policy or cash it in, your family can use the proceeds to pay for funeral costs and other final expenses.

VARIATIONS ON A THEME

Insurance companies offer a raft of policies that are variations on whole-life and term insurance. Generally, these variations cost more and offer less protection for each premium dollar

Whole-life insurance policies are usually much more costly than term policies.

Part of your premiums is used to build up a · cash value.

Variations on whole-life and term insurance cost more and offer less protection.

The more you borrow against the policy's cash value, the more it cuts into the insurance proceeds.

With the "fifth dividend option," part of your dividend is used to buy one-year term insurance.

than regular whole-life or term insurance. Here's how some of these other kinds of insurance stack up:

A *minimum deposit policy* is usually sold as a painless way to finance your life insurance. In reality it's a premium paying technique that's tied to a high cash-value insurance policy. Basically, you borrow against the cash value that the policy accumulates to pay for part of your insurance premium—instead of paying all of it out of your own pocket. As a result, interest charges, which may be tax deductible, form part of the cost of carrying the policy. (These interest costs are tax deductible only if you pay four of the first seven premiums without borrowing from the policy to pay premiums.) The entire deal hinges on the cash value of the policy growing enough each year for you to borrow against it to pay the premiums. If it does not grow fast enough you'll have to make up the difference yourself.

However, borrowing from the policy's cash value to pay for the premiums is like robbing Peter to pay Paul. The more you borrow against the policy's cash value, the more it cuts into the insurance proceeds your beneficiaries will get. That's because the insurance company will deduct the outstanding balance of your loans from the face value of the policy when it pays the policy's proceeds to your beneficiaries.

To make sure your beneficiaries get proceeds equal to the policy's face value you have to take out term insurance protection to make up the difference. If it's a participating policy (one that pays out dividends), you can use the "fifth dividend option" to obtain the term protection so that there's no additiomal out-of-pocket expense to you. With the "fifth dividend option," part of your dividend is used to buy one-year term insurance to close the gap in your minimum deposit insurance.

But in 15 or 20 years, the price of covering your loan with a term policy becomes greater than the dividend payout. Reason: As your loan gets larger, you'll need an ever-increasing amount of term insurance. And the premiums for that term insurance will zoom as the amount of coverage rises and as you grow older. As a result, the insurance company will stop insuring the entire loan and you'll have to buy a term policy on your own—providing you can get one. If you can't, you'll be stuck with paying more and more for less and less insurance. What's more, after 20 years or so, your actual cash outlay will begin to outstrip the deductible interest costs.

The only time minimum deposit insurance seems to make any real sense is if you're 50 or older when you take the policy out. That's

Minimum deposit life insurance bought at 50 or older compares well with the best term insurance.

An endowment policy doesn't stack up to term insurance or even regular whole-life.

An endowment policy makes sense only if you live long enough to collect its face value.

because it takes at least 15 years for any of the problems we've mentioned to develop. Minimum deposit life insurance bought at 50 or older compares well with the best term insurance, says George C. White, a Chartered Life Underwriter in New York. In fact, many insurance consultants say that people should consider converting their term insurance to a minimum deposit plan as they grow older—especially if they're in a high tax bracket and can use the tax deductions they can get for the interest payments.

An *endowment policy* provides only temporary protection. It is taken out for a specified time, say 10 or 30 years, or until you reach a set age, say 60 or 65. At the end of the policy term you collect the full face value of the policy. If you die before the end of the term, your beneficiaries will get the policy's full face amount. The so-called endowment at 85 or variations of it are in effect similar to a whole-life policy.

In terms of pure insurance protection per premium dollar, an endowment policy doesn't stack up to term insurance or even regular whole-life. For example, 20-year endowment policy with a face value of $100,000 taken out at 45 costs $4,200 a year as against the $2,330 a year it would cost to buy a similar whole-life policy at that age, or the $1,440 needed to purchase a 20-year term policy.

And since the cash value of an endowment policy builds up very rapidly—it equals the face amount of the policy when the policy ends—you quickly become, in effect, a coinsurer of the policy. (As the cash value builds up, the amount the insurance company has to pay drops.) After 15 years, about two-thirds of the proceeds your beneficiaries will get comes from the cash value you've built up.

To put it bluntly, an endowment policy makes sense only if you live long enough to collect its face value. And even if you do, you'll still have to find a new insurance policy if you need continuing coverage. Although your policy will always include a change-of-plan clause, the insurance company will likely ask you to show proof of insurability. So, you can't count on that to come to your rescue.

A *limited-life insurance policy* is similar to a regular whole-life policy, except that you can stop paying premiums after a set period of time—often worked out to coincide with your retirement. In other ways, a limited-life policy is just like a regular whole-life policy—the premiums remain level and the policy will usually stay in force until you reach 100—the age at which all whole-life insurance policies pay off, just as if you had died.

The premiums for a limited life policy are much higher than those for a regular whole-life policy—especially at older ages. For example, a $100,000 whole-life policy taken out at 45 and paid up at 65 costs $3,200 a year in premiums, as against the $2,330 it costs for a $100,000 whole-life policy taken out at the same age. And since the cash value builds up more quickly than it does in a regular whole-life (but more slowly than in an endowment policy that lasts as long) you coinsure more of the proceeds than with a regular whole-life policy.

O A POLICY ON PARTICIPATION

One of the biggest debates among life insurance experts is whether a participating policy is better than a nonparticipating (guaranteed cost) policy. (A participating policy pays dividends which can be used to offset the out-of-pocket costs of premiums.) Life insurance agents bandy about a host of facts and figures to support their points of view. However, since numbers can be easily juggled, you have to look at the assumptions behind them to find out how these different kinds of policies really stack up.

The premiums for nonparticipating policies are some 20 to 30% lower than those for participating policies. For example, a $100,000 nonparticipating whole-life policy taken out at 45 costs $2,380 a year as against the $3,126 premium for a $100,000 participating policy taken out at the same age.

The counterargument made by most insurance agents is that dividends from a participating policy will eventually reduce out-of-pocket cost of premiums to a point where they're lower than those for a nonparticipating policy. (While dividends are by no means guaranteed, most companies have paid dividends consistently for more than 50 years.) But what some insurance agents don't tell you is that dividends paid by a participating policy should really be looked at as a refund of an overcharge. Even the Internal Revenue Service recognizes this and doesn't tax the dividends.

What's more, the aggregate cost of a participating policy becomes lower than that of a nonparticipating policy only after it has run for 10 to 15 years or so. What it all boils down to is that a nonparticipating policy is your best bet if you take out insurance at an older age or if you want it for only a short period of time or for a limited purpose—say, to cover mortgage payments or your children's college education.

The claim that participating policies eventually become less costly

Numbers can be easily juggled.

Dividends paid on a participating policy should really be looked at as a refund of an overcharge.

*Participating policies
only seem cheaper.*

than nonparticipating policies is dubious at best. Participating policies only seem cheaper—until you figure in (as you should) the time value of the money you'd save by purchasing the cheaper policy and set off that amount against the dividends the insurance company gives you. For example, assume you put the money you could save on the cheaper premium into a savings account where it earned only 5½% interest. Here's how it would work out:

	Dividend-paying policy	Nondividend-paying policy
Annual cost of policy at age 45	$ 3,126	$ 2,380
Amount annually placed into savings account	–	746
Total paid over 20 years	62,520	62,520
Return-of-premium compounded in the policy	20,581	–
Savings ($746 a year) from lower premiums compounded at 5½% (interest is taxable)	–	27,685
Policy cost net of return-of-premium proceeds or net of proceeds from savings	41,939	34,835
Cash value after 20 years	43,851	43,500

As you can see, the participating policy builds up a bigger cash value, which is obvious since you paid more money into it. And as we've said before, building up a big cash value is not all that great. Note also that the $20,581 built up in the participating policy is an untaxed return-of-premium; but even after taxes on the interest earned on $746 a year, the cheaper policy will come out ahead. (Cost comparisons are at net cost without waiver of premiums.) If you want to lay out more on life insurance, buy a nonparticipating policy with a higher face value—or, better, a term policy offering even more protection for your money.

However, those people who don't have the discipline to salt away the savings in premiums might well consider a participating policy. While there are a number of dividend options, your best bet is to use the dividends to reduce the premium costs of the policy, says George C. White, a Chartered Life Underwriter in New York. Alternatively, you could use the dividends to buy paid-up additional insurance at bargain rates—the company won't tack on overhead or commission charges. The company will do this even if you were unable to buy

*There are a number of
dividend options.*

insurance at any price because of health reasons. Even so, the "fifth dividend option" is overrated and its vitality is grossly misunderstood, says White.

CENTS AND NONSENSE

Comparison shopping for an insurance policy really pays. The cost of identical term policies can vary by as much as 140% over the life of the policy and the difference between whole-life policies can be as great as 170%. The difference in cost between a term and whole-life policy can be even greater. However, trying to find out which policy gives you the most coverage for your premium dollar is difficult at best. Every insurance agent should be able to whip out facts and figures that show his or her policy is better than the ones offered by competitors.

The usual sales ploy is to convince you of the policy's low *net cost—* which agents define as the total premiums you pay, less the cash value built up and any dividends paid. (Note that term policies don't build up a cash value and only participating policies pay dividends.) With this method, the net cost can actually fall below zero—which would mean that the insurance company is paying you to carry the policy. The truth of the matter is that your cost for any insurance policy is more than the mere difference between your premiums and the policy's cash value and dividends, if any.

What's more, the net-cost method ignores the time value of money. Even if you ignore inflation, a dollar is worth more today than it will be in the future—especially if current dollars are invested for a current return. Hence, while the costs of two seemingly identical policies may add up to almost the same amount at the end of 20 years, the policy that costs less in the early years makes more sense than one whose premiums are initially high but reduced later on.

Since people have become more sophisticated shoppers, the insurance community came up with the *interest-adjusted* method of calculating the cost of a policy. It takes the time value of money into account all right—but it still deducts the cash value of your policy to come up with an interest-adjusted net cost. And since the cash value of your policy does nothing to reduce your costs (unless you cash the policy in), the interest-adjusted method is only slightly more useful than the "net-cost" method. The fact is that cash value makes the insurance you buy more expensive.

Comparison shopping for an insurance policy really pays.

The policy that costs less in the early years makes more sense.

Furthermore, the net cost is only an abstraction based on the assumption that a person is going to drop his or her insurance. A more accurate way of determining or comparing prices is the simple or interest-adjusted method. It measures the net outlay (premiums less and dividends) since it measures the cost of keeping insurance in force, not the cost of terminating it.

The *company-retention* method is the best system for figuring out just how much bang you're getting for your insurance buck. Devised by Professor Joseph Belth of Indiana University, it measures how much of your premium dollar goes for insurance protection and savings (cash value plus interest) and how much is retained to cover the company's expenses and profits. Belth's approach differs from the others in that he uses mortality tables and lapse rates to take into account the effect on the company of a policyholder letting the policy lapse or dying while it is in force. As a rough rule of thumb, you can figure that the less the company retains, the lower your costs will be, says Belth.

The less the company retains, the lower your costs will be.

The differences in retention figures for companies offering exactly the same policy are sometimes huge. For example, take a $100,000 whole-life policy issued at age 35. Over 20 years, Bankers Life (Iowa) retains $3,141 as against the $5,394 retained by Connecticut General. It's small wonder that the annual premiums for the Bankers Life policy are $310 lower than the one sold by Connecticut General. Note that Belth suggests disregarding small retention differences—say, 10% of the larger figure over the life of the policy—when it comes down to deciding which policy is best. Retention is then just one of many factors used to determine which policy offers you the most for your money. You should also consider the services rendered by the company and agent, and variations in the insurance contract itself.

Also consider the services rendered by the company and agent.

When you compare policies, make sure that you compare participating policies with other participatimg policies, and not with nonparticipating policies. Reason: The dividends paid by a participating policy affect the comparison. And keep in mind that you have to figure that the dividend from a participating policy is really a return of some of the premium payments you made. Although these policies cost more in premiums, Belth says that the return of premiums through dividend payments in a policy with low company retention will eventually reduce the cost below that of a nonparticipating policy.

Take into account the time value of money.

But, as we pointed out earlier in this chapter, that doesn't take into account the time value of money. Nonparticipating policies cost less to begin with—and it takes a good 10 to 15 years for the cumulative cost of a participating policy to become cheaper. In the meantime, you could be putting the difference between the two premiums in a bank each year. The combination of savings account and cheaper policy would probably put you ahead. Or you could use the difference in rates to buy more insurance.

You can get detailed rankings of the different insurance policies from Joseph Belth's book, *Life Insurance: A Consumer's Handbook* (Indiana University Press, $7.95). While insurance agents prefer to use comparisons that show their policies in the best possible light, they can probably dig up the retention analysis figures on their policies if you press hard enough.

WHEN SWITCHING PAYS

What should you do if you find out you're not getting the protection you're paying for with one of your insurance policies? There are no easy answers. Whether switching insurance policies pays or not depends on how overpriced your present policy is, what the premiums on a new policy would cost, your age, and other factors such as the policy's incontestability, policy loan interest rates, settlement option rates, and so on.

Following Joseph Belth's advice, only consider switching if your policy has a company retention rate that's 10% greater than a comparable policy.

Following Joseph Belth's advice you should only consider switching if your policy has a company retention rate that's 10% greater than a comparable policy. The higher the retention, the larger the premiums usually are—and the less insurance protection you're getting for your money.

Consider buying a policy that has a smaller face value.

If you are thinking of switching policies, you should consider buying a policy that has a smaller face value—especially if you're switching from one cash value policy to another. For one thing, you'll probably need less insurance protection because the assets you accumulate as you grow older should be able to cover more and more of your family's needs. For another, when you switch from one whole-life policy to another, you can cash in the policy you now own, put the proceeds in the bank, and buy a new policy that equals the face value of your original policy minus the cash value.

Here's how the numbers from two actual whole life policies with a $100,000 face value issued by different companies work out:

Age at purchase:	COMPANY A			COMPANY B		
	Annual premium	Cost per $1,000	Cash value[a]	Annual premium	Cost per $1,000	Cash value[a]
35	$1,811	$18.03		$2,183	$21.75	
40	$2,201	$21.93	$ 5,200	$2,552	$25.44	$ 7,700
45	$2,705	$26.97	$14,300	$3,111	$31.03	$17,400
50	$3,314	$33.06	$24,100	$3,858	$38.50	$27,100
55	$4,136	$41.28	$34,400	$4,838	$48.30	$37,200

[a]Cash value buildup is based on a policy taken out at age 35. The amount of cash value refers to buildup reached when policyholder reaches the age at left.

Analysis: You can leave your beneficiaries the same amount of insurance proceeds they now have at a lower cost by purchasing a new policy that has a face value equal to your present policy, less the cash value you'll get when you cash in your policy. For example, if you cash in company B's policy when you're 45, you'll get $17,400 in cash value. Put that money in the bank and take out a new policy with a face value of around $83,000—that way your beneficiaries will still have $100,000 of protection.

Here's how the numbers work out: At $26.97 per $1,000 of insurance, an $83,000 policy purchased from company A will cost $2,238 a year—which is only $55 dollars more than what you're now paying. However, if you earn 5½% interest om the $17,400 you salt away in the bank, you'll make $957 a year. Apply that against the annual premiums of your new policy and your net insurance costs will fall to $1,281 a year.

In fact, the longer you delay before switching, the lower the net cost of the new policy will probably be. That's because you'll have much more cash value coming to you, so you can get by with less and less insurance. Also, the greater the amount you put into the bank, the more interest it will earn. Hence, if you switch policies at 55, the net cost of the new policy with a face value of $63,000 will come to only $554 a year.

Switching from one policy to another may make even more sense if you cash in a whole-life policy and buy a renewable term policy. Even if you purchased a term policy with the same face value as your whole-life policy, you could probably save plenty on premiums. For example, a $100,000 whole-life issued by a company with a low

The longer you delay before switching, the lower the net cost of the new policy will probably be.

Cash in on a whole-life policy and buy a renewable term policy.

retention rate costs $1,811 a year if you take it out at 35. A $100,000 term policy taken out at 45 would cost $1,440.

Some final tips. □ While we're great believers in term insurance, we think you'd be wise to have some whole-life insurance as well. Term insurance usually can't be renewed after you reach 65 or 70. □ Never cancel a policy until you have actually purchased a new one. The medical examination for an insurance policy can throw some wicked surprises. □ One of the major drawbacks to switching policies is that you'll have to wait out the customary two-year incontestability period all over again. This is provided for in a clause, which is standard in every life insurance policy. It states that during the policy's first two years the insurance company may cancel the policy or refuse to pay the proceeds to your beneficiaries if you materially misrepresented facts when applying for the policy. After two years, you're home free.

U ESTATE PLANNING TACTICS

Unless you're careful, a large chunk of the insurance protection you've purchased for your family could be eaten up by federal estate taxes. And since life insurance is probably one of the major assets that you're leaving your family, getting insurance policies out of your estate will probably boost its net after-tax value.

But before you get the policy out of your estate, find out what effect it will have on the estate of the person who winds up with it. Most people transfer their life insurance policies to their spouses. That may save taxes on their own estates, but it may boost the amount of taxes for which the spouse's estate will be liable. Your best bet is to check these estate planning ramifications with your accountant or lawyer.

Transferring ownership of a policy you now own to someone else is relatively simple. All you have to do is file a notice of assignment (available from your broker or agent) with your insurance company. Note, however, that the ownership of group policies can be transferred only if the insurance company and your employer allow it. When you transfer the policy, make sure that you clearly state on the notice of assignment that the transfer is a gift and not a sale. If the IRS should for some reason consider it a sale, the new owner of the policy will have to pay ordinary income taxes on most of the policy's proceeds.

Life insurance is probably one of the major assets that you're leaving your family.

Transferring ownership of a policy you now own to someone else is relatively simple.

You have to give up all "incidents of ownership."

You'll probably be liable for a gift tax.

Consider setting up an irrevocable insurance trust.

When you assign ownership of a policy to someone else you have to give up all "incidents of ownership". That means you have to give up the right to: (1) change the beneficiaries or provisions of the policy; (2) cancel or surrender the policy for its cash surrender value; (3) assign or revoke a prior assignment of the policy; (4) use the policy as collateral for a loan, or borrow against the cash surrender value of the policy; and (5) change any settlement options (which are ways the beneficiaries can take the proceeds of the policy.)

Of course, giving the policy away means that you'll probably be liable for a gift tax based on Treasury tables and the cash surrender value of the policy at the time that it's transferred. (That's only a problem with whole-life; term insurance has no cash surrender value and so there's usually no gift-tax liability.) You can probably cover part of the gift-tax liability with your annual $3,000 gift-tax exclusion. What's more, you can also take advantage of the gift-tax marital deduction—which allows you to make a gift of up to $100,000 to your spouse tax free. Note also that you can reduce the gift tax liability by borrowing as much as you can against the policy's cash value before you assign the policy to someone.

If you're thinking of taking out a new policy, you may be able to avoid any gift-tax liability by having your spouse sign the application. That way he or she will own the policy from the start, even though it's on your life. The person who takes out the policy should pay the premiums in order to help substantiate his or her claim of ownership. If you want to help pay for the policy, give your spouse some cash to make the payments with. You can always use your annual gift-tax exclusion to shield yourself from the gift tax liability. Note, however, that the amount you give should not be directly related to the amount of the insurance premiums. In fact, you should avoid making the gift at times when the premiums have to be paid.

While you may be able to get the policy's proceeds out of your estate, the premiums you help pay for with gifts will probably be taxed in your estate—thanks to the Tax Reform Act of 1976.

If you don't want to saddle your spouse with the burden of managing the policy's proceeds, you might consider setting up an irrevocable insurance trust. That way a trustee chosen by you can manage the assets for your spouse and any other beneficiaries you name. What's more, the assets of the trust will pass on tax free to your children and other beneficiaries of the trust when your spouse dies. (If your spouse owned the policy, the proceeds would be taxed in his or her estate.) Naming more than one beneficiary is also a good way of making sure the trust won't land back in your estate if your spouse dies before you do.

Discuss legal considerations with your attorney when you set up a trust.

Some legal considerations to discuss with your attorney. When you set up the trust, add a clause stating that your spouse and other beneficiaries can withdraw any money added to the trust during the year. That makes the trust, as well as any money added to it, a gift of a present interest. (You can only use your annual $3,000 gift-tax exclusion on gifts of a present interest.) The clause should also limit the amount the beneficiaries can withdraw to, say, a maximum of $5,000 or 5% of the trust's assets. That avoids a complicated legal problem which could result in your beneficiaries being socked with a gift tax on part of what you put into the trust each year.

If you die within three years of giving away a life insurance policy, its proceeds will be taxed in your estate as a gift made in contemplation of death. If you should die more than three years after giving away the policy, only those premium payments made within three years of your death will be taxed in your estate.

Some final tips. □ If your spouse owns a policy on your life, make sure that someone other than you is named as successor owner. Otherwise, if your spouse dies before you do, the policy will land back in your estate. □ Also, make sure that your children are not named as beneficiaries of the policy you've assigned to your spouse. When you die, the IRS will hit your spouse with a gift tax on the entire amount of the policy's proceeds. □ Before you have your spouse own a policy on your life, calculate how the policy's proceeds will affect her estate tax burden. □ If you have ever lived in a community property state, transferring ownership of a policy can be a dicey business. Consider the advice of a lawyer who's skilled in the community property laws of that state. □ Finally, the cardinal rule of personal financial planning is: Remember your objectives, don't be misled by tax savings or gimmicks.

I DISABILITY INSURANCE

Most people carry ridiculously little disability insurance.

If you have enough disability insurance you're a rare person with great foresight. Most people carry ridiculously little disability insurance because they are so appalled by the thought of being disabled that they avoid thinking about the

Social Security and any group disability policies probably will not be enough to cover your needs.

The proceeds from a disability insurance policy are tax free.

possibility altogether. And even though the chances of being disabled are slim, it's not worth gambling about.

The fact of the matter is that the monthly income you get from Social Security and any group disability policies you now carry probably will not be enough to cover your needs—unless you've stashed away a sizable nest egg. The reason is quite simple. Many group plans subtract Social Security, workmen's compensation, and sick pay from the benefits that they pay you, says Von R. Smith of Oakland Financial Group in Charlottesville, Virginia. That could dramatically decrease the proceeds you anticipated from the plan, he says.

What's more, a group policy may pay benefits for only two years or less. Taking a chance on how long you may be disabled is a fool's wager. You can generally figure that the older you get, the greater the chances are that a disability will last for more than two years, says Smith.

Hence, you should strongly consider taking out an individual disability insurance policy. It will generally pay you as much as 60% of your gross salary, up to a maximum of $3,500 a month. That may not seem like much—until you consider that the proceeds from a disability insurance policy are tax free. Here are the most important features to check out in an individual disability policy:

Disability should be defined as an inability to perform your regular occupation or specialty—for as long as possible. That way, you'll still get full disability payments even if you eventually become well enough to work at a less demanding job—say, as a part-time consultant.

The policy should cover you for both accident and sickness until you reach 65 for both accident and sickness, says Robert Waldron of the Health Insurance Institute. Some policies will cover you up to 70 or 75, or your retirement. Of course, these policies carry higher premiums that will probably go up each year.

The elimination period—the time between the occurrence of the disability and the first scheduled disability check—should be as long as you can afford to go without benefits, states Waldron. The longer the elimination period, which can range anywhere from one day to two years, the lower your premium costs. If you have money coming in from continuing salary and some group coverage, you can save a bundle in premiums by opting for a longer elimination period, say 90 days, instead of the normal 30 days. For instance, if you're 50 years old, a disability policy with a 90-day elimination period that pays

Your best bet is a noncancelable policy.

Don't let an insurance salesperson talk you into buying a return-of-premium disability policy.

You'd be far better off buying a cheaper policy.

$1,000 a month until you reach 65 will cost $589 a year. The same policy with a 30-day elimination would run you $760 a year.

Your best bet is a noncancelable policy. The premiums can never be raised and the policy can't be canceled for anything less than failure to pay the premiums. While it may sound similar, a guaranteed renewable policy—which must be renewed by the company regardless of changes in your health or occupation—is not quite as good as a noncancelable policy. An insurance company can raise premium rates on a guaranteed renewable policy as long as they do it to the entire class, say, for everybody in your profession.

Whatever you do, don't let an insurance salesperson talk you into buying a *return-of-premium disability policy*—which gives you a chance to get all or some of the premiums you paid back when you retire or cancel the policy. As tempting as that may sound, it just doesn't stack up all that well.

For one thing, a return-of-premium policy costs roughly twice as much as a regular disability policy. For example, if you're 50 years old, it would cost you $1,200 a year to get $2,000 a month of disability coverage. (This assumes a 90-day elimination period—the time between the occurrence of the disability and the first scheduled check.) By contrast, a return-of-premium disability policy offering exactly the same coverage would run you around $4,200 a year.

For another, getting back all the premiums you paid into the policy is pretty "iffy" when you read the fine print. (1) If you receive any disability benefits from the company, the amount you will receive when the policy ends will be reduced by the benefits you received and (2) If you drop the coverage before you reach 65 you'll only get a percentage of the premiums back. For example, if you took out a return-of-premium policy at 50 and dropped it at the end of five years, you'd only get back $9,300 of the $21,000 you paid in premiums. And that's assuming you never received any disability benefits—which would reduce the amount you'd get further.

Robert Osler, an independent health insurance consultant with Life Underwriters in Indianapolis, Indiana, thinks you'd be far better off buying a cheaper policy and investing the difference. You'll get just as much disability protection and a bigger nest egg later on—even if you invest the money conservatively, he says. After all, a return-of-premium policy only gives back what it took from you—and without interest.

A good disability policy will have some of the following optional benefits: □ A partial disability clause. It entitles you to as much as one-half of the total disability benefits even if you're only partially disabled. Benefits, however, will usually last for only six months. □ A residual disability clause. If, after a qualifying period of three months or so, you can't earn, say, 80% of what you were earning before being disabled, the company will supply the difference up to 80% for the length of the policy if necessary. □ Waiver of premium. After 90 days of disability, you no longer have to pay any premiums for the length of your disability and the company will refund any premiums already paid. □ A homemaker disability clause. It pays enough to hire a housekeeper if your spouse is disabled by an accident or sickness. □ Coverage for a recurrent disability. If you have a disability, return to work within four to six months, and are then disabled again for the same or a similar reason, you'll receive disability benefits immediately. The elimination period won't be applied. However, the duration of benefits (if it is limited to a fixed number of years) will be reduced by the benefits paid earlier.

Make sure that any disability policy you take out allows you to purchase additional coverage at certain imtervals without proof of health. Some companies offer a cost-of-living rider that lets you increase the amount of your coverage by about 5% a year. However, that could add as much as $100 a year in additional premium costs.

Read your policy very carefully. It should cover you for any disabilities other than those caused by wars or acts of God—both of which are normally excluded from coverage. If the protection isn't that broad, it's not the policy for you, says Robert Osler, a health insurance consultant based in Indianapolis. Read the fine print again if a policy costs $100 or so less than other policies. It's a good tip-off that the coverage is probably not as broad as it should be. Finally, remember that there's nothing to prevent you from mixing different policies to get the kind of protection you feel you need.

Some companies offer a cost-of-living rider.

Read your policy very carefully.

THOMEOWNER'S INSURANCE

The cost of having adequate insurance coverage on your home and its furnishings is rising dramatically. For one thing, insurance companies are boosting their premiums in order to make up for their higher claims losses and dwindling cash reserves. For another, you probably have to increase the coverage of your homeowner's policy because it probably doesn't even begin to cover the inflated replacement cost of your home and personal possessions.

The average price of a house has jumped some 17% in just the past two years.

That's especially important because all homeowner's policies have an 80% clause which covers losses to the building itself (not to your furnishings or other possessions). The 80% clause penalizes you for not keeping up with inflation because you'll be paid the full replacement cost of any loss only if you're insured for 80% or more of the house's current replacement value. If you're insured for less, you'll get less than the replacement value—either the actual cash value of the loss (replacement cost less depreciation) or an amount based on the percentage formula determined by your actual insurance coverage.

The 80% clause penalizes you.

Example: Say you have $50,000 of insurance coverage on a home now worth $100,000 and you have a fire that destroys property with a replacement value of $10,000. The way it's figured, you'd only collect $6,250, unless the actual cash value of the loss was larger than that amount. Had you maintained the 80% ratio, or $80,000 of insurance, you'd get the full $10,000 replacement cost. Note that some companies don't apply the 80% clause to losses of less than $1,000 or less than 5% of your insurance. They reimburse you for full replacement value.

Protect yourself against the 80% clause.

You can protect yourself against the 80% clause by purchasing an inflation-guard endorsement which automatically increases your coverage by about 1% every three months. It costs from 5 to 8% extra. Nevertheless, you may still be inadequately covered, since construction costs have been rising by around 8% a year. You should check your home's value now and then and increase your coverage when necessary.

Alternatively, you can offset increased premium cost for a higher assessment on your home by trading down to a less comprehensive policy. There are three basic types of homeowner's policies (HOs): basic (HO-1), broad (HO-2), and comprehensive (HO-5). Each is more sweeping and costly than the previous one:

There are three basic types of homeowner's policies.

Basic (HO-1) covers 11 perils—including fire, theft, windstorm, hail, explosions, smoke, vandalism, and civil commotion. It's quite restrictive: Explosions, for example, do not include sonic booms or electric arcing. Smoke coverage doesn't include damage from fireplace smoke.

Broad (HO-2) the most popular policy, adds seven more perils, including falling objects, building collapse, damage caused by the weight of ice and water, and the freezing of plumbing, heating and air conditioning systems. However, damage to pavements, fences, patios, and pools caused by freezing, thawing, or the weight of ice or water is not covered.

Comprehensive (HO-5) protects you against *all perils* except earthquakes, tidal waves, nuclear radiation, and floods. Note that you can have earthquake coverage written into the policy, and get flood insurance through the government.

If you now have a comprehensive policy, trading down to one with broad coverage could save you 30 to 40% on premium costs. And it won't cost you that much in protection. It will cover you for damage to your home caused by most common perils. Note, however, that damage to your furnishings and personal possessions aren't covered so thoroughly as they would be under a comprehensive policy. Don't be tempted into saving even more money by dropping down to a policy with "basic" coverage—which is around 15% cheaper than a policy with broad coverage. The saving in premiums isn't worth it because a basic policy's coverage is limited.

Reduce your premiums by boosting the amount of the deductible.

You can also reduce your premiums by boosting the amount of the deductible on your homeowner's coverage. For example, boosting the deductible to $500 from $50 could save you as much as 40% in premium costs. Similarly, you could save some more money by increasing the deductibles on the personal property riders to your homeowner's policy. (Personal property riders cover your furnishings and personal effects.) Note that you can usually save money by lumping a number of personal possessions under one policy rider instead of taking out separate riders for each item. You'd be wise to look over what you're insuring with the personal property rider. Some things, such as jewelry that's never worn or coin collections, can be kept more safely and cheaply in a safe deposit box.

You can save money by purchasing a package policy.

If you have your property insured to the limit, you can save money by purchasing a package policy that combines homeowner's, personal property, and auto insurance coverage. If the policy limit is high enough, say $250,000 or more, you could save substantially compared with what you'd pay for three separate policies. For example, a $250,000 package policy will probably cost a good 10 to 20% less than the total premiums on separate homeowner's, auto, and personal property policies.

If you find that your homeowner's premiums are still too high for your budget, shop around for one with another company. Chances are that you'll be able to cut your costs by switching insurance companies. (Warning: Some companies will penalize you for not staying with them for the full term of your policy.) For example, Maurice Blond, who heads his own agency in New York, found a comprehensive policy for a client that was cheaper than one he owned that just covered fire damages.

Premium rates vary widely.

Premium rates vary widely depending on your home's location and the construction of the house—fire-proof building materials, naturally, lower your premium. Broad costs roughly 15% more than basic; comprehensive, 30 to 40% more than broad. Some companies offer a 12% discount if you prepay three years worth of premiums. You might get a lower rate if you install sprinkler or alarm systems or fire extinguishers. Most policies have a $50 deductible clause. You pay a declining share of the loss between $50 and $500. Comprehensive policies have $100 deductibles.

What to look for in the fine print. □ Read your policy carefully so you'll know exactly which situations are covered and which are not. For example, you're not insured for the extra expense if replacement costs rise because of a new building ordinance. □ Only 10% of your insurance applies to structures such as detached garages, tool sheds, and so on. But you can increase this coverage if necessary. □ In new policies, insurance against vandalism, broken glass, and frozen or cracked plumbing will lapse if you vacate your house for 30 consecutive days. □ If you have an office at home and lose business income because of some disaster, you're not covered unless you buy a separate business interruption policy. □ The company may refuse to renew your policy if you rent your home for an extended period.

To assure payment, notify the insurance company immediately of all losses, board up the windows to protect your property from further damage, give the company a household inventory as well as proof of damaged property, and sort out the damaged goods from the undamaged. If you think the company's appraisal of your property is too low you can insist on a three-man arbitration panel consisting of the company's appraiser, your own consultant, and an umpire. Majority rules.

You can insist on a three-man arbitration panel.

PERSONAL PROPERTY

There's a good chance your personal property is also underinsured. Inflation steadily increases the current replacement cost of many items. And as you grew wealthier, your insurance probably failed to keep pace with your personal property accumulations. Moreover, homeowners' policies insure certain items for only minimal amounts, and exclude others from coverage entirely.

Homeowners' policies—basic, broad, and comprehensive—

automatically insure most personal property against fire, theft, and other perils for 50% of the coverage carried on your house. (Insurance pays the actual cash value—replacement value minus any depreciation—of damaged or stolen property.) But 50% may be far less than enough. You'd be surprised at how many items you've probably overlooked—sports and hobby equipment, records, vanity sets, automobile accessories, musical instruments, household appliances, tools, and so on. Ask your agent for a personal inventory checklist, and compute the original and estimated present value of all your possessions. Keep the inventory list up-to-date, and buy more coverage when necessary.

You'd be surprised at how many items you've probably overlooked.

Keep the inventory list up-to-date.

Most motorized vehicles, aircraft, pets, valuable paintings and sculpture, and business samples aren't covered at all. Trees and shrubs are only insured up to $250 each; cash, bank notes, coin collections, and silver bullion up to $100 in the aggregate; securities, deeds, stamp collections, jewelry, watches, furs, and gems up to $500 in the aggregate; manuscripts up to $1,000; and boats up to $500 each. However, you can boost your coverage on any of these items by purchasing a special *personal property floater*—separate insurance for the full value of a specific article. "Floaters" usually cover you against all risks, not just those listed in your homeowner's policy. Rates vary widely depending on where you live and the item you want insured.

You're even more vulnerable when you take property away from home. If, for example, the valuable clothing and camera equipment you take with you on vacation are stolen or destroyed, you're only covered for up to 10% of the insurance on your house under "basic" and "broad" policies. Moreover, the 10% "off-premises" limit applies to the property of a house-guest or a resident employee, like a housekeeper, when they're *on the premises*. For a higher premium you can increase *off-premises insurance*. Comprehensive policies and personal property floaters insure you fully on a worldwide basis.

You're even more vulnerable when you take property away from home.

Apartment dwellers, who don't have to worry about insuring the building itself, can get a variation of the homeowner's policy (HO-4 for tenants) which just insures the contents of the apartment. But if you own a condominium apartment, you can get a tenant's policy that covers improvements you've made up to 10% of your personal property insurance. Such "improvements" insurance works as "excess" coverage, paying you for losses not covered by your building's insurance.

The scope of tenant's coverage is similar to the broad policy—most of the same perils and exclusions apply, including the 10% off-

You can apply for federal crime insurance.

Theft insurance under a homeowner's or tenant's policy has some special wrinkles.

premises limit. There are, however, some differences. For example, a homeowner's policy stipulates that insurance against vandalism and malicious mischief lapses if you vacate your home for 30 consecutive days, but that doesn't apply to tenants. You may want a special leasehold endorsement, so that if fire or some other catastrophe forces you to move into a more expensive apartment, the insurance will cover the difference in rent for the amount of time left on your old lease.

It's now much easier for tenants to get theft coverage, even in high-crime cities. But if you can't get adequate protection through regular private channels, you can apply for federal crime insurance. The rates and coverage are comparable with those for private insurance, but you may have to install special protection devices (police locks, alarm systems, and so on) to qualify. Note: You might get 10% or more off on regular insurance if you install a burglar alarm system or other device.

Theft insurance under a homeowner's or tenant's policy has some special wrinkles: □ You're fully covered even if your property is in a safety deposit box, warehouse, or some other public place of safety. □ Under the "basic" policy, you're not covered for "mysterious disappearance"—a situation where something is missing but you can't prove theft. "Mysterious disappearance" is covered under "broad" and "comprehensive." □ No policy insures against losses due to the theft of a credit card or check. Nor are forged checks or promissory notes covered. You can buy a "credit card and depositor's forgery" endorsement for a few dollars a year. □ Theft of materials used for construction or repair of your home is not covered. □ "Basic" and "broad" policies don't insure the loss of a precious stone from its setting unless you can prove theft. And they don't cover theft from an unattended boat or trailer, unless you can prove "forcible entry" into a locked compartment. You can get an endorsement to eliminate the "unattended" clause from the "broad" policy.

Some clauses to watch for in the policy: □ You need a specific endorsement to cover incidental business equipment or supplies needed to run an at-home professional business or studio. □ Unlicensed motor vehicles like golf carts, for use off-premises, aren't covered unless you buy a "floater." □ If you move, personal property is covered for 30 days at the new location. □ Personal property lost or damaged while someone else rents your home is not protected.
□ "Consequential losses"—say a power line on the next block blows

down, cutting off electricity and spoiling your food—are not covered. But if the line blew down on your property, you'd be covered, because the incident occurred "on premises." □Property lost in the mail is not insured. □Losses due to a "friendly fire" (one confined to where it's supposed to be) are not covered.

If you drop a watch in the fireplace, you're out of luck.

A POLICY AGAINST LIABILITY

Accidents do happen. You never know when a perfect stranger will pick your front steps to break his leg on, or when junior might throw a beanball at the girl next door. Should someone sue you, they'll likely go after every cent they can wring out of you. Unless you have enough liability insurance you could lose your shirt and still owe some more.

Sold as part of a homeowner's or tenant's policy, liability insurance can be written to give you as much protection as you need. An extra few dollars a year in premiums can pay for a lot of sleep at night. The insurance protects you against any actions or claims involving you or your family personally, on or off premises. The bodily injury or property damage, of course, must stem from causes that were personal, not related to your business, and unintentional—unless the "guilty party" is less than 13 years old.

In addition to your family, the insurance covers non-relatives who live in your dwelling and who are under 18 or 21—depending on the laws of majority in your state. (Older resident nonrelatives can be covered with an endorsement to the policy.) Also covered are the actions of pets, others using your property for non-business purposes, and domestic employees in the course of their work for you. If you have more than two domestics, you'll have to pay extra. Here's how your coverage works:

The company will defend you in court and pay claims for bodily injury (including disease, loss of use, death, and medical costs) or property damage (including loss of use). However, there is no coverage or defense for criminal actions. In addition to defending you, the company will take care of costs such as bail bonds, interest on judgements you want to contest, and may even reimburse you for lost income due to court appearances.

Should you be proved legally liable for the incident, the insurance company will pay for the damages—up to the limit of your coverage.

If you drop a watch in the fireplace, you're out of luck.

Accidents do happen.

You could lose your shirt and still owe some more.

The insurance company may settle the claim out of court.

If the amount awarded by the court is greater than the amount of your coverage, you'll have to make up the difference yourself. Alternatively, the insurance company may settle out of court.

Hence, if a rotten oak tree topples over and demolishes your neighbor's new car, the insurance company will take care of removing the debris, pay for the damage, and defend you in court, whether it's your fault or not. You're also covered for fire, explosion, and smoke damage to property you're renting or borrowing. The policy also protects you against any liability you assume in written nonbusiness contracts. For example, you rent a ballroom for a big party and your guests tear the place apart. The company will pick up the cost of the damage.

Excluded from your personal liability coverage are most business activities as well as all professional services and any failure to perform them. Note, however, that the policy may be endorsed to cover incidental office occupancy—say you give piano lessons in your den—for a slight increase in premium. No vehicle licensed to operate on a public highway is covered, nor are dragsters, go-carts, racing cars, or aircraft. Snowmobiles can be covered through an endorsement either to your homeowner's or to your automobile insurance policy. Unless you get a special endorsement, motor boats of more than 50 horsepower and sailboats longer than 26 feet aren't covered when off premises. Note that motor boats of more than 25 horsepower are also excluded, unless you buy the boat after you get the policy. However, you'll pay an extra premium when the policy is renewed.

You'll pay an extra premium when the policy is renewed.

Whether you're found legally liable or not, *medical payments insurance* covers doctors bills, surgery, x-rays, dental bills, ambulance, hospital, nursing, and even funeral costs. It covers situations on or off your premises as well as accidents caused by an employee in the course of his duties.

Medical payments may only go to nonrelated persons who are not residents of your home. (Also covered are domestic employees, even though you were required to have workmen's compensation and didn't.) People hurt on your property will be reimbursed for first-aid expenses, whether they were there on business or not.

Supplementary coverage is meant to cover minor physical damage to someone else's property.

Supplementary coverage, under your homeowner's policy, is meant to cover minor physical damage to someone else's property. It doesn't depend on your legal liability, but is rather designed for situations where you feel morally obliged to pay—say you borrow a friend's table and it's damaged at a party. All you'd have to do is file a claim with your company.

You're covered up to $250 per occurrence, but note that this can't be increased. Motor vehicles, aircraft, watercraft, and trailers are excluded from supplementary coverage.

Some other points. □You're still covered under personal liability insurance if you use part of your house as a studio or office. □You're covered while away from the premises—say while you're on vacation. □Any additional property acquired while the policy is in force is automatically covered without notice to the company. However, your rates may go up slightly when you renew the policy. □You're covered if you're found legally liable for the actions of a contractor or his workers when your house is under construction or renovation. □Unattached boats, camping or home trailers are covered, as are unlicensed vehicles such as dune buggies and lawnmowers when they're on your premises—even if it's a 300-acre farm.

Unattached boats and camping or home trailers are covered.

INSURANCE WORKSHEET 1

ANALYSIS OF FAMILY ASSETS AND LIABILITIES

Assets	Liquid	Nonliquid	Combined	Annual income
CASH AND BANK ACCOUNTS	$ _____	$ _____	$ _____	$ _____
ACCOUNTS RECEIVABLE	_____	_____	_____	_____
RESIDENCE(S)	_____	_____	_____	_____
HOME FURNISHINGS	_____	_____	_____	_____
SECURITIES	_____	_____	_____	_____
CASH VALUE OF INSURANCE	_____	_____	_____	_____
BUSINESS INTEREST(S)	_____	_____	_____	_____
PERSONAL EFFECTS	_____	_____	_____	_____
COMPANY BENEFITS[a]	_____	_____	_____	_____
MISCELLANEOUS	_____	_____	_____	_____
Total	$ _____	$ _____	$ _____	$ _____

Liabilities	Short-term	Long-term	Combined	Annual debt[b] service
NOTES TO BANKS	$ _____	$ _____	$ _____	$ _____
ACCOUNTS PAYABLE	_____	_____	_____	_____
MORTGAGE(S)	_____	_____	_____	_____
INSURANCE POLICY LOANS	_____	_____	_____	_____
DEBTS TO OTHERS	_____	_____	_____	_____
PLEDGES TO CHARITY	_____	_____	_____	_____
TAXES	_____	_____	_____	_____
Total	$ _____	$ _____	$ _____	$ _____
Net surplus (deficit)	$ _____	$ _____	$ _____	$ _____

[a]Limit to "living" and "vested" benefits (i.e., excluding those amounts payable only on death, or which are forfeitable). Generally, such benefits are not assignable. This data should be verified with employer's Personnel-Benefits Department.
[b]Interest and principal payments.

INSURANCE WORKSHEET 2

JOINT INCOME CASH FLOW

Income	Self	Spouse	Combined
SALARY	$ _____	$ _____	$ _____
BONUS	_____	_____	_____
COMMISSIONS	_____	_____	_____
INTEREST AND DIVIDENDS	_____	_____	_____
OTHER	_____	_____	_____
Total	$ _____	$ _____	$ _____

Expenses

RENT/MORTGAGE (PRINCIPAL AND INTEREST)	$ _____
FOOD	_____
CLOTHING	_____
UTILITIES (GAS, ELECTRICITY, PHONE) AND FUEL	_____
FURNISHINGS, REPAIR AND OTHER HOME MAINTENANCE	_____
HEALTH-CARE (MEDICAL, DENTAL, DRUGS, GLASSES, INSURANCE) EXPENSE	_____
LIFE AND DISABILITY INCOME INSURANCE	_____
OTHER INSURANCE	_____
INCOME TAXES	_____
REALTY TAXES	_____
SALES AND OTHER TAXES	_____
PERSONAL ALLOWANCES (MEALS, AUTO, TRAVEL, DUES AND MISCELLANEOUS EXPENSE)	_____
EDUCATION	_____
GIFTS AND CHARITY	_____
RECREATION AND VACATIONS	_____
DEBT REPAYMENT (EXCLUDING MORTGAGE)	_____
SAVINGS AND INVESTMENT	_____
MISCELLANEOUS	_____
Total	$ _____
Combined income	$ _____
Total expense	$ _____
Surplus (Deficit)	$ _____

DATE: _____

THE IMPACT OF DISABILITY OR DEATH

Generally, total and permanent disability (i.e., ordinarily, of six continuous months' duration) will have no appreciable effect on either assets or liabilities. Exceptions to this might include (a) under Assets, the payment of certain principal sums on account of disability. (This, however, is more customary in employer-group disability insurance and, is usually, limited to specific losses—e.g., for dismemberment, loss of sight, etc.) (b) under Liabilities, the waiver of debt service and/or debt cancellation on account of total and permanent disability, where such debts are covered by (group) creditor disability insurance.

Aside from these two exceptions, net worth and its qualitative character remains unchanged on becoming disabled.

On death, however, major changes do take place in the amount and composition of assets and liabilities. Perhaps this is more easily explained by the following steps:

INSURANCE WORKSHEET 3

Assets	Liquid	Nonliquid	Combined	Annual income
1. TOTAL (FROM WORKSHEET 1)	$ _____	$ _____	$ _____	$ _____
2. SUBTRACT INSURANCE CASH VALUE[a]	_____	_____	_____	_____
3.	_____	_____	_____	_____
4. "GROSS" DEATH BENEFITS OF INSURANCE[b]	_____	_____	_____	_____
5. ADD ADDITIONAL AMOUNTS OF COMPANY BENEFITS PAYABLE ON DEATH	_____	_____	_____	_____
6. *Adjusted total assets*	$ _____	$ _____	$ _____	$ _____

Liabilities	Short-term	Long-term	Combined	Annual debt service
1. TOTAL (FROM WORKSHEET 1)	$ _____	$ _____	$ _____	$ _____
2. SUBTRACT ANY NOTES AND/OR ACCOUNTS PAYABLE COVERED BY (GROUP) CREDITOR LIFE INSURANCE	_____	_____	_____	_____
3.	_____	_____	_____	_____
4. SUBTRACT ANY OTHER DEBTS OR PLEDGES EXTINGUISHED ON DEATH	_____	_____	_____	_____
5.	_____	_____	_____	_____
6. ADD ESTIMATED "DEATH TRANSFER COSTS" (I.E., PROBATE/ADMINISTRATION EXPENSE, AND ESTATE/INHERITANCE TAXES)[c]	_____	_____	_____	_____
7. *Adjusted total liabilities*	$ _____	$ _____	$ _____	
Adjusted net surplus (deficit)	$ _____	$ _____	$ _____	

[a]On the life of the decedent.
[b]Face Amount, less any additional amounts attributable to dividends—if any. Do not take loans into consideration, since they are included in Liabilities.
[c]On the life of the decedent.

DATE: _____

139

ANALYSIS OF ANNUAL FAMILY INCOME AND EXPENSES

The Joint Income Cash Flow revealed the composition of these components of cash flow. To determine the financial impact of disability or death, the figures must be recast, as follows:

A. DISABILITY *(lasting at least six months or more):*

Income	*Self*	*Spouse*	*Combined*
1. TOTAL (FROM WORKSHEET 2)	\$ _____	\$ _____	\$ _____
2. SUBTRACT COMPENSATION[a]	_____	_____	_____
3.	_____	_____	_____
4. ADD PERSONAL DISABILITY INCOME INSURANCE BENEFITS[b]	_____	_____	_____
5. ADD EMPLOYER GROUP DISABILITY INCOME INSURANCE BENEFITS[c]	_____	_____	_____
6. ADD SOCIAL SECURITY, VETERANS, AND OTHER STATUTORY BENEFITS	_____	_____	_____
7. *Adjusted total income*	\$ _____	\$ _____	\$ _____

[a]Sum of salary, bonus and commissions.
[b]Regardless of "waiting" and "benefit" periods, lump all such income on person's life—excluding limited benefits from "hospital cash (confinement)" insurance.

[c]Group policies should be accounted for separately because such coverage may not be available when needed (e.g., if employer has terminated plan or, on change in employment, if new employer doesn't offer coverage).

Expenses

8. TOTAL (FROM WORKSHEET 2)	\$ _____
9. LESS ANY INSURANCE PREMIUMS WAIVED DURING DISABILITY	_____
10.	_____
11. LESS ANY CURTAILED EXPENDITURES[a]	_____
12.	_____
13. PLUS ANY INCREASED EXPENDITURES[b]	_____
14. *Adjusted total expenses*	\$ _____

Adjusted combined income   \$ _____

Adjusted total expense   \$ _____

Adjusted surplus (Deficit)   \$ _____

[a]For example, disabled person's discretionary expenses for such things as dues, gifts and charitable contributions; and possible reductions in clothing, meals and travel expenses. In addition, this might include waived debt payments, where there is (group) creditor disability insurance coverage.

[b]For example, expenses for such specialized help as therapist's or "practical nurse's" where not covered by insurance; and increased clothing, meals, travel and similar costs if non-disabled spouse must go to work (in which event, Adjusted Total Income must be corrected to include such earnings).

B. DEATH

Income	Self	Spouse	Combined
1. TOTAL (FROM INSURANCE WORKSHEET 2)	\$ _____	\$ _____	\$ _____
2. SUBTRACT DECEDENT'S COMPENSATION[a]	_____	_____	_____
3.	_____	_____	_____
4. ADD ANY AUGMENTED POST-MORTEM INCOME FROM ANALYSIS OF FAMILY ASSETS AND LIABILITIES	_____	_____	_____
5. ADD SOCIAL SECURITY, VETERAN'S, AND OTHER STATUTORY BENEFITS	_____	_____	_____
6. ADD ANY OTHER INCOME NOT INCLUDED PREVIOUSLY (E.G., SURVIVING SPOUSE IF PREVIOUSLY UNEMPLOYED)	_____	_____	_____
7. *Adjusted total income*	\$ _____	\$ _____	\$ _____

[a]Sum of salary, bonus and commissions.

Expenses	
8. TOTAL (FROM INSURANCE WORKSHEET 2)	\$ _____
9. LESS ANY INSURANCE PREMIUMS ON DECEDENT'S LIFE	_____
10.	_____
11. LESS ANY CURTAILED EXPENDITURES[a]	_____
12.	_____
13. PLUS ANY INCREASED EXPENDITURES[b]	_____
14. *Adjusted total expenses*	\$ _____

Adjusted combined income	\$ _____
Adjusted total expense	\$ _____
Adjusted surplus (Deficit)	\$ _____

[a]For example, decedent's expenses for travel, clothing, meals, and such discretionary items as dues, gifts and charitable contributions. This would include debt service which was extinguished by (group) creditor life insurance.

[b]For example, any increased personal expenses if surviving spouse first goes to work (in which event, Adjusted Total Income should have been corrected to include these earnings). In addition, this would include imputed "debt service arising from payment of death transfer costs.

DATE: _____

7. RETIREMENT PLANNING

INSURANCE IN
RETIREMENT

YOUR RETIREMENT
INCOME

PENSION PLANS

INDIVIDUAL
RETIREMENT
ACCOUNTS

KEOGH PLANS

HOW TO INVEST IN A
RETIREMENT
NEST EGG

TAX STRATEGIES
FOR PEOPLE ABOUT
TO RETIRE

ANNUITIES

VARIABLE
ANNUITIES

ESTATE PLANNING
FOR RETIREES

HOW TO FIND A
PLACE IN THE SUN

WORKSHEETS

Almost everybody looks forward to retiring, but very few people plan for it. Most people try to put their finances in order a year or so before they retire. That's a pity, because they're only short-changing themselves: The sooner you start planning for it, the more comfortable your retirement will be.

Start by running a projected cash flow on yourself. To do that you'll have to figure out what your income and expenses will be when you retire. You'll have to rework these calculations from time to time in order to take into account changes in your salary, pension and fringe benefits, social security payments, investments, savings, and the cost of living. You'd also be wise to include an estimate of the taxes that will have to be paid on your retirement income, says Carlos Betancourt of Betancourt, Hummel and Co. The tax rate on your income may stay the same or change dramatically, depending on how you plan to receive your retirement income. Under the new Tax Reform Act of 1976, your pension, deferred bonuses, and profit-sharing annuity payments will be taxed at no more than a 50% tax rate, just like your present salary. But, if you add in a large income from dividends or capital gains in the year you retire, you may wind up with too large a tax bill. It would probably be better to stagger receipts as much as you can over several years. Figuring out your projected cash flow is not so hard as it sounds. Once you have your cash flow, all you'll have to do is plug in new numbers.

The best way to figure out your retirement expenses is by writing down all your current outlays and culling out those that won't exist after you've retired. For example, you probably won't have to pay for your children's education or support. You can also scratch off job-related expenses such as some clothing bills, the cost of commuting to work, and lunch tabs. Note, however, that you may have to add in the cost of some of the fringe benefits—like the use of a company car, free medical checkups, and so on—that you'll lose when you retire, says J. Chandler Peterson, who heads his own financial planning firm in Atlanta.

Most of your other retirement expenses will depend on how you want to live. And that means you're going to have to take a hard look at the cost of some of your choices. Take housing, for example. If you want to hang on to your present home because you figure your children will visit frequently, you had better allow for rising maintenance costs, property taxes, and all those other expenses that you now have to bear. That may not be worth it when you consider what you'd likely save by moving into a smaller apartment or condominium.

After you've worked out your budget in terms of both you and your wife, you should also break out a separate retirement budget for your wife. True, it's difficult for her to sit down and figure out how she wants to live if she becomes a widow—but, it's necessary if you're not to leave her unprotected.

For your retirement expenses you'll have to factor in inflation.

Once you've figured out your retirement expenses in current dollars, you'll have to factor in inflation. You can get a rough idea of how your expenses will be affected by picking a figure like 6% (or whatever you feel is reasonable), and applying it to each year you have left until retirement. You'll want to revise this estimate as each annual consumer price index comes out. That way, your estimate of expenses will grow more accurate the closer you get to retirement.

HOW TO INSURE YOUR ECONOMIC HEALTH

If you don't have adequate health insurance coverage, just one painfully long illness could wipe out your nest egg and possibly cut into some of your retirement income. (That's not an idle statement. Doctor's bills have soared some 9% over the past year and hospital costs have doubled in the past five years.) Should that happen, your well-laid retirement plans would be demolished.

Just one painfully long illness could wipe out your nest egg.

Sure, you'll get Medicare when you qualify for Social Security at age 65. But generous as it seems, Medicare isn't enough. Here's what we mean: Under part A of Medicare, which covers hospital costs, you'd pay the first $84 of the bill and Medicare would pick up the rest of the bill for up to 60 days. If you're in for more than 60 days, you have to pay $26 a day over the next 30 days with Medicare paying the rest. After that, you'd have 60 more days where your portion of the bill would be $50 a day. Note: Care in a psychiatric hospital has a 190-day life-time limit. However, part A doesn't cover your doctors' bills, private duty nurses, private custodial care or the cost of such amenities as a telephone or television set.

You can fill in some gaps with part B of Medicare.

You can fill in some of these gaps with part B of Medicare—which is optional and costs only $7.20 a month. It will pay 80% of your doctor bills after you pay the first $60. Trouble is, the coverage under part B is based on a nationwide "usual and customary fee"—normally a year or so behind actual costs. Note that part B of Medicare doesn't cover the cost of drugs and medicine administered outside the hospital, routine physical check ups, false teeth, or glasses.

A major medical policy is the best way to cover yourself against the threat of serious health problems. It is designed to help cover the high cost of major surgery, doctors, hospitals, and medical expenses (like medicine) in and out of the hospital. Check the policy for what are considered "covered expenses." Also find out what its scheduled limits, if any, are on surgical procedures, daily room and board rates, and so on. If your major medical policy was purchased some years ago, it's a good bet that the policy has low ceilings for each sickness or accident. Some of the newer major medical policies have unlimited benefits—which means they pay 100% of the covered expenses (even in some rare ones the cost of routine dental work).

Most new policies avoid costly duplications of benefits.

All major medical policies are sold with a deductible—which means the first $500 or $1,000 of the bill won't be reimbursed by your major medical policy. The company then picks up a percentage of the rest—usually around 80%. Generally, the higher the deductible, the lower your premium costs will be. You can minimize the cost of a major medical policy and maximize your coverage, by having the deductible on it correspond to the coverage you get from your basic hospitalization plan. Most new policies avoid costly duplications of benefits by coordinating your medical policies into a cohesive whole.

If you're still working, you probably already have some form of group major medical insurance provided by your employer. Many companies will keep retired employees in their major medical group plans without any loss of benefits, except that the benefits and the deductible will adjust to Medicare payments. And in some states, such as Iowa and New York, you have the legal right to convert group major medical insurance to an individual policy when you leave your company for whatever reason. However, the benefits will then be reduced.

Make sure your policy coverage will continue after you reach 65.

If you own an individual policy, make sure its coverage will continue after you reach 65. Also find out if there are any restrictions on the policy. With some policies, for example, you're only covered if you maintain a residence in the United States, Canada, Guam, or Puerto Rico. If you retire to sunny Spain, you'll be out in the cold.

If you don't already own a policy, try to get one as soon as possible. Should you not be able to get into your company's group plan because of a disqualifying illness, look into the group plans that might be offered by your lodge, religious or fraternal organizations, or professional societies. They often have open enrollment periods when a physical examination is not required. The rub is that these policies may be abruptly cancelled if the group experience is poor.

If you're close to retirement now, you can buy a hospital and medical policy that is especially designed to supplement Medicare. This kind of policy, which will cost you roughly $115 a year, picks up where Medicare leaves off and adds some items not covered by Medicare at all. Because these policies are geared to Medicare and are issued to older persons, you'll find it very hard to get one without some limits on the coverage.

Because these supplemental hospital and medical policies have low benefits, you should consider taking out an excess major medical policy as well. It usually doesn't cost very much and there's generally no insurability requirement for excess coverage under an umbrella liability policy. However, the deductible is usually the greater of $10,000 or the benefits you receive from your other health insurance policies. By getting one with a face value of $100,000 you can be fairly certain no health calamity will cut into your savings. An individual excess major medical policy with $100,000 maximum benefit and $10,000 deductible bought at age 64 will only cost you $52 a year.

Consider taking out an excess major medical policy.

INCOME YOU CAN FEEL SECURE ABOUT

Once you have a handle on your major retirement expenses you should get a fix on where the money to cover them will come from. Your Social Security payments are the best place to start because they're guaranteed and tax-free. Hence, you should consider using this income to cover some of your basic, recurring retirement expenses, like mortgage payments and real estate taxes.

Here's how to figure out what you're likely to receive from Social Security: The maximum amount you can get from Social Security is based on the average of your earnings that were hit by Social Security taxes over 18 years or so—depending on when you were born. The greater the average, the larger your maximum benefits will be. Since the early 1950s the maximum amount of earnings covered by

The greater the average, the larger your maximum benefits will be.

this tax has been climbing steadily—from $3,600 in the early 1950s to $16,500 in 1977. That trend will likely continue. Hence, even if two people always earn the maximum, a person who retires ten years from now will likely get a larger check than a person who retires five years from now.

If you always paid the maximum Social Security tax, and retire in 1977, you will receive $412.70 in monthly benefits. If your wife is also 65, she shall receive $206.35—giving you both a total of $619.05 a month. If your wife is younger, your total will be lower. Couples over 65 get 150% of what a single person receives. Wives who have worked get benefits based on what they've earned or what they would have gotten as a nonworking spouse.

Don't count on Social Security escalators to keep you even with inflation.

You'll probably get even more because your Social Security payments will rise whenever the Consumer Price Index (CPI) rises by 3% or more during the year. For example, if the CPI rises 8%, your benefits will go up 8%. Even though there's a year's lag, that's a lot better than not having a cost-of-living escalator. But don't count on it to keep you even with inflation. The CPI is based on the average spending pattern of an urban wage earner's family—and that may well be a lot different from the way you'll spend your money during retirement. Note that Congress can override the automatic CPI escalator and increase benefits at any time, except in a year in which benefits go up automatically.

If you decide to retire at 62 (which is when you first become eligible for Social Security), your monthly check will be reduced by 20%. For one thing, the average amount you've been taxed on over your working life will be lower. For another, the payments will be reduced because the Social Security Administration figures the checks will be spread over a larger number of years. For example, if you're 62 and retire in 1977, your maximum benefits will be $319.40 and your wife would get no more than $149.70—giving you both a total of $469.10 a month.

You'll get hurt even more if you retire before you turn 62.

You'll get hurt even more if you retire before you turn 62. That's because your average earnings subject to the Social Security tax will be even lower. For example, here's how you would have been penalized if you had retired at the beginning of 1967 when you were only 55. If you didn't start getting a social security check until this year, you and your wife (assuming she's your age) would get $544.10 a month instead of the $619.05 a month you'd both get if you had waited until this year to retire.

On the other hand, you'll also have to consider how continuing to

Consider how continuing to work after 65 will affect your Social Security check.

work after the "normal" retirement age of 65 will affect your social security check. You can earn up to $230 a month or $2,760 a year, and still collect your full benefits. However, for every $2 you earn above that amount, your check will be reduced by $1. Your monthly benefits will be reduced only if your income for the month exceeds the monthly limit or when your income for the year exceeds the annual limit. When you reach 72, you're allowed to keep your full social security check, regardless of how much you earn.

If you continue to work (and haven't collected any Social Security checks), you get a special credit that adds 1% a year to your benefit until you start collecting your checks or you reach 72. If you wait till you're 72, that could mean a 7% increase in benefits. You'll also be paying Social Security tax on your earnings—but you'll probably be able to count on more years of relatively higher covered earnings which will raise your benefits.

YOUR NEW IMPROVED PENSION PLAN

Your pension benefits will be almost as safe as Social Security payments.

Thanks to the Employee Retirement Income Security Act (ERISA) of 1974 your pension benefits will be almost as safe as social security payments. (Up to $750 of monthly pension benefits will be insured under the act.) Here's how to figure out how much you stand to get from your pension.

Chances are, your company already sends you an annual statement listing the benefits you can expect to get from your pension plan. (Under the act, companies offering pension plans must give their employees clearly written annual statements.) Problem is, the benefits listed on that statement normally are based on your current salary; what you'll get at retirement is usually based on your average salary over your last five working years. That means you have to factor in any raises you can reasonably expect to get between now and the time you plan to retire.

Factor in any raises you can reasonably expect before you retire.

To get a fix on what your pension payments will be, you also have to find out what kind of formula your company uses to figure your pension benefits. The results can be as varied as fingerprints. For example, your company might figure your pension on the basis of anywhere between 1% and 1¾% of your final average compensation for each year of service. If you were allowed 1% of your final average compensation (say, $50,000) you'd get $500 for each year of service. If you've been with the company for 30 years, your pension would amount to 30 times $500, or $15,000 a year. Had your company used a 1.5% formula, you'd get $22,500 a year.

If you haven't been with your company very long, your benefits will likely be much lower. But under vesting provisions of the new law, you may be able to carry over some of the benefits you earned in earlier jobs—which will raise your total pension benefits somewhat.

Your pension will be affected by changes in Social Security.

If your company's pension plan is integrated with Social Security, it will be more difficult to determine how much you'll get at retirement. Reason: Your pension will be affected by changes in Social Security. There are two basic types of integrated plan: □ In some plans, a portion of your Social Security payments reduces or offsets what you'd get from the pension plan. But note that any increases in Social Security benefits after you retire won't reduce your pension payments. □ In other plans, the percentage formula used to figure out your pension is based on the portion of your earnings subject to the Social Security tax. For instance, the formula might give you 1% of the first $16,500 of annual earnings and 1¼% of anything over that.

Unless you've built up a very sizeable nest egg, you should think twice about retiring early. It not only reduces the amount you'll get from Social Security but also shrinks your pension payments. Here's why: (1) You'll have fewer years of service credited to your pension. (2) You have to figure that your last five years of salary (on which your pension will likely be based) won't be as large as it would have been had you worked longer and perhaps gotten some raises. (3) Your check will be lower because the payments will be spread over a greater number of years.

All plans now have to provide survivor's benefits.

All plans now have to provide survivor's benefits—which give your spouse 50% or more of your pension benefits if you die after you've retired. It's automatic unless you opt otherwise. Note, however, that the amount you collect each month will be lower than what you would have gotten if you had chosen to forego the survivor's benefits. But unless you've provided for your spouse in some other way, it'll pay to choose the survivor's benefits. What you lose in monthly pension benefits will likely be less than what you'd have to shell out for an insurance policy that paid your spouse as much.

You should find out how much of your pension will be left after it's

Find out how much of your pension will be left after it's hit by taxes.

Be very conservative in your estimate.

hit by taxes. If you choose a lump-sum payment (and your company contributes all the money), you'll pay capital gains taxes on pension contributions for your years of service up to 1974, and ordinary income taxes on anything after 1973. However, under the new pension act you may be able to use a special 10-year averaging rule to soften the tax burden. Under the Tax Reform Act of 1976, you can now choose to have the entire amount taxed as ordinary income subject to the special 10-year income-averaging provision. If you decide you want the money in the form of a regular monthly check, it will be taxed as ordinary income each year. What's more, under the new tax law, monthly payments will now be taxed at no higher than a 50% rate as against the 70% rate that it was subject to before the Tax Reform Act of 1976. If you've contributed to your company's pension plan, you have to pay income taxes only on that portion of the pension check that represents your company's contributions as well as anything that's earned by the contributions you or the company put into the plan.

You can also count on getting a lump-sum payment (which can be used to buy an annuity) from any thrift or profit-sharing plan in which you're accumulating money tax free. You'll get an annual statement showing how that money has fared in terms of investments, but it's almost impossible to figure out how much you'll get when you retire. The stock and bond markets, where that money is likely invested, are just too erratic for anyone to come up with even a semireasonable guess. Hence, retirement counselors suggest that you be very conservative in your estimate of what you'll get from these plans. Note that early retirement will again cut down what you'll get from them because you'll have had fewer years to accumulate money.

The Pension Act has also boosted the amount a self-employed person can put away tax-free into a Keogh plan. You can now sock away up to 15% of your annual income or $7,500 a year, whichever is less—which is appreciably higher than the old limits of 10% or $2,500. Usually you pay the funds into a trust account with a mutual fund, insurance company, or bank.

When you retire, you get the money as a lump sum. However, you can use that money to buy an annuity which will give you a regular monthly income. If you decide to do that, have the trust send the check directly to the company from which you buy the annuity. That way, you won't be taxed on the entire lump sum, only on the amount you receive each year.

*Get the plan best suited
to your present and
future needs.*

*You may be able to
contribute even more to
a Keogh plan by
switching over to a
"defined benefit plan."*

SOME CHOICE DECISIONS

ERISA could make your retirement pot considerably sweeter—regardless of whether you're covered by a regular corporate retirement plan. But you're going to have to make some hard decisions to get the plan best suited to your present and future needs.

If you're self-employed, you can sock away up to the lesser of $7,500 or 15% of your annual earnings before taxes in a Keogh plan. (That's up from the previous annual limit of $2,500 or 10%.) If you do some moonlighting, you may be able to salt away some money in a Keogh plan. Note that if you go into a Keogh, you can still lock up high yield savings account interest rates, which are dropping elsewhere.

You may be able to contribute even more to a Keogh plan by switching over to a "defined benefit plan" that became available in 1976. Under this type of plan, you may be able to make higher than normal contributions (set by a Treasury Department formula) in order to get a specified amount of annual retirement benefits. But there's a catch: You have to fund a defined benefit plan whether you have profits or not. If you have a bad year, you'll probably have to borrow money to make the payments—or play "catch up" later on to make up a lower than usual contribution.

If you're an employee, but don't participate in any qualified retirement plan, you can put as much as $1,500 or 15% of your earnings before taxes, whichever is less, in an individual retirement account (IRA) next year. If your spouse works part time, he or she can put part of what is earned into an IRA to fatten that retirement nest egg. Under the Tax Reform Act of 1976, you can also put money in an IRA for a nonworking spouse. That raises your maximum contribution to $1,750.

If you're an owner-employee of a business, say a partnership, you have a variety of choices: □ A Keogh plan can be set up as long as it covers all full-time employees with more than three years of service. □ You can set up an IRA for yourself alone or one that also allows selected employees to participate. □ Or you might consider incorporating so that you can get even lusher retirement benefits. But before you incorporate, you should weigh additional costs such as special taxes and administrative expenses.

Regardless of the type of plan you go into, you'll have to figure out

Figure out how much money you can comfortably lock up in a retirement plan.

how much money you can comfortably lock up in a retirement plan. These Keogh and IRA plans are by no means a way of saving money for a rainy day. Unless you're disabled, there's no way you can get the money out of one of these plans—or even borrow against it— before age 59½ without being hit with a fairly heavy penalty. (Note that this does not apply to corporate pension or profit-sharing plans.)

If you withdraw funds from an IRA prematurely, the plan is terminated. Bingo! All its assets will be taxed as ordinary income that year—which will probably boost you into a much higher bracket. And as if that isn't enough, you'll also be hit with a 10% penalty tax on the IRA's assets.

If you prematurely withdraw money from a Keogh plan, you'll be hit with a 10% penalty tax on the amount you withdraw—all of which will be taxed as ordinary income.

Look at your own tax bracket before you choose a plan.

If you're an owner-employee, you should look at your own tax bracket before you choose a plan, say the pension experts. They figure an IRA makes the most sense if you're under the 25% tax bracket; a Keogh plan if you're in the 25% to 50% tax bracket; and a corporate plan if you make more than $50,000. They reason that you can contribute more (and hence shelter more income) to a Keogh than an IRA, and even more to a corporate plan.

But there are other factors you should plug into your calculations. For example, you have to figure that a Keogh will cost your company or partnership a bundle if you have a large number of eligible employees. That's because your business has to make contributions to the plan on their behalf. And since the Keogh plan has to cover all eligible employees uniformly, that could come to a tidy sum. If you were to contribute, say, 15% of your salary to the plan, your business has to contribute an amount equal to 15% of their salaries to the plan. (With a defined benefit Keogh plan, this would vary according to the age mix of your employees.) If you find the cost to your business is too high, you might consider setting up an IRA for just yourself and giving raises to a few valued employees for them to fund their IRAs.

Consider how the payout of the plans will be taxed when you retire.

You'll also have to consider how the payout of the plans will be taxed when you retire. With a Keogh or corporate retirement plan, you may get a tax break by taking your benefits as a lump sum and using a special 10-year averaging provision to ease the tax bite on what you receive. (If you're already in a Keogh or corporate plan, part of your payout can be taxed as capital gains.) The payout of an IRA is taxed as ordinary income.

No matter what type of plan you go into, you'll have to decide how

*Consider diversifying
your investments.*

you want your retirement money invested. You should consider diversifying your investments, pension consultants say. You can do that by setting up separate Keoghs or IRAs or by putting your contributions into one of the newer "master" plans that offer a variety of investments.

If you decide you want to join a prototype trust to handle your investments (most people do), insist that the trust instrument give you the right to: (1) name a beneficiary for your Keogh, (2) switch investments, (3) receive the money either in a lump sum or in installments when you retire, and (4) choose how long a payout if you want installments. You should also make sure that you and your employees have the right to make voluntary contributions under a Keogh—that way you can contribute up to an extra $2,500 or 10% of your income (whichever is less). Those dollars won't be tax deductible, but the earnings on them will accumulate tax free.

INVESTING IN A STANDARD OF LIVING

Generous as they might seem, your pension plan and Social Security will probably pay out less than half of what you make during your last working years. If you run a projected cash flow on yourself, you'll probably find that your retirement income falls way short of your anticipated expenses. That means your standard of living will fall drastically unless you pull in some extra money from investments to augment your retirement income.

*You'll probably find that
your retirement income
falls way short of your
anticipated expenses.*

Problem is, it takes a lot of investment capital to generate just a little annual income. For example, if you're a male, 65 and about to retire, it will cost you $112,275 to buy a sole-life annuity that pays out $12,000 a year. (At current prices, you can figure on shelling out around $9,350 for every $1,000 of annual income from a sole life annuity.) Now consider this: That's the current price of about the cheapest kind of annuity around; you can figure on paying a lot more for it some years from now because of medical breakthroughs in cancer and heart disease—which will increase longevity.

*Socking money away
regularly is the best
way.*

Socking money away regularly is the best way to build up a retirement nest egg. The earlier you start, the less you'll have to put away each year. Management consultants Towers, Perrin, Forster & Crosby were asked to work out a table that shows you how much you have to invest each year at 6 or 8% to accumulate $1,000. If you figure that you'll need a nest egg of $100,000 in 15 years you'll have to put away around $4,180 a year at 6%, according to the chart below. (Of course, you'll likely need to put away more than that to make up for inflation.)

Annual savings required to accumulate $1,000 over various periods of time:

Number of Years	Interest Rate	
	At 6%	At 8%
1	$973.51	$965.10
5	172.70	164.51
10	73.86	66.62
15	41.82	35.54
20	26.46	21.09
25	17.74	13.20
30	12.29	8.52

Note: The table is based on the assumption that payments are made monthly and that the interest rate is net after taxes.

Shelter your retirement income from taxes.

You can shelter much of this income from taxes by investing through one of your company's qualified retirement plans, says J. Chandler Peterson, of Atlanta. Some companies will let you contribute up to 10% of your annual salary to one of their voluntary retirement plans. What's more, most of them will let you decide (within certain limits) how your money is to be invested—in stocks, bonds, or whatever. Some companies will even let you specify Treasury bills or a no-load money-market fund. If you later need the money for an emergency or to invest in a better deal, you can withdraw your contributions from the voluntary retirement plan at any time.

Set up a retirement plan of your own.

If your company doesn't have a contributory retirement plan or if you don't like the way the company's plan is managed and you have the option to get out (or if there isn't one), set up one of your own. Under ERISA you can put up to 15% of your annual salary or $1,500 (whichever is less) into an individual retirement account. While not as much can be put into such a plan, you get more investment freedom and control, while getting all the tax advantages of a regular, contributory retirement plan. What's more, the Tax Reform Act of 1976 lets you put an extra $250 a year into an IRA if your spouse does not work.

If you're self-employed, you can establish a tax-free Keogh retirement plan.

If you're self-employed, or earn income from a source outside your company, you can establish a tax-free Keogh retirement plan. Under ERISA, you can now put away up to 15% of what you earn each year from self-employment or $7,500 (whichever is less) into one of these plans. You can probably put in even more if it's a "defined benefit" plan.

The Keogh plan you set up will probably be run by a bank or a trust company, which has to maintain a fairly conservative investment posture. However, they should be willing to put your money into one of the better, well-established money-market funds when interest rates are rising and the stock market is plunging. Later, when short-term interest rates drop, you can ask your Keogh plan's administrator to pull your money out of the money-market fund and invest it in, say, stocks or medium-term (two- to five-year maturity) bonds.

LOOKING AHEAD WILL SAVE YOU TAXES

Why lose more money than necessary to taxes?

You'll probably need every cent you can lay your hands on when you retire. So why lose more money than necessary to taxes? Herb Paul, director of tax services for the New York office of Touche Ross, says you should ask your tax advisor to draw up a tax plan at least three years before you retire. Here are some points to consider:

You have to decide whether to take the payout offered by profit-sharing or thrift plans (as well as by some pension plans) as a lump sum or in the form of monthly checks. If you opt for a monthly income you'll have to pay ordinary income tax on that portion of the check that covers your company's contributions and what the plan has earned. You get back tax-free any money you put into the plan yourself. What's more, under the new tax law, the maximum tax rate on profit-sharing payout has been reduced to 50%.

The maximum tax rate on the profit-sharing payout has been lowered to 50%.

Most people decide to take whatever they have coming to them from a profit-sharing or thrift plan as a lump sum. For one thing, they worry that inflation will steadily whittle down the purchasing power of money spread out over a number of years. For another, they may get a tax break by taking the plan's payout as a lump sum. Any money that's attributable to the years you were in the plan up to the end of 1973 may be taxed at long-term capital gains rates, and anything after that as ordinary income. However, under the 1976 Tax Act, you can elect to take the whole sum as ordinary income.

You can also get a big tax break by taking at least part of the payout in your company's stock.

Here's how it works: Assume you were in a plan for 10 years, five of which fell before 1974. That would mean that half the payout you get can be taxed at long-term capital gains rates. The alternative tax on capital gains—25% on the first $50,000 and 35% on anything over that—will more than likely be lower than your income tax bracket. The other half of your payout is taxed as ordinary income, but you can use a 10-year forward averaging provision to soften the tax burden—providing that you've been in the plan for at least five years.

You can also get a big tax break by taking at least part of the payout from your profit-sharing or thrift plan in your company's stock. That's because you'd have to pay tax only on what the securities cost the plan even if the stock has since tripled in price. Of course, when you sell the stock, you'll have to pay a capital gains tax on the difference between what it cost the plan and the price at which you sell it. Any other kind of securities will be valued at the fair market price on the date they're distributed to you. That might mean that some of the appreciation in the shares will be taxed at ordinary income rates if some of the payout is attributable to years after 1973.

If you're self-employed or an employee-stockholder of a Subchapter S corporation and own 10% or more of the company's stock, you can accumulate retirement income tax-free under a Keogh plan. The payout is taxed under the same rules as are the distributions of a regular corporation's pension or profit-sharing plan. If you set up an individual retirement account as an employee not covered by any other kind of plan, any payout you get will be taxed as ordinary income, regardless of whether you choose a lump-sum or a monthly income.

If you decide to take your profit-sharing or pension plan as a lump sum, consider holding off selling any assets until the year after you retire. That lets you take full advantage of the capital gains alternative tax rate. Deferral may even make sense if you select 10-year income averaging for the entire distribution.

Let's say you'll get $30,000 in capital gains from your profit-sharing plan, and expect a gain of $60,000 from the sale of property. If you take both capital gains in the same year, the first $50,000 will be taxed at the 25% rate and the remaining $40,000 at 35%. That comes to a $26,500 tax bill. However, if you take the capital gain from the profit-sharing plan the year you retire, it will all be taxed at the 25% rate. You can then sell the property a year later when you'll pay 25% on the first $50,000 of your gain, and 35% on only $10,000. That comes to a $23,500 tax bill, which means you've saved $3,000 in taxes.

Shift investment income to a low tax bracket member of your family.

Some states will reduce taxes on your house.

You might also consider putting some income-generating assets into a Clifford Trust—which runs for at least 10 years and a day or for the life of the beneficiary. The idea is to shift investment income to a low tax bracket member of your family while you're earning a lot of money. By timing it right, you can set up the trust so that it ends when you start your retirement—at which time you'll get the property back.

When you reach 65, you may be able to get two tax breaks on your home. First you may be able to lower your property taxes. Some states, such as Vermont and Michigan, will reduce the amount of tax paid if the tax exceeds a certain percentage of your total income. Other states, particularly in the South, will cut the assessment on your house or exempt a fraction of the assessment once you reach age 65.

You may also qualify for a one-time-only federal tax break if you sell your house after you reach age 65. (To qualify you have to own the house for eight years, and to have lived in it for five of the eight years preceding the sale.) If you meet the requirements, you can exclude all or part of the gain when you sell the house. And, of course, if you were to buy another house within 12 months, or build another house within 18 months, you could postpone paying tax on any of the gain not excluded.

CAN YOU LIVE WITHOUT AN ANNUITY?

Many people approaching retirement turn to the life insurance annuity as a financial security blanket. But at current rates of inflation, fixed income from a traditional annuity may hardly amount to a fig leaf. Some financial advisors suggest you might be better off creating your own more lucrative retirement nest egg through flexible financial planning. However, if you're going to get a lump of cash from your profit sharing plan when you retire and don't want to be saddled with managing it, you might consider purchasing an annuity. Similarly, an insurance company will let you "trade in" your policy's cash value in exchange for an annuity. The advantages are that the "exchange" rate may be more favorable than the current "open market" rate because there isn't a sales charge or a premium tax—which some states levy on this kind of transaction.

Fixed annuities pay a fixed monthly amount for life. How much depends on how much you invest, your age, and your sex (annuities

There are several annuity options.

Once annuity payments begin, your investment is generally locked up for life.

for women pay less because women live longer) and on the type of annuity you select.

There are several annuity options: □ *A sole life annuity* stops paying when you die. If that happened just months after the payments began, the entire investment would be lost. □ *A life annuity with "years certain" provision* costs more, but guarantees that when you die payments will continue to your beneficiary for some fixed period—usually 10, 15, or 20 years. □ *Refund annuities* promise that if you die before recovering your total investment, the balance will be returned to your beneficiary—either in a lump sum or in installments. □ *A joint and survivor annuity* guarantees a regular income to two persons—usually a husband and wife—as long as either one is alive. It's the most expensive option and comes in several versions. For example, a joint and two-thirds survivorship means that the surviving spouse collects two-thirds of the original amount for life.

You can buy immediate or deferred annuities. If you purchase one that's immediate, you invest a lump sum and payments begin right away. Deferred annuities can be purchased with one payment or investment and the annuity payouts start at whatever future age you choose. In the interim, your paid-in premiums earn interest at a guaranteed rate, which may be increased at the discretion of the insurance company. With a deferred annuity, you can cash in the funds you've paid into your accumulation fund any time before annuity payouts begin.

Fixed dollar annuities of any kind have a number of serious drawbacks. They fail to protect you against inflation precisely when you're most vulnerable—during your retirement years. Illiquidity is another problem. Once annuity payments begin, your investment is generally locked up for life. You can't cash it in even in an emergency. Moreover, plunking down a bundle in an annuity may leave your heirs with nothing—especially if you buy a sole-life annuity which ends when you die. Some annuity contracts with "certain" or "refund" benefits let you take out some cash from the policy. What you get is actually the commuted or discounted value of future payments. Hence, the annuity won't pay you until you've lived past the time these payments were scheduled to stop.

Even that most sacrosanct annuity feature—guaranteed income for life, no matter how long you live—is less than it seems. With a sole-life annuity that started at age 65, it would take about 12 years for your annuity income to exceed your original investment. But the average 65-year-old is only expected to live an additional 14.4 years.

A simple savings account can match the payout on most annuities.

By contrast, even a simple savings account can last well beyond normal life expectancy, and still match the payout on most annuities. For example: A representative sole-life annuity guarantees $100 a month at age 65 on an investment of about $12,500. A savings account earning 5¼% could pay out $100 a month for around 16 years (well beyond a normal life expectancy) before exhausting the $12,500 in capital. Of course, there's no guarantee that a savings account will pay 5¼% or any other rate for an indefinite length of time. And you may live much longer than your "life expectancy." After all, 50% of us will still be around at our life expectancy age.

Until recently, deferred annuities were especially bad. The guaranteed rate of accumulation, after sales charges, was often less than 3%. There are few ways to do worse. The after tax return on a 6% savings account, for example, is 4% for someone in the 35% tax bracket. An investment in tax-exempt municipals, a tax-exempt bond fund, or even U.S. savings bonds might accumulate even more rapidly. Moreover, because of the front-end sales load, cash value accumulations in the average deferred contract didn't equal paid-in premiums until the sixth year or later. If you need to cash it in early in the accumulation period, you may sustain a loss.

Fixed annuities do enjoy some tax breaks.

Despite all the drawbacks, fixed annuities do enjoy some tax breaks. Interest in a deferred annuity accumulates tax-free like the cash value in a life insurance policy. And payouts on both immediate and deferred annuities are partially tax-exempt, because they represent a return on invested capital. For example, if you invest $50,000, and it's assumed, given your life expectancy, that you'll eventually collect $100,000, then 50% of each monthly payment is nontaxable. This "exclusion ratio" continues to operate even after you've recovered your full $50,000 investment. In addition, dividends from a participating policy may augment benefits.

Shopping tips. □Stay away from deferred annuities, especially at early ages. You can do better investing in tax-exempts, and buying an annuity later on. □Select the plan best suited to your liquidity and estate needs. For example, even if you're married, you still might purchase a sole-life option and use the extra money to buy additional life insurance. □Compare prices and payout rates on immediate annuities. The cost spread between different companies is large and changes often. For example, a life annuity paying $100 a month at age 65 might cost anywhere from $12,000 to $14,000, depending on the

Shop the market.

Payout rates may be far better elsewhere.

company. □Shop the market. One company may do poorly on a sole-life annuity, but do much better on a "years certain" option. □Check out the Canadian companies. They often outperform their U.S. competitors. □Don't automatically convert the cash value in your life insurance policy into an annuity. Although your initial acquisition costs may be lower with your old company, payout rates may be far better elsewhere. □Don't buy an annuity from a company that isn't licensed by the state in which you now live or the one you expect to retire to. The state's insurance or banking department can give you this information.

GETTING A FIX ON VARIABLE ANNUITIES

The big problem with most conventional sources of retirement income is that they don't protect you against inflation. So someone came up with the idea of a variable annuity—which is tied to stock market performance and is hence supposed to act as an inflation hedge.

Unlike a fixed annuity, the variable contract guarantees nothing.

But unlike a fixed annuity which pays a fixed monthly amount for life, the variable contract guarantees nothing. Your premiums are placed in a variable account (a pooled account just like a mutual fund) which the insurance company invests mainly in common stocks. If the common stock portfolio does well, you may eventually receive more than you would have from a fixed annuity; if it does poorly, you'll probably receive less. Moreover, if you need to cash in the annuity contract during the "accumulation period" before you begin receiving annuity income you may sustain a loss if the variable account does poorly with its investments.

Except for its mortality and administration guarantees, a variable annuity promises no more—and no less—than a mutual fund accumulation-withdrawal plan. However, the average mutual fund is a more flexible vehicle because you can alter the rate or amount of your withdrawals or liquidate shares when you please. With a variable annuity, on the other hand, you can't liquidate your investment once you begin receiving annuity income, and the rate of withdrawal is fixed in the contract.

The singular advantage the variable annuity has over most mutual funds is that it provides you with tax-free accumulation of investment income. But note that if you cash in part of or all the annuity, any gain will be taxed as ordinary income.

Since most insurance companies have only recently introduced the individual variable annuity, measuring performance is difficult. A Prudential Insurance Co. spokesman admits that over the last three to four years its individual variable annuity hasn't done so well as a savings account. Of course, you might want to start investing in a variable annuity when stock prices are low. Then when the market rebounds, you'll enjoy the benefits of dollar cost averaging over the long term. Some shopping tips are as follows:

1. If you're interested in an annuity at all, you should combine the variable product with a fixed annuity both during the accumulation and pay-out periods. By including a fixed annuity, you can at least count on some definite amount of retirement income—and hope that the variable annuity does well enough to act as an inflation hedge.

2. Study the variable annuity prospectus carefully. Policy provisions vary widely from company to company. Look first at the sales charge. A heavy front-end load can make a big difference in net accumulation in the early years. Aetna Life and Casualty, for example, hits you with a sales charge of as much as 20% a year over the first 12 years. Most companies charge between 8 and 10% over the life of your contributions.

3. Check out the management fees and the mortality expense charges—by which insurance companies cover themselves for a margin of error in their actuarial tables. These can amount to 1 to 2%. Although the charges may seem small, they're deducted throughout the accumulation and pay-out periods and are charged against the investment performance of the variable account.

4. Investigate the *death benefit clause.* If you die before the pay-out begins, some companies will only refund the current accumulation value of your account. If the market's off, your beneficiary may receive less than you invested. For a slight additional charge, companies like Hartford will guarantee to refund either the current value of the account or the total paid-in investment, whichever is greater.

5. Make sure the contract includes a *waiver of premium rider* which

With the individual variable annuity, measuring performance is difficult.

Look first at the sales charge.

Investigate the "death benefit" clause.

promises that if you're totally disabled before age 60, the company will credit regular premiums to your account up to age 65.

6. Watch out for the assumed interest rate used by the company to figure out your first month's payout. It may be just a sales gimmick. If the company uses a high assumed rate, you'll get a fat pay-out in the first month. But it's highly unlikely that the variable account will do well enough for future payments to match that or rise above it—as they should if they're to be an inflation hedge.

Two recent innovations in variable annuities are worth considering. The *cost-of-living annuity,* which is offered by Colonial Penn Life and Dominion Life (Ontario, Canada), is a hybrid of fixed and variable annuities. Colonial Penn's policy promises an automatic 3% annual increase in annuity benefits through age 90. Although it may seem less at first than average annuity benefits, by age 70 the annuity pays out more than does a fixed one.

First Investment Annuity Co. of America sells *an investment annuity* which gives you (instead of the insurance company) control over investment decisions, while preserving the tax advantages of a normal variable contract. The investment annuity allows you to vary your investment objectives, and might be ideal if you have the time and competence to manage your own equities portfolio—or can afford having a portfolio manager do this for you.

Don't completely swallow the sales pitch made by investment annuity salespersons.

But don't completely swallow the sales pitch made by investment annuity salespersons. Some of the assumptions need to be examined. For one thing, most investment annuities have a front-end fee of 2 to 4%—depending on the insurance company offering it and the assets used to fund it. In addition, there's an annual administrative fee that amounts to between .50 and .85% of your assets in the annuity. Some companies will also hit you with a custodial fee of $1.50 for each asset in the annuity. And finally, there's a transaction fee, which can be as high as $15. If you sell one bond to buy another, you could be slammed with as much as $30 in fees on the deal. This could be a real killer—considering how volatile the stock and bond markets can get.

As for the tax shelter, it's a little elusive.

As for the tax shelter, it's a little elusive. You're liable for any capital gains realized on assets in the annuity—and at corporate rates. Hence long-term gains are taxed at a 30% rate and short-term gains are taxed at a 48% rate. Furthermore, you'll have to pay a regular income tax on the rest when the gain is finally paid to you.

LOOKING AFTER AFFAIRS OF ESTATE

As you approach your 50s, you'd be wise to shift some of your attention from estate planning, and start focusing on building up a fat living estate that will make your retirement years more comfortable. Here are some points to consider:

Trusts. Unless you're extremely well off, shy away from setting up an irrevocable trust once you've reached middle age, says Frank Berall, an attorney with the firm of Copp, Brenneman, Tighe, Koletsky & Berall, in Hartford, Conn. Irrevocable trusts are a standard way of getting property permanently out of your estate so that it won't be gouged by estate taxes. But the problem is that you can't touch any assets put into an irrevocable trust, even if you should need to raise money for some unexpected emergency.

However, if you're in a high tax-bracket, you could use a short-term irrevocable trust like the Clifford trust, says Steven A. Lampert, a Chicago attorney with the firm of Katten, Muchin, Gitles, Zavis, Pearl & Galler. It allows you to shift income to a low tax-bracket family member or friend for at least 10 years and a day or the life of the beneficiary. When the trust ends—say, the year you retire—you'd get all the property back.

You have to decide carefully how the death benefits from your pension or profit sharing plan are to be paid out to your widow. The choices are: (1) a lump sum or (2) installments over a minimum of two to three years. If you choose a lump-sum distribution, it will be included in your estate where it will be subject to estate taxes. However, you can use your marital deduction to shelter part or all of the estate tax liability. On the other hand, there is an income tax advantage. Lump sum distributions will be taxed as capital gains or qualify for 10-year income averaging. If you opt for the installment method of distribution, the payout will not be hit by estate taxes—except for the amount attributable to your contributions to the plan. However, all the payout would be taxed as ordinary income—which would be taxed at no higher than the 50% maximum tax rate. What's worse, your spouse will not be able to use 10-year income averaging to lighten the tax load on the payout.

Revocable trusts—which let you take back the property you've put into them—are also well worth considering. (If you die while the trust

Shy away from setting up an irrevocable trust.

If you want to manage the trust's assets, name yourself as trustee.

is in force, the property will be taxed in your estate, but could avoid probate.) And you can use the estate-tax marital deduction to shelter part or all the trust from estate taxes. For example, you could set up a retirement trust to receive and manage the lump-sum payout from your profit-sharing or pension plan. That way, you'd get all the income tax breaks of a lump-sum payout but not the burden of having to manage what could amount to a mini-fortune. The trustee you pick manages the fund's assets for you. If you want to manage the trust's assets, name yourself as trustee.

The beauty of a retirement trust is that it will shield the survivor's benefits of your plan from being taxed in your estate if you died before retiring. It works this way: You name the trust as the designated beneficiary of your plan's benefits and your spouse (or whomever) as the trust's beneficiary. If you die before retiring, the trust will receive the plan's benefits free of estate taxes (as long as the plan's payout is not a lump sum) and your spouse will get the income generated by the trust's assets. You can also arrange it so that your spouse can dip into the trust's capital. Note, however, that the trust cannot use any of the money it gets to pay your estate's expenses.

After you retire, you should use a convertible trust.

If you do plan to manage your investments after you retire, you should use a convertible trust. You name yourself trustee and someone whose management ability you respect as co-trustee. That way, you get full control over the investments. However, if you become seriously ill or incompetent or no longer want to manage the trust's assets, the cotrustee can step in and take over.

Life insurance. As you grow older, your life insurance needs diminish—especially if your spouse is in line to get the survivor's benefits of your retirement plans. And while you'll need some insurance, it makes little sense to tie up a bundle in cash-value insurance. The purchasing power of the cash value that's being built up is constantly being eroded by inflation. Hence, many insurance consultants say that you'd be better off buying a cheaper term insurance policy and investing the money you save conservatively to build a fat nest egg. However, as you approach your 60s, you should consider converting some of your term insurance (which will usually end when you're 65 or 70) to a cash value whole life policy.

Update your will regularly.

Wills. You should update your will regularly—especially if you're thinking of moving to or from a community property state after you retire. For example, if you move from a non-community property state to one of the community property states—Arizona, California, Idaho, Louisiana, Nevada, New Mexico, Texas or Washington—a house or anything else you buy in that state will be considered community property. All these changes in the ownership of your property have to be reflected in your will.

HOW TO FIND A PLACE IN THE SUN

It's amazing how many people spend hours on end dreaming of the place to which they'll retire, but spend hardly any time checking the place out. They just leap, then wonder why there's trouble in Paradise. Here are some things you should look into before you move:

Living costs. You can get an idea of relative prices in various U.S. cities from *Three Budgets for a Retired Couple in Urban Areas of the U.S.*, published by the Bureau of Labor Statistics.

In a rural area, prices will be around 10% lower than the closest urban area.

If you're thinking of a rural area, you can generally figure that prices will be around 10% lower than the closest urban areas. One of the best ways of getting a handle on costs is to subscribe to newspapers in the areas you're thinking of retiring in. The ads will give you a clear picture of the cost of food, clothing, and housing.

Pay particular attention to your insurance.

If you're thinking of retiring overseas, ask the country's consulate for a breakdown on living costs. (Most countries maintain consulates in San Francisco and New York.) If you take a vacation in one of these countries, stop at the American consulate; they usually have up-to-date information on costs and retirement problems for Americans. And pay particular attention to your insurance—it may not cover you if you live abroad.

Get a good fix on the tax burden you'll have to carry.

Taxes. There are various ways of getting a good fix on the tax burden you'll have to carry. The difference might surprise you. For instance, Alaska has the heaviest state and local per capita burden ($2,781.78), and Arkansas the lightest ($727.55). You can put the taxes of the place you like in perspective by getting the state-by-state breakdown of per capita tax burdens that's published by the Tax Foundation (50 Rockefeller Plaza, New York, New York).

You can also write to a state's Department of Taxation to get specific figures on income tax rates, sales taxes, as well as inheritance and estate taxes. That's particularly important if you're going to own property in more than one state after you move or are moving to or from a state that has community property laws.

Once you've picked specific communities in a state that interests you, ask the local Chamber of Commerce about property taxes. It should be able to tell you if property taxes are expected to rise because of new schools or sewer systems. Also find out if you're eligible for any special property tax breaks for people over 65. Some states, like Texas, have homestead exemptions that will ease the tax burden, and some places even exempt you from paying school taxes once you reach 65.

Find out if you're eligible for any special property tax breaks for people over 65.

If you're planning a move overseas, ask the country's consulate for tax information. While some countries tax U.S. Social Security payments, others, like Costa Rica, not only don't tax retirement income, but will forego customs duties and sales taxes for your first few months as a resident.

However, as with everything else, tax considerations should not be the tail that wags the dog. Remember that you'll be living in the place for the rest of your life. The tax picture may change for the worse while you're there. So don't get suckered into moving to a place because taxes are low if it's otherwise less preferable than another area you've looked at.

Medical Care. Because you're more likely to need good medical care after you retire, you'd be wise to check out health facilities. Ask the county medical society what kinds of doctors—and how many of each kind—practice in that area. This way you avoid moving to an area that is well stocked with pediatricians, but has few or no cardiac specialists.

You should also find out if a good hospital is nearby. If your proposed new home is 50 miles from the nearest hospital, you may find yourself out of luck during a medical emergency. Sounds like good common sense, doesn't it? Then consider this: Most adult communities aimed at a population that's over 50 years old are located relatively far from hospitals. Because of their size, they have to build on outlying land. Newer retirement communities, however, are starting to include health-care facilities within their boundaries.

Find out if a good hospital is nearby.

If you retire abroad, you'll lose your Medicare protection. However, some countries like Britain and Sweden will let you join their national health plans if you're in good health when you get there. (If you're ill

If you retire abroad, you'll lose your Medicare protection.

or have a medical problem, you'll have to fork over money for your care.) You can find out which countries are generous with their health care by sending for *Social Security Programs throughout the World*, ($4.20, from the Superintendent of Documents, U.S. Government Printing Office, Washington, D.C.).

RETIREMENT PLANNING WORKSHEET

MONTHLY INCOME[a]

	Self	Spouse	Combined	Widow/Widower
SOCIAL SECURITY	$ _____	$ _____	$ _____	$ _____
PENSION PLAN	_____	_____	_____	_____
PROFIT SHARING	_____	_____	_____	_____
PRIVATE ANNUITY	_____	_____	_____	_____
LIFE INSURANCE[b]	_____	_____	_____	_____
SAVINGS ACCOUNT	_____	_____	_____	_____
STOCK OR BOND DIVIDENDS	_____	_____	_____	_____
OTHER INVESTMENTS	_____	_____	_____	_____
Total	$ _____	$ _____	$ _____	$ _____

ASSETS THAT COULD BE SOLD AND CONVERTED TO INCOME

	Current value	Income[c]
HOME	$ _____	$ _____
OTHER REAL ESTATE	_____	_____
LOW YIELD SECURITIES	_____	_____
ART	_____	_____
COINS	_____	_____
ANTIQUES	_____	_____
OTHER COLLECTABLES	_____	_____
CARS	_____	_____
CASH VALUE IN LIFE INSURANCE	_____	_____
Total	$ _____	$ _____

[a]List only income that's secure—that you're certain of receiving.
[b]The calculations for income from life insurance proceeds should be conservative—for example, assume you can get 5% interest on the insurance proceeds. If need be, you can always dip into the principal to make up a shortfall of income.

[c]Be conservative. Assume you'll put the proceeds into a savings account where they'll earn 5% interest.

MONTHLY EXPENSES

	Current	Estimated[a]	Revised estimate[b]
MORTGAGE OR RENT	$ _____	$ _____	$ _____
GAS AND ELECTRICITY	_____	_____	_____
FOOD	_____	_____	_____
TELEPHONE	_____	_____	_____
CLOTHING	_____	_____	_____
TRANSPORTATION	_____	_____	_____
LAUNDRY AND CLEANING	_____	_____	_____
MAINTENANCE AND REPAIRS	_____	_____	_____
CAR	_____	_____	_____
OTHER TRANSPORTATION	_____	_____	_____
TOILETRIES	_____	_____	_____
OUT-OF-POCKET MEDICAL	_____	_____	_____
ENTERTAINMENT	_____	_____	_____
Total	$ _____	$ _____	$ _____

Total combined income $ _____

Less total estimated expenses $ _____

Surplus or (shortfall) $ _____

[a] In your estimate make adjustment for the fact that some costs will be lower and others slightly higher. For example, your clothing costs will be lower after you retire because you won't need a wardrobe for your job. On the other hand, your out-of-pocket medical costs as well as your entertainment expenses may be slightly higher.

[b] Since you also have to take inflation into account, you will probably have to revise your estimates from year to year. Still, you will have a running fix on what you'll have to spend in retirement—and that puts you much further ahead than most people who tend to wait until a few months before their 65th birthday to even think about retirement planning.

8. ESTATE PLANNING

HOW TO SET UP AND
UPDATE YOUR
ESTATE PLAN

AN INVENTORY OF
ASSETS

THE ROLE OF LIFE
INSURANCE

HOW TO PROTECT
INSURANCE
PROCEEDS

COMMUNITY
PROPERTY
PROBLEMS

THE MARITAL
DEDUCTION AND
GIFTS

WILLS

THE MANY KINDS
(AND USES) OF
TRUSTS

HOW TO FIND A
GOOD TRUSTEE

HOW TO PAY THE
PIPER

WORKSHEETS

If you're like most other high earners, you'll spend thousands of dollars and hundreds of hours figuring how to increase your wealth. But odds are you have no rational plan for conserving what you've so laboriously made. Should you die tomorrow, your wife and children might see their inheritance eaten up by unnecessary estate taxes. If you've put off making a will (which is inexcusable), your wife might wind up with only one-third of your estate, with the remainder held under court supervision for your children until they're 21. Even if you have a will, you may not have revised it for years. Inflation and affluence have probably vastly increased the value of your property, and with it your potential estate-tax liability.

Under the 1976 Tax Reform Act, your estate will have an automatic tax credit in 1977 of $30,000—which will shelter about $120,000 of your assets from estate taxes. (By 1981, the tax credit will stabilize at $47,000, which will cover about $175,000 worth of assets.) What's more, you can leave your spouse up to one-half of your estate, or $250,000, whichever is greater. Anything that can't be sheltered is taxed at a rate between 30 and 70%. But most people pay far more than they have to in estate taxes, simply because they haven't disposed of their assets properly.

Your first step in sorting out your personal financial affairs is to draw up an accurate property inventory for all members of your family. This sheet will tell you how big each person's estate would be on his or her death—and should suggest ways to shift ownership so as to minimize estate taxes.

Your worksheet should include a column for yourself, your spouse, and each child, plus a column for jointly held property. On separate lines under the proper headings, list the value of all properties each family member owns or has an interest in, including such things as savings accounts, insurance proceeds, stocks, bonds, houses, furnishings, fine art, automobiles, trust income, and the equity in your house and other real estate. Don't forget possible inheritances. For jointly held property, indicate who paid for each item (important in deciding how much, if any, of the property is excludable from one joint owner's estate.) List any debts that would significantly reduce your estate, and also indicate the amount and terms of any mortgages.

Next, you have to determine how much income you've provided for your family. Start with a schedule of your employee benefits (such as

Start with a schedule of your employee benefits.

pension and profit-sharing plans, stock options, deferred payments, bonuses, and the death benefits from your employment contract), including their present value and value at retirement. If you're a principal in a business, estimate the value of your interest—what it's worth on sale, at your death, what income it will throw off for retirement and, if there's an agreement to sell your stock on death, what it provides for your surviving spouse.

Include income due from Social Security—which you get tax free. Your local Social Security office will tell you the exact payments due you or your survivors (benefits were vastly increased last year, and a cost-of-living clause was added). As a rough estimate, you can figure that you and your wife together will get the equivalent of $5,200 a year in today's dollars if you retire in 1985 at age 65. If you died today at age 50, leaving two minor children, the family would get about $6,832 until the children reach 18 (or 22, if they're students).

You can prepare a pretty accurate income schedule.

With all this information, you can prepare a pretty accurate income schedule—including your present income from all sources, your expected income at retirement, and your family's income in the event of your death or disability. (For the latter two, estimate a fair return on all your assets, assuming they're invested conservatively and that any salable business interests or speculative real-estate positions are disposed of.)

Next you need a life insurance schedule. List by policy and company: the amount payable on your death, partial disability, or total disability; annual new premium (after dividends, if any); type of policy (such as term, group, ordinary, endowment); present cash surrender value, if any; and who "owns" the policy. Policy ownership can make a big difference to your estate-tax bill. The full amount of your policy is included in your estate, even if payable to your wife, unless she herself applied for the policy on your life or you assigned your policy over to her.

Don't forget special expenditures.

Now compare the income schedule with what you know your family needs to live on—both now, and after the children are grown. Don't forget special expenditures like graduate school, weddings, and medical bills. If your income falls short, you'll need more insurance to protect your family. Your long-term goal, however, should be to accumulate enough assets and sources of income in order not to need insurance protection after you retire.

Be realistic in all your appraisals. An estate plan is only as good as the information put into it. And only as good as the imagination and ability of your estate-planning advisor.

IT'S A GOOD POLICY TO HAVE INSURANCE

Your first concern in constructing an estate is for the immediate welfare of your family if you are no longer bringing in income. This means an adequate insurance plan—including both life and disability coverage. But you'll have to plan carefully if you hope to get your money's worth from this costly purchase. Most people spend too much for too little insurance leaving their families underprotected.

Do not buy insurance by some "rule of thumb," like three times or four times your annual income. If your family needs all the money you make, what would they do when the three or four years were up? A better approach is to determine realistically how much monthly income your family would need if you had died yesterday. Total up all their probable expenses, including mortgage payments, utility bills, medical costs, food and clothing, college tuition, even entertainment. Deduct from this total the amount they would get from Social Security—you checked this out when you did your personal financial inventory. What's left is the insurance your family needs, per month, until the children are grown.

Of course, they'd probably have other sources of income, including the payout from your employee group insurance, pension or profit-sharing plan, real estate, savings, and investments. But if you can afford it, you should consider this income your family's inflation hedge, while you provide for their basic expenses with an insurance policy.

Now comes the prickly question of what kind of life insurance to buy: term or ordinary life. Because term is pure insurance—it pays only death benefits—the premium is relatively low. Ordinary life policies cost substantially more because only part of the premium goes for insurance; the rest builds up a cash value that you can get if you turn the policy in.

It would be prohibitively expensive to try to provide your family with many years of insurance protection through an ordinary life policy. If they needed $1,000 a month from insurance proceeds, a $50,000 policy would last them only four years and it would cost you a lot of money. For a much lower amount, you could buy a decreasing-term policy—which provides a specified dollar amount per month until a specified ending date. Hence you might purchase a decreasing-term policy guaranteed to provide $1,000 a month for as long as it's

Do not buy insurance by some "rule of thumb."

The kind of life insurance to buy is a prickly question.

needed—say, until the year your youngest child is expected to graduate from college. At that point, your policy would terminate.

Decreasing-term insurance, which has level premiums throughout the life of the policy, is even less expensive than renewable term— which you must renew periodically at a higher price each time.

It is most efficient, in terms of cost and coverage, to purchase decreasing-term insurance. Make sure your policy includes a waiver of premium if you become permanently disabled, and the right to convert into an ordinary life policy, regardless of health, if it should seem prudent to do so. *Renewable term policies* are useful for special, short-term coverage; make sure your policy permits you to renew until age 65, after which most term coverage ceases. Some insurance buyers also like to keep a small, ordinary-life policy to meet contingencies after their term insurance expires. Here, you'd be wise to include a double indemnity clause for accidental death. The cost is small and the potential benefit considerable.

Once you've settled your life insurance, you should review your total disability coverage. It's just as important that your family have a guaranteed source of income if you can't work, as it is to have income at your death. The best policies pay off when you are unable to perform your usual job (don't tie up with an insurance company that insists you be a basket case to collect). It might also be useful to have partial disability coverage, for when you can work part-time but are unable to carry a full schedule.

Medical coverage is the third point in your insurance triangle. If you don't have a top-flight major medical policy, a serious illness might wipe out your savings entirely. If you can't get adequate coverage through your employer, by all means purchase a policy directly from a private carrier. (See Chapter 6 for a much fuller picture of insurance.)

HOW TO PROTECT INSURANCE PROCEEDS

Once you've arranged for enough life insurance to cover your family's needs, you have to make certain that none of the proceeds is lost to estate taxes. If you leave a large estate, these taxes could siphon off up to 30% of the proceeds from your insurance policies. And since your insurance is probably one of the major assets you're leaving your family, you'll boost the net after-tax

Decreasing-term insurance is most efficient.

The best policies pay off when you are unable to perform your usual job.

Make certain that none of your life insurance proceeds is lost to estate taxes.

worth of your estate substantially by getting the insurance proceeds out of it.

You remove your insurance from your estate by having someone else own the policy. That means you have to give up all "incidents of ownership" over the policy. Note that these rules apply to anything you try to remove from your estate either through gifts or through a trust. According to the Internal Revenue Service these include: (1) the power to change the beneficiary; (2) the ability to surrender or cancel the policy; (3) the right to assign, or revoke an assignment of, the policy; (4) the right to pledge the policy for a loan, or borrow from the insurance company against the policy's cash surrender value, (5) the right to change any settlement options (which are ways the beneficiaries can take the policy proceeds.) If you keep any of these powers, your estate will have to pay taxes on the insurance proceeds.

Some tax courts have held that after surrendering ownership, you can use your former policy as collateral.

While the new owner of the policy gains absolute control over it, some tax courts have held that you can use your former policy as collateral for a loan—with the new owner's permission—yet not retain an "incident of ownership." Before you do it, check with your attorney; he'll be able to tell you what your district tax court thinks about this.

You transfer ownership by assigning the policy to someone else— your spouse, child, a close friend, a charity, or a trust. This is done by filing a notice of assignment with your insurance company. (Your insurance broker will send you the forms.) Be certain that the company's records show the assignment is a gift, not a sale. If the policy transfer goes down on the books as a sale, the recipient of the policy may have to pay ordinary income taxes on the proceeds.

Term insurance has no gift-tax value, but a whole-life policy does.

When you give an insurance policy away, you may be liable for gift taxes. Term insurance has no gift-tax value, but a whole-life policy does (it approximates the cash-surrender value; ask your insurance company to compute it for you). If the value comes to less than $3,000, you won't owe any taxes. If it's less than $6,000 and you're giving the policy to your spouse, you'll also get away tax free, since one half of the gift is covered by the marital deduction and the other half by the gift tax exclusion.

If you're taking out a new policy you can avoid the gift-tax problem entirely by having someone else sign the application. Although the insurance is still on your life, your spouse (or child, or friend) will own it from the start. The owner should always pay the premiums, to help substantiate his or her claim to ownership. You can use your annual gift allowance to give the recipient money to meet the bills. If you've given away the policy, but continue to meet the premiums yourself (even through your joint checking account), the IRS will include the last three years of premium payments in your estate.

In most states, you can assign your employee-group insurance policy to someone else—even it it's paid for by your company. But note: Some insurance companies don't permit the assignment of their group policies. Check this out with your company's benefits officer.

If you assign the policy to your wife, advise her to leave the proceeds to someone else—say your children—either directly or in a trust. If she leaves all her property to you and dies before you do the insurance policy will land right back in your estate. Should that happen, you'd have to go through the whole assignment procedure again. If you want to get the policy out of your estate but aren't sure to whom to give it, you can set up a trust to receive the proceeds. Consult an attorney on this.

WHAT'S YOURS IS MINE, BUT SHOULD IT BE?

Many couples think they're doing themselves a favor when they buy or own property jointly. Often, however, they're laying themselves wide open to estate or gift taxes, as well as creating other problems. (Couples who live in one of the eight community property states face special joint ownership problems— which we discuss in the next section.)

The big problem with owning property jointly is that half of it is likely to be taxed twice. As a rule, it's taxed in the estate of the first joint owner to die and again when the second owner dies. That considerably reduces the amount you have left to pass on to your heirs.

However, any property that one owner can prove he or she paid for personally will be removed from the estate of the other. If the wife dies first, the husband generally has little trouble proving he was the financial mover and shaker. But if the husband dies first and the widow helped pay for the house, she'd better be able to prove it right down to the last canceled check. In the absence of proof, courts will often assume that a wife's earnings or other funds went toward luxuries rather than toward the down payment on your home. If she can't find every relevant document, the entire house may needlessly be taxed in the husband's estate.

You can assign your employee-group policy to someone else.

If you want to get the policy out of your estate, set up a trust to receive the proceeds.

The big problem with owning property jointly is that half of it is likely to be taxed twice.

On joint investments you may both have to agree before anything can be sold.

If you put stocks or bonds in joint names, but you paid for them, you make a gift of one-half the investment's current value. And you owe the gift tax right away, not after the stocks and bonds are sold.

When you and your spouse own investments jointly, you may both have to agree before anything can be sold. This is fine as long as you're getting along. But if one spouse walks out in the middle of a bear market, the other might not be able to sell the stock unless they've both signed a special agreement with a broker permitting one owner to act. Should one spouse become incompetent, the other would probably have to get a court order before any jointly held property could be sold.

In many states, all joint property is frozen on the death of one joint owner until the will is probated. Unless the law makes special provision for a widow without funds of her own, she may be unable to write checks on a joint bank account, or draw money from joint savings, for many weeks after your death. Hence, it's a wise idea for a wife to have some emergency funds in her own name.

There are some other estate planning problems with jointly owned property.

There are some other estate planning problems with jointly owned property. You won't be able to set up the estate as a separate taxpayer with its own exemptions. If you and your spouse should simultaneously die in the same accident, one half of the jointly owned property lands in each of your estates. That's fine as long as your wills mesh. If they don't, or if one of you doesn't have a will, your fraternal lodge and her favorite charity may wind up owning equal shares of your house and other jointly held property.

You can reduce your estate taxes by giving some of your property to your spouse, rather than owning it jointly. For example, you can put the house in your wife's name. If you do it at the time you buy the house, you'll be liable for a gift tax only on the amount of the down payment you put up. If you transfer the house later, the gift value will equal the amount of equity you have in the house. Once your wife owns the house, she should make the mortgage payments and pay other house related costs. If she doesn't have her own funds, you can give her the money she needs, probably without incurring any gift-tax liability. You can give a spouse $6,000 untaxed every year.

You and your spouse can take title as "tenants in common."

If you don't want to give up control of your house by giving it away, you and your spouse could take title as "tenants in common"—which means that each of you pays for and owns one-half of the house. Hence, only half of the house's value will be taxed in each of your estates. Note, however, that if you give your wife the money to buy her share of the house, and you die within three years of giving it, that amount will be taxed in your estate as a gift made in contemplation of death.

There are other considerations besides taxes involved in deciding who should own the property. Ownership means control, and you may not want to give your property away. The ages and sources of income of any couple are a factor in settling on property ownership. If one spouse is more exposed to possible liability suits, it might be wiser to have the bulk of the property in the other's name. But note that shielding assets from creditors can be tricky. Courts pay close attention to when and under what circumstances title to the property is passed. If you want to make any changes in who owns what property in your family, make sure you consult a lawyer, so you won't inadvertently fall into tax or legal traps.

ESTATE PLANNING IN COMMUNITY PROPERTY STATES

You have some special estate planning problems if you live, or have *ever* lived with your spouse in one of the community property states—Arizona, California, Idaho, Louisiana, Nevada, New Mexico, Texas, and Washington. Except for gifts and inheritances, all property acquired by a couple while they're married and residents of one of these states is equally shared by each spouse. You may think you're not affected by these laws because you moved out of a community property state. But note: Once an asset becomes community property it stays community property, no matter where in the United States you go.

If you move from a noncommunity property state to one with community property, the ownership status of property you've already acquired generally won't change. The status of personal property depends on the laws of the state in which you live at the time the property was acquired. The status of real property, on the other hand, is determined by the laws of the state in which it's located.

Note, however, that California is a major exception. Its inheritance laws are clouded by something called "quasi community property." Personal property separately acquired while you were a resident of a noncommunity property state is treated in California as community property. The "quasi community property" rules also apply to real

Once an asset becomes community property it stays community property.

The ownership status of property you've already acquired generally won't change, but California is a major exception.

property purchased by either party while you were residents of a noncommunity property state.

Since community property is equally owned, only one-half of its value will be taxed in the estate of the first person to die, giving you in effect an automatic marital deduction. Separately owned assets in a community property state get the same tax treatment as assets in a non-community property state. However, if you can't segregate community property from separately owned property, everything will likely be treated as if it were community property. You'll need a good lawyer who's familiar with the community property laws of your state to advise you on the status of all your property and how to prove who owns it.

What you and your spouse earn is treated as community property.

What you and your spouse earn is treated as community property by all these states. Each of you must pay half the income taxes, whether you file joint or separate returns. In some states, this applies even if the couple is separated. In others, however, the earnings of a wife who is separated from her husband are treated as separate property. By the same token, damage awards for personal injuries you've suffered may be treated as community property by some states, and separate property by other states.

The income and profits from separately owned property is treated differently by the various community property states. Idaho, Louisiana, and Texas treat the income from separate property as community property, although if the property is sold, the capital gains would go to the individual owner. But in California, Arizona, and Washington, income generated by a separate property stays separate. In California, Arizona, New Mexico, and Nevada it becomes even more complex. The income from an individually owned business stays separate as long as the income is a return on invested capital. However, if you actively engage in the business, the income becomes community property.

It's extremely important to determine whether income is separate or community property. Reason: Anything purchased with separate funds becomes separate property and anything bought with community funds becomes community property. A couple can agree to make the property purchased with community funds the separate property of one spouse. But the spouse giving up ownership in the property may be liable for a gift tax on half the property. You can use your $3,000 annual gift tax exclusion to cover part of the gift tax liability. But note that you can't use the gift-tax marital deduction because half the property already belongs to your spouse.

You can convert existing community property into separate property.

You and your spouse can also convert existing community property into separate property. The simplest way is to split the community property into two equal shares. Because neither spouse gains a greater interest in the property, there's no gift tax liability—and no sale or exchange, so no capital gains liability. You can also convert community property into separate property by giving your 50% interest in the property to your spouse and paying a gift tax. In some states, you can even enter into an agreement with your spouse to make all present and future possessions separate property. State law will determine the estate and gift tax treatment for this type of arrangement.

Property conversions can also go the other way. You can convert separate property into community property by giving your spouse one-half your property. If you do this, you'll have to pay a gift tax on one-half your property. Yet it should qualify for the gift tax marital deduction. If you and your spouse give community property to someone else, say your children, you'd share the gift tax liability. Normally, giving community property to someone else will get the property out of both your estates.

Couples who live in community property states must take some special measures to get the proceeds of a life insurance policy out of their estates. If the policy is bought with community funds, up to one-half the insurance proceeds might be taxed in your estate—even if you've made your spouse the policy's owner.

Have your spouse own the life insurance policy.

You can make sure that none of the insurance proceeds are lost to estate taxes in your estate by having your spouse own the policy and pay for the premiums with his or her separate funds. If your spouse doesn't have enough money, give some of your separate funds to him or her. File a gift tax return on those gifts even if they're covered by your annual exclusion. The tax form serves as proof that your spouse paid for the policy. If your insurance policy has already built up a cash value when you transfer it, make sure your gift tax return is based on the cash surrender value.

Life insurance in a community property state is no simple matter.

Dealing with life insurance in a community property state is no simple matter. You need an experienced lawyer's help. If you don't know exactly what you are doing, you or your spouse could get clobbered by taxes. For example, if you buy an insurance policy on your life with community funds and name your child as beneficiary, your spouse might have to pay a gift tax on one-half the proceeds when you die.

On your death, your half of whatever community property you own falls into your estate, as well as all your individually owned property. You can reduce the estate tax burden, however, by taking a marital deduction on that part of your estate that remains after deducting community property plus debts and expenses.

Keeping good records is a must.

Keeping good records is a must. You have to be able to prove that separate property is in fact separate. That means having a file of all mortgages and deeds, receipts, income and gift tax returns, and documents attesting to gifts and inheritances. You also should keep track of all insurance premium payments and maintain separate bank accounts for receipts and expenses from separately owned property. Above all else, you need a lawyer who knows all the ins and outs of laws for your particular state.

MARITAL DEDUCTION AND GIFTS

The marital deduction and life-time gifts will vastly increase the money you can leave to your heirs.

Marital deduction and lifetime gifts are two of the most important factors in a well-laid estate plan. Used wisely, they can cut federal estate taxes sharply—which will vastly increase the money you can leave to your heirs.

The marital deduction lets you transfer up to one-half your adjusted gross estate, or $250,000 whichever is greater, to your spouse tax free. (Your adjusted gross estate is what's left after deducting debts, administration expenses, and any community property, severed or owned). For example, if your adjusted gross estate came to $400,000, you could leave your spouse a maximum marital deduction of $250,000. Your taxable estate would drop to $150,000—the federal estate tax on that would come to $38,800 from which you could deduct the estate tax credit of $30,000—leaving an estate tax liability of $8,800. If you hadn't used the marital deduction, your estate would have paid $91,800 in estate taxes. Note, that you can leave your spouse less than the full amount allowed under the marital deduction.

You can leave property to your spouse directly or in trust.

You can leave the property to your spouse directly or in trust. If you leave it in trust, ordinarily your spouse must (1) get the income for life and (2) have the absolute right to dispose of the principal. Your spouse has to have full power to dispose of the trust at death, with no strings attached. Should you have a binding agreement specifying how the money is to be spent or distributed at your spouse's death, the bequest won't qualify for the marital deduction—and hence would be taxed in your estate.

Give the trustees the right to invade principal.

The first $3,000 of any outright gift you make can still be excluded from gift taxes.

There's no gift until you complete delivery of the property.

The marital deduction defers estate taxes, but doesn't avoid them. Eventually, the money you've bequeathed your spouse, or whatever is left of it, will be taxed in his or her estate. If your spouse should die soon after receiving the bequest, the increased tax cost to the second estate could far outweigh the savings to the first. However, if you're both young and healthy, you'll have to assume that the surviving spouse will live on for many years, so it's well worth arranging to defer taxes.

Nevertheless, make sure you figure the effect of the marital deduction on both estates before deciding to use it. If your spouse's estate is as large as yours, it might be wiser (from a tax point of view) to skip the marital deduction. Instead, leave your estate to your children, either outright or in trust, with the income payable to your spouse for life. You should give the trustee the right to invade principal for your spouse, if the need arises.

The Tax Reform Act of 1976 has deep-sixed gift giving as an effective way of reducing federal estate taxes. (Under the old law, any gifts you made were removed from your estate where they would have been clobbered by the federal estate tax. While you were liable for a federal gift tax, it was roughly 25% lower than the estate tax rate. And that's assuming you couldn't shelter the gift tax through an annual gift-tax exclusion or $30,000 lifetime exemption—which no longer exists.) Now the federal estate and gift tax have been unified—between 30 and 70% depending upon the amount. Note that 16 states levy gift taxes. You should ask your lawyer how these state taxes will affect your estate plans.

The first $3,000 of any outright gift you make can still be excluded from gift taxes. That means you can give away tax-free every year as many $3,000 gifts to separate recipients as you like. If you're married the exclusion can be doubled—which means that you and your spouse can jointly make annual gifts of $6,000, regardless of whose funds are used to make the gift. When you make joint gifts, both you and your spouse have to sign the gift tax return. But note that for tax purposes there's no gift until you complete delivery of the property.

While giving income earning assets makes income tax sense, it will no longer help reduce your estate's tax burden. Any gifts you make will now be taxed in your estate even though you no longer own the assets. And if you die within three years of making the gift, the IRS will include any gift taxes you may have paid as part of your gross estate. Which means that your estate will have to pay a tax on a tax you paid.

You also have a gift-tax marital deduction.

You also have a gift-tax marital deduction—which allows you to give your spouse a total of $100,000 tax free. Furthermore, half of any additional gifts to your spouse are also tax free. And of course, you can always use your annual $3000 gift tax exclusion to shelter small gifts to your spouse from gift taxes.

The gift tax is figured on the fair market value of the gift at the time it's made. If you don't want to pay the gift tax, you can make it a net gift. That means the gift is made on condition that the recipient pays the tax. Note however, that for gift tax purposes, the value of the gift is reduced by the amount of tax the recipient pays. Hence, if you gave $10,000 and the gift tax came to $2,000, your estate would be reduced by $10,000, since you get credit for gift tax paid.

WHERE THERE'S A WILL, THERE'S A WAY

Unless you have a carefully drawn will, all your estate planning gambits will have been for naught. If you die intestate (without a will) the state you live in will use some sort of formula to divide up your estate. Under some state formulas, your spouse would share the estate equally with your children. If you have three children, your spouse will get only one-fourth of your estate—which probably won't be enough to live on. And since intestacy favors your closest relatives, some members of your family, friends, and favorite charities will receive nothing from your estate.

Leaving no will favors your closest relatives.

Your will lets you choose your beneficiaries, what they'll get and when they'll get the bequest. Hence, your will is a major estate planning tool that can save your estate a considerable sum in taxes and fees. For example, you can use your will to set up the marital deduction. That lets your spouse get up to one-half of your adjusted gross estate tax-free. If you die intestate, your spouse will likely get less than half of your adjusted gross estate, and your estate won't get the maximum tax advantage of the marital deduction—which means that your heirs will get less.

Name a successor trustee in case the original trustee dies.

A will is an absolute must if you have children who are minors. Chances are you'll leave half your adjusted gross to your spouse, and most of what's left in trust for your children. When you pick a trustee to manage their assets, make sure you also name a successor trustee who can step right in and take care of things if the original trustee dies or becomes incompetent. Alternatively, you can give someone else the power to name a successor trustee if you die before the trustee does. Otherwise, the court will have to pick a trustee.

If you die intestate, your children will inherit the money outright, and the court would likely appoint a guardian to oversee their assets. The administration costs of a guardian can be steep, especially if the children inherit a large, complex estate. The guardian may have to post a bond guaranteeing your children's assets, as well as give periodic accountings to the court of the money under his control. What's more, the court appointed guardian may not be able to protect your children's assets from the ravages of inflation—a guardian is often severely restricted in the way he or she invests your children's funds. He may even have to get a court order to spend the children's money, even if it's on their behalf.

A will lets you name whom you want as your estate's executor—the person responsible for seeing that the terms of the will are carried out, the assets gathered and the expenses paid. Note that you should also appoint substitute executors. Many people name their spouse as executor but neglect to provide for a substitute. If you both die in the same accident, or within a short time of each other, the court would step in and appoint an executor. The trouble with a court appointed executor is that he or she may not measure up to the person you could have picked for the job. What's more, controls imposed by the court may hamper the executor's administration of your estate.

You can hold down your estate's administration expenses by stating that the executors, guardians and trustees need not post fidelity bonds—used to protect the assets they're managing. The bond premium is paid for out of your estate's funds. Most bonding companies claim the right to co-sign all estate checks. If you've chosen competent and reliable guardians, executors, and trustees, give them the freedom to manage your estate's assets as they see fit.

Some points to consider. Your will should be drafted by an attorney who is knowledgeable regarding your state's inheritance laws. Ask your attorney how many wills he's drawn and the size of the estates he's handled. Your friends, accountants and bank may be able to suggest a capable estate lawyer. You can also contact your local bar association—they'll usually have a list of attorneys specializing in estate planning. *Don't try writing your own will.* An amateurish, do-it-yourself job could cost your estate 10 times what you would have paid a lawyer to draft the will.

Provide for a substitute executor.

Don't try writing your own will.

Estate planning is a family matter. Your will and your spouse's should be planned together to achieve maximum tax savings and the proper disposition of your combined estates.

You'll want to review your will with your attorney as your circumstances change—and make sure your attorney keeps you abreast of any changes in the tax laws. They may alter your estate plans. You can reconsider, revise, or revoke your will at any time.

W WITH A TRUST, YOU SAVE

Well-designed trusts can reduce your estate's tax burden, lower your income taxes, and get property to your heirs with a minimum of delay. While trusts can be quite complex when set up, the principle is basically simple. You place some property under the control of one or more trustees of your choice who pay out the income from the property to a particular person, say your spouse. When your spouse dies, the trustee distributes the principal to specified beneficiaries such as your children. (In all states, trusts can be designed to accumulate income and pay their own taxes. However, this type of trust is now out of favor—the Tax Reform Act of 1969 drastically reduced the tax breaks a beneficiary could get with an accumulation trust.)

Regardless of the type of trust you choose, you should make sure that the trust's principal can be invaded to take care of any beneficiary's maintenance, support, and education. If you don't include a provision allowing this, an unforeseen emergency could leave your spouse or children strapped for funds. You should also give your trustees broad powers of investment. It's impossible to anticipate all the needs of your beneficiaries—hence any limitations you place on the trust's uses may eventually hurt the very people you meant to protect.

There are basically two types of trusts: (1) *Testamentary trusts*, set up by your will and thus not effective until your death; (2) *Inter vivos or living trusts* formed during your lifetime and effective as soon as they're made. You'll want to consult an attorney experienced in estate and income tax planning before you decide which kind to use. Most estate planners recommend testamentary trusts. Reason: You maintain control over your assets and can change beneficiaries at any point during your lifetime.

A testamentary trust can save your estate plenty in taxes as well

---

You can reconsider, revise, or revoke your will at any time.

Trusts can be complete but the principle is basically simple.

A testamentary trust can save your estate plenty.

Place the rest of your property in a remainder trust.

With an irrevocable life insurance trust, the proceeds can be paid to your children.

as reap other benefits. A *marital deduction trust* lets you give your spouse up to one-half of your adjusted gross estate, tax free. If you give the property outright, you'll saddle your spouse with administration and investment burdens that he or she may not be able to handle. You can relieve your spouse of these burdens and still get the tax break by leaving the property in a marital deduction trust. To keep the bequest out of your estate, you must make certain that your spouse gets the income for life and has the absolute right to dispose of the principal at death.

If you don't think the income from the marital deduction trust will give your spouse enough money to live on, you can place the rest of your property in a remainder trust. Your spouse will get to use the income from the remainder trust for the rest of his or her life. When your spouse dies, the principal in the remainder trust will go to the beneficiaries you've named without being taxed in your spouse's estate—which can be quite a saving in federal estate taxes.

Many people who use both a marital deduction trust and a remainder trust have set them up so that the trust principal can be used to take care of emergencies. However, they specify that the principal of the marital deduction trust must be used before the remainder trust can be touched. That makes a lot of sense: Cutting into the principal of the marital deduction trust reduces the amount of property in your spouse's estate—and hence lowers his or her estate taxes.

Some other provisions in trusts well worth considering: (1) *a "sprinkling" trust provision* which allows the trustee to distribute the income to your spouse as well as to any other beneficiary you name; (2) *an irrevocable life insurance trust,* to get the proceeds of your life insurance policy out of your estate as well as out of that of your spouse. The income can be paid to your spouse for life, and the principal used for her maintenance and support. On your spouse's death, the proceeds could be paid to your children.

A living trust can be either revocable or irrevocable. You can end a revocable trust at any time, and get the property back—hence the trust will be included in your estate. If income from the trust is paid to someone else, you'll be liable for a gift tax on that income. A revocable trust is often used to test the ability of someone being considered as a trustee of a testamentary trust.

An irrevocable trust will get the property out of your estate if you make a complete gift of the property and don't retain any interest in the income or principal. In addition to reducing your federal estate taxes, you'll also save your estate certain administration expenses and probate fees. And if you give away income-producing properties, you'll lower your income taxes. Note, however, that you're liable for a gift tax when you set up the trust.

One living trust that makes sense for income tax purposes is the Clifford trust—which lets you shift income to a person in a low tax bracket. A Clifford trust is a short-term irrevocable trust—you can get the property back after 10 years and a day, after the property is put in the trust, or if the trust beneficiary dies. Because you get the property back, most of the trust will be taxed in your estate if you die while the trust is in force. Note that you'll be liable for a gift tax when you set the trust up.

GUIDE TO FINDING A GOOD TRUSTEE

When you set up a trust, you have to make sure that you pick a good trustee. The economic well-being of your beneficiaries depends on your trustee's ability to handle the administration, investment, and distribution of trust assets.

A bank is there in perpetuity, with a trust department trained to administer trust funds cautiously. While some banks are excellent trustees, others follow an extremely conservative investment policy that may not be suitable for your beneficiary. For example, an investment in high-yielding bonds might not serve the true interests of a beneficiary who has a high income of his or her own.

You can test a bank's trust department by setting up a revocable trust—which can be cancelled at any time and has no tax ramifications. If the bank has a common trust fund for all its smaller estates, find out how the fund has performed over the past few years.

When you interview trust officers at the bank, skip the older officers—they'll probably retire before your trust becomes effective. You should speak to the junior members of the trust department who will likely run your trust. Find out what kind of training they're getting and what the staff turnover is. And don't be bashful about asking questions—it's your heirs' money they're going to be dealing with.

An individual trustee will likely give the trust's assets and beneficiaries more personal attention than a bank or trust company would. However, you should make sure that the person you choose has

With a Clifford trust you can get the property back after 10 years and a day.

A bank is there in perpetuity.

Skip the older officers.

Your child can be named trustee.

the financial expertise to handle the trust assets. You should also name one or more alternate trustees who could take over the trust duties if the original trustee dies, becomes incompetent or resigns. Some people name a friend and a bank as co-trustees. The way they figure it, the friend will stay tuned to the needs of your beneficiaries, and the bank will watch over your investments.

Your child can be named trustee. However, he can't be the sole trustee if he's a beneficiary of the trust's income or principal. You could name your spouse, child, and bank as co-trustees—which would allow them a hand in deciding how the trust's assets are to be invested. Note that your child can not have a say in how the assets will be distributed. If an individual trustee wants to waive his commission he must do so when he qualifies and before he acts as trustee. Otherwise the trustee will be taxed on the amount of commissions he's entitled to, even though he doesn't receive them.

Once you've picked a capable trustee, give him or her broad investment powers. You can't anticipate all the needs of your beneficiaries. What might seem like a sound investment program today could be a disastrous one a decade from now. Note that unless you specifically give your trustee these discretionary powers, state law may tie him or her to a very conservative program of investments. However, you can't stipulate how the trust principal is to be invested or distributed. If you do, the trust will likely be taxed in your estate.

Invade principal for "maintenance, support, and education."

The trustee should have the power to dip into the principal for the benefit of any of the beneficiaries. Common standards for the invasion of principal include "maintenance, support, and education" of the beneficiaries. When you provide for the invasion of principal, it's up to the trustee to decide whether the request is reasonable. Usually, he won't quibble with the just demands of a spouse.

Set limitations on an income beneficiary's power to withdraw principal.

You can guarantee a beneficiary's right to invade principal by giving him or her the power to withdraw every year a set percentage of principal or a fixed amount of cash. For example the trust could be set up so that a beneficiary has the right to take 5% of trust or $5,000—whichever is greater. However, you have to set some limitations on an income beneficiary's power to withdraw principal. Otherwise, the entire trust may be taxed in his or her estate.

Some final tips.   □ You want a trustee who will stay tuned to the investment needs of your spouse. Hence you want a trustee who can be conveniently reached by your beneficiaries. □ Make sure that the trust document has a clause releasing the trustee and successor trustee from any requirement to post a fidelity bond. □ Advise your beneficiaries that a trustee can be held liable for fraud or willful misconduct.

A HOW TO PAY THE PIPER

A clever estate plan can bring your estate taxes down to a minimum. But it almost never eliminates them entirely. No matter how much you hate the tax collector, it's rarely practical to dispose of all your major assets before death. So you have to provide for enough ready cash to meet the taxes, as well as administrative and funeral expenses.

If you don't, your heirs may have to cover these costs by selling some of the estate's liquid assets, such as stocks and bonds. This could deprive them of property that has great appreciation potential, or that provides the most reliable income. Also, a forced sale can take property out of your estate that might benefit from alternate valuation (which permits the estate to be valued either as of the date of your death or six months later, whichever is more advantageous to your heirs). Generally, the estate must pay federal estate taxes within nine months; however, extensions are available in cases of undue hardship or for reasonable cause (defined in the IRS regulations). When you get an extension, you pay interest on the unpaid balance— 7% for either undue hardship or reasonable cause.

Before you can take steps to protect your estate from the depredations of estate taxes, you need a fix on what the taxes will probably be. Do this by adding up the value of all the property you own and deducting debts, funeral expenses, community property, and the expected administrative and legal fees connected with your estate. This gives you your adjusted gross estate. If you're married, you then subtract the marital deduction, which permits you to leave up to one-half your adjusted gross estate or $250,000 (whichever is greater) to your spouse tax free. At this point, you add back in your half of any community property. Anything left over is your taxable estate and will be taxed on a sliding scale. However, your estate now has a tax credit of $30,000—which would cover a taxable estate of around $120,000. Note that the tax credit will rise to $47,000 in 1981. That would cover a taxable estate worth $175,000.

For most people, an insurance policy is the most practical way to

It's rarely practical to dispose of all your major assets before death.

Take a fix on what the taxes will probably be.

An insurance policy is the most practical way to cover expected estate taxes.

cover expected estate taxes. You get the most inexpensive coverage with renewable term, convertible at a later age into straight life. Your spouse should own this insurance policy; otherwise the proceeds will fall into your estate, making the estate taxes even higher.

To preserve your estate intact, you'll also want your insurance to cover funeral and administrative expenses. Even if you owe no federal estate taxes at all, it's often a good idea to provide your survivors with the money they'll need for legal and funeral costs. An inexpensive $5,000 policy should do it. Many insurance companies offer a guaranteed insurability policy which you can take out without submitting to a physical examination.

Consider buying flower bonds.

If your tax bill is going to be large, you might consider buying flower bonds. These are certain Treasury bonds which sell at a discount but are redeemable at par for estate tax reckonings. For example, a par $1,000 bond selling for $750 is worth $1,000 if presented to the government in payment of estate taxes—and there is no state or local income tax liability on the $250 you picked up. The beauty of flower bonds is that they can be bought literally on your deathbed, and still be redeemed at par at the tax collector's office. However, you have to be fully competent when you make the purchase. If you're not, the bonds will not be redeemable at their par value. Any flower bonds not used for estate tax purposes are taxed in your estate at current market value, just as any other bond would be.

SUMMARY OF PRESENT DISPOSITIVE PLANS

MINE	What property?	Value	How?[a]

BY WILL

To _____ _____ $ _____ _____
To _____ _____ _____ _____
To _____ _____ _____ _____
To _____ _____ _____ _____

BY SURVIVORSHIP[b]

To _____ _____ $ _____ _____
To _____ _____ _____ _____
To _____ _____ _____ _____
To _____ _____ _____ _____

BY CONTRACT[c]

To _____ _____ $ _____ _____
To _____ _____ _____ _____

SPOUSE'S	What property?	Value	How?[a]

BY WILL

To _____ _____ $ _____ _____
To _____ _____ _____ _____
To _____ _____ _____ _____
To _____ _____ _____ _____

BY SURVIVORSHIP[b]

To _____ _____ $ _____ _____
To _____ _____ _____ _____
To _____ _____ _____ _____
To _____ _____ _____ _____

BY CONTRACT[c]

To _____ _____ $ _____ _____
To _____ _____ _____ _____

[a]Outright and/or in trust.
[b]Property which bypasses probate, such as jointly held property.

[c]Life insurance beneficiary designation, Totten (i.e., "in trust for—" account) trust, custodial account (e.g., under Uniform Gifts to Minors Act).

9. BASICS OF PERSONAL FINANCIAL PLANNING

TAKING IT ALL INTO
ACCOUNT

HOW TO PROTECT
WHAT YOU'VE GOT

FRINGE BENEFITS

BONUSES

PROFIT-SHARING
PLANS

SUPPLEMENTAL
RETIREMENT PLANS

LEVERAGE

WHAT IT TAKES TO
INVEST
SUCCESSFULLY

THE PROS YOU NEED
ON YOUR TEAM

WORKSHEETS

Alot of people keep an eagle eye trained on their company's finances, but are blind as a bat when it comes to their own money. Income isn't the problem, says Herb Paul, a partner with Touche Ross—one of the big eight accounting firms. "These people are very good at increasing their earnings. They simply lose sight of how much they're spending." Hence, they have to scramble for funds to pay their taxes, lose out on stock options because they can't come up with the exercise price, and have to roll over debts constantly. The cost of all their debts and missed opportunities adds up to a tremendous loss of financial security.

Your first step in solving the problem is to run a cash flow on yourself, says Paul. Now is the perfect time to do that. You know exactly how much you made last year and you've probably run through all your expenses looking for tax deductions. Even if it's just to satisfy your own curiosity, subtract all your expenses (including taxes for the year) from what you made in 1976. If you have a deficit or just a pittance left over, you've got a problem.

The next step is to find out where the problem lies. Sort your expenses into broad categories such as mortgage payments, household costs, food, vacations, entertainment, and so on. Chances are you'll find that one or more of these categories is much higher than you thought. Now get a fix on your true cost of living—that is, your basic fixed expenses, not the endless luxuries. You'll likely find that this is a lot lower than you thought it would be. That means that you've got plenty of room to play with.

Setting up a strict budget would be your wisest course. However, if you're not the type who can stand a structured life, there's an easier way—forget about the basic expenses and concentrate on cutting back those inessential costs that were so much higher than you thought. Then, three months from now, do another cash flow on yourself to see if you actually managed to save some money. Paul recommends doing a cash flow quarter by quarter, but says the fine tuning is up to you.

The beauty of the cash flow is that it lets you forecast how much discretionary income you'll have for various purposes. That means you'll be able to set up a rational financial plan. For example, you'll know how much money you can annually set aside for investments. As your assets and income grow, you'll be able to time your receipt of income—which will let you do some fancy tax planning. And you'll have the financial flexibility to carry out your estate planning goals.

You can find out if your finances are improving by calculating each year your net worth—which is the true measure of your wealth. You simply add up the market value of all your personal assets and subtract your obligations. If your net worth rises from year to year, you're making financial progress.

HOW TO PROTECT WHAT YOU'VE GOT

It doesn't take much to be financially wiped out today—thanks to inflation. The cost of repairing or replacing your house has soared. Doctors and hospitals want the sky in fees. And liability settlements are going through the courthouse roofs. The only way you can protect yourself is by having enough insurance.

It doesn't take much to be financially wiped out today.

Homeowner's insurance. It's more important than ever to make sure you have enough homeowner's insurance to cover the soaring costs of repairing or replacing your home and personal property. Construction costs alone have leaped some 50% during just the past five years. But we'll wager that your homeowner's coverage is way behind these inflationary times. Hence, you should have your home appraised to get a handle on its present replacement costs—and then get enough homeowner's insurance to cover that amount. Note: Every few years you'll need a new appraisal.

You'll also want an inflation guard endorsement.

You'll also want an inflation guard endorsement. It boosts your coverage by 1% every three months, or 4% a year. That extra insurance should keep you above your homeowner's policy's 80% requirement—the insurance company won't pay the full replacement cost unless you're insured for 80% or more of the home's current value. If inflation has driven the cost of your house significantly higher, you may find that you're at present insured for less than 80% of its current replacement value. If that's the case, the insurance company will only pay part of the cost of repairing or replacing your home.

Your homeowner's insurance also covers your personal property. But note that some of this property may be only minimally covered, and other items may be excluded from coverage entirely. Hence, you should consider getting a "personal property floater"—separate insurance which covers the full cost of a specified piece of valuable personal property, like art or jewelry. Because of inflation, you should have such items reappraised from time to time. It usually costs very little to have personal property appraised.

Health Insurance. If you don't have good medical insurance, one painfully long illness could wipe out your life savings. Doctors' bills have risen 68% over the past five years, and hospital costs have soared 87%. Doctors' bills are expected to increase another 8% and hospital bills another 10% this year.

You probably have some sort of company-sponsored medical insurance, but don't let that lull you into a false sense of security. The policy may be vastly inadequate for today's sky-high medical costs. Compare your insurance coverage to that of Blue Cross—generally considered the best health insurance you can buy. It covers 100% of the cost of most health services. Trouble is, it's usually difficult to buy Blue Cross except through a group plan. If you don't have Blue Cross, try to buy a health insurance policy that says it will pay 100% of the "customary and usual fee" for the treatment of a large number of illnesses. That type of insurance covers you regardless of how high medical costs rise.

Disability insurance. You need a policy with a "cost-of-living" rider. You're guaranteed the original amount of benefits you signed up for—say $1,000 a month, plus however much the consumer price index has gone up in any one year. Such policies usually allow your monthly pay-out to double or even triple before the insurer stops increasing it. However, make sure that you get the benefits if you can't practice your own profession—even though your disability would allow you to get into another line of work.

Liability insurance. If you don't have enough coverage, you're liable to lose your shirt. Liability awards and settlements are probably rising faster than the rate of inflation, some lawyers say. For as little as $50 a year you can get a personal umbrella liability policy—which extends your homeowner's, auto, and other liability coverage to $1 million or more for each occurrence. You can also get a professional umbrella liability policy either separately or as an endorsement to a personal umbrella policy. Its premiums are much more expensive because potential damage awards are very high.

Company-sponsored medical insurance can provide a false sense of security.

Get benefits if you can't practice your own profession.

Without enough liability insurance you can lose your shirt.

THE SALARY WITH THE FRINGE ON TOP

Don't take your company's fringe benefits for granted.

Don't take your company's fringe benefits for granted. You can sometimes negotiate improvements to suit your particular needs. In many cases, you can only get some kinds of valuable insurance coverage through a company-sponsored group plan. If you're a stockholder-employee in a closely-held corporation or a partner in a partnership, you'll want to see that your outfit sets up something that offers the protection you need. Some points:

Medical insurance. As good as your company's basic medical coverage may be, it won't cover all costs. Hence, you should try to get a company-paid medical reimbursement plan—which will pay you back for expenses that may not be covered by your company's insurance. Most reimbursement plans will pick up the tab for blood, special nursing care, long-term sick pay, and so on. Some very good plans will pay for dental work, eye care, psychiatric help, and nursing home care.

Individual policies covering these expenses are either prohibitively expensive, or impossible to buy. Note also that you generally can't convert a group medical reimbursement plan to individual coverage—especially if the company self-insures the benefits. If you decide to leave your present company, make sure the firm you join offers comparable medical fringe benefits.

The premium is lower for the group plan than for a separate medical insurance policy.

If you're a shareholder-employee in a closely held corporation, you and your colleagues should be able to get all the group medical insurance you want through the corporation. But if you're a partner, you can't be legally recognized as an employee of the partnership—which means you will lose out on a lot of free fringe benefits. However, if you pay the premium yourself, you can join the partnership's employee basic medical plan. Still the premium for the group plan is lower than what you'd pay for a separate medical insurance policy. Note that partners can't get a medical reimbursement plan.

You want a supplemental disability plan with payments that reflect your present salary.

Disability Insurance. Many companies have policies that base disability payments on the average salary you earned while working there. That kind of policy would give you very little if you started with the company at a low salary and worked your way up to a significantly higher one. Hence, you want a supplemental disability plan with payments that reflect your present salary.

If you're a shareholder-employee, you can get the same type of supplemental disability coverage. But if you're a partner, you can't. What's more, it may not even be worthwhile to contribute to the partnership's group disability plan. Reason: The plan's payment schedule is pegged to the salaries of partnership employees, which may be much lower than what you're making. Your best bet is to get enough extra income from the partnership to cover the cost of buying a good disability insurance policy on your own.

Life Insurance. Your company probably provides you with life insurance amounting to one or two years' salary—which is much too little. You can get up to $50,000 of group life insurance without any income tax consequences. But, you do have to pay income taxes on the "economic benefit" you get from life insurance exceeding $50,000. However, the tax, which is based on IRS tables, is lower than what the premiums would cost you if you bought the extra insurance elsewhere.

If you're an executive or a stockholder-employee, you should look into split-dollar insurance. The company pays most or all of the premiums, but the proceeds are split between your estate and the corporation—which gets back the premiums it paid. (Again, you're taxed on the "economic benefit" you receive.) Note that split-dollar insurance doesn't make sense for partners because the partnership has to use after-tax dollars to pay the premiums. A corporation also pays the premiums in after-tax dollars, but when the insured person dies, it gets back the premium payments tax-free.

As a partner, you have to pay a premium to join your employees' group life plan—whereas your employees receive it as a free fringe benefit. Still, the cost of group life insurance is a lot lower than what you'd have to lay out for an individual policy.

Partners and stockholder-employees should also consider having their firms take out key-man insurance—which is taken out on the lives of people considered essential to the business. Key-man insurance will strengthen the partnership's or corporation's ability to get credit, since creditors know that the policy's proceeds will provide capital needed to keep the business running even if a key man has died. What's more, if you're one of the key men, the cash value of the policy taken out on you can be used to fund some of your retirement benefits.

As a partner or shareholder, you'll also want to take out a business life insurance policy on each owner of the business. That will give

With split-dollar insurance you're taxed on the "economic benefit" you receive.

You'll want a business life insurance policy on each owner.

your firm enough money to fund a buy-sell agreement in the event a partner or shareholder dies. The agreement sets a fair value on each person's interest—which is backed up by the proceeds of the insurance. The surviving partners or shareholders will get enough cash to buy out the interest of the heirs without having to liquidate the business. The insurance will also give your heirs enough ready cash to pay estate taxes and other expenses. Note: Make sure that the value you set on your interest is revised upward as the business prospers.

FRINGES THAT FEATHER YOUR NEST

Cash bonuses are becoming more popular because the money can be used right away. And even though the stock market is doing well, many executives are still very wary of options because they've had the misfortune of being granted options that could never be exercised.

Cash bonuses are becoming more popular.

What's more, cash bonuses can now be deferred and the tax rate on them won't be higher than the 50% maximum tax—thanks to the Tax Reform Act of 1976. (In the past, deferred bonuses were subject to an income tax of up to 70%.) And that has made deferred bonuses immeasurably more attractive.

Deferring a cash bonus makes the most sense if you're fairly sure that you'll fall into a lower tax bracket when you receive it. You'll have to do some careful calculations to verify that your tax bracket will indeed fall. It may not, especially if you expect to cash in on a pension plan, other fringe benefits, as well as get some income from other sources. Some other factors to consider: (1) The Social Security Administration recently ruled that you have to pay social security taxes on the deferred cash you receive—even if you've been paying these taxes all your working life. (2) If you leave the company, there's no guarantee you'll ever get the money. (3) Deferred compensation may be eroded by inflation.

Tax deferral can make a lot of sense.

However, there are some valuable fringe benefits where tax deferral can make a lot of sense. Because some of the funds contributed to such plans are in pre-tax dollars, you'll have more money working for you. But you have to examine the plan carefully before you decide to participate. Here are some common plans and what to look for:

Check into your company profit-sharing plan's vesting provisions.

Qualified profit-sharing plans defer taxes on the company's contribution along with the appreciation of funds in the plan. Your contributions to the plan may be voluntary or mandatory. The amount you and your company put in is then given to a trustee who invests the funds for you.

A good profit-sharing plan will let you choose how you want your contribution to be invested. Generally, your choices include investments in a fund of government bonds, common stocks, your company's stock, or a combination of all three. Before you join your company's profit-sharing plan, check into its vesting provisions. In some plans, you'll lose your share of company contributions if you leave the company within, say, five years of joining the plan. The better plans will give you a vested interest a year or two after you join. If the vested interest comes in at 20% a year, you could get your entire share in the plan five years after vesting begins.

The taxes on a profit-sharing plan are complicated. Company contributions made before 1974, along with the appreciation on that money and on your own funds will be taxed as long-term capital gains—if you take it as a lump-sum payout. Employer contributions made after 1973 are taxed as ordinary income and you can use a special income averaging provision to reduce your taxes. Under the Tax Reform Act of 1976, you can elect to have the whole lump sum treated as ordinary income, subject to the special 10-year averaging provision. That choice would eliminate any minimum tax problem and may result in overall lower taxes. Or you can get your share in the plan on the installment method. That would stretch the payments out and help reduce your tax burden each year. Before you choose a method, you'd be wise to work both of them out on paper to see which one gives you the best tax break.

A supplemental retirement income plan is very similar to a profit-sharing plan. You contribute anywhere from 2 to 6% of your salary, and the company contributes, say, half of what you do. In some plans the company will contribute a percentage of its annual profits—which is shared on a pro-rata basis by the members participating in the plan. Again, you want a plan that gives you a choice of investment, as well as one that gives you vesting rights. The payout on these plans is taxed in the same way as the proceeds from a profit-sharing plan.

Find a plan that gives you a choice of investment.

A savings (or thrift) plan gives you a lot of individual leeway. You can decide how much you want to contribute, how the money will be invested, and when you want the funds to be distributed. Here's how it works: You contribute anywhere from 2 to 10% of your salary and

The larger your contribution to the plan, the greater your benefits will be.

the company matches 25 or 50% of your contribution. The larger your contribution to the plan, the greater your benefits will be. For example, if you contribute 10% of your salary, say $5,000, and the company matches half of that, you've in effect boosted the amount of money you make by $2,500. When you get the payout, it's taxed in the same way as on a supplemental retirement income plan or a profit-sharing plan.

If you're a partner, you can't participate in any of these capital building programs because you can't be legally recognized as an employee. If you're a shareholder-employee in a Subchapter S corporation, you can set up this kind of program. But the income that can be used to determine what the contributions will be is limited to $100,000 a year.

But if you're a stockholder-employee in another type of closely-held corporation, your company can form any of these plans. You have more control over the type of plans and how they're structured—which lets you boost your benefits.

LEVERAGING WORKS TO YOUR CREDIT

If you handled your personal finances with the care you do your business affairs, you'd likely be a wealthier person. Take leverage, for example. Chances are you use it to finance your company's growth, but shy away from it when it comes down to your own assets. Many people fear that a leveraged position would necessarily leave them strapped for funds if an emergency came up. Not true. You can keep a leveraged position absolutely liquid. Even though you keep your capital fully invested for income and growth, you can quickly convert it to cash if the need arises. Here are some leverage possibilities:

You can keep a leveraged position absolutely liquid.

(1) You've probably built up a lot of equity in your house. But the dollars you've sunk into your mortgage are lying fallow instead of earning money for you. Some financial consultants suggest you refinance your mortgage and use the money you raise to work for you elsewhere.

Refinance your mortgage.

Your monthly mortgage payments will be higher but the interest segment is tax-deductible. If you invested in good high-yield situations you could more than cover the increased mortgage costs on an after-tax basis. And over the long term, your investment should grow.

It may make you nervous to think of having higher mortgage payments in case trouble strikes and you lose your job. But consider: If you're out of work, no banker will give you the extra $20,000 on your house. Whereas if you have money in, say, oil stocks, you can sell the stocks to raise emergency cash or put them up as collateral for a loan. The more of your assets you have deployed in good liquid investments, the better off you'll be in troubled times.

If you're lucky enough to have a mortgage with an open-end clause, the bank will simply tack the additional financing on to your existing mortgage. The interest rate on the old mortgage stays the same; only the additional financing should carry a higher interest rate. If your mortgage doesn't have an open-end clause, you'll have to get a new one with a higher interest rate on the full amount of the mortgage. You will also have to pay the closing costs.

Raise your income by assigning the mortgage as collateral for a loan.

(2) Say you sold some property when money was really tight and had to help the buyer out with a purchase money mortgage. That's a private financing arrangement whose terms are worked out between the buyer and you. You can raise the income you're getting by assigning the mortgage to a bank as collateral for a loan. Since the property stands behind the loan, the bank will likely charge you a fairly low interest rate.

(3) You can borrow against the cash value of your whole-life insurance policy and sink the money into bonds—now yielding 8½% and better. The insurance company will charge you 5% if you bought the policy before August 1, 1970 (loans on policies bought after that date cost 6% everywhere except for New York's 5%). If you borrowed $10,000 at 5% and bought a bond paying 9%, you'd make $400 annually. The insurance company will deduct the amount you borrowed from the policy's face value if you die while the loan is still outstanding. Hence, consider using part of your profits to buy $10,000 worth of renewable term insurance to cover the loan. You're making a little on the side, and your beneficiaries will get the full value of your insurance policy, plus the $10,000 bond.

Borrow against the cash value of your whole-life insurance policy.

One more idea: You could cash in your insurance policy, invest the entire proceeds and use the yield to fund the purchase of another policy. At your death, your heirs would receive the insurance proceeds plus whichever high-yield investment you chose—two inheritances for the price of one.

(4) You can write (sell) options on any of your stocks that are

*You can make money
three ways.*

represented on the Chicago Board Options Exchange or listed on the American Stock Exchange. When you write a call, you're selling the right to buy 100 shares of stock at a set price, within a specified time. You can make money three ways: □ You make 5 to 15% of the stock's price by charging the buyer a premium for the call. □ If the call is exercised, you'll likely have made a profit on the underlying stock because the stock generally won't be called until it hits a price higher than the current market price. □ You get to collect all the stock's dividends until it's called away from you. Of course, if the option expires you'll have pocketed the premium money and you'll still own the stock.

(5) If you really have to, you can leverage against any of the assets you own but have never thought of as negotiable property. For example, you can sell the rights to several years worth of rent from income-producing properties, pledge jewelry and paintings as collateral, or even leverage an option on land.

WHAT IT TAKES TO INVEST SUCCESSFULLY

You have to be savvier than ever to find an investment that pays off. The good old days when amateurs could dabble in real estate or the stock market without losing too much are over and won't likely return for some time to come. Inflation, the energy crunch, commodities shortages, and political uncertainties have turned most amateurs into big losers.

The name of the game today is selectivity, with an emphasis on long-term values. The only way you can consistently pick a winner (or keep your investment advisor honest) is by becoming an expert in an investment area that interests you—whether it's the stock market, real estate, or scotch whiskey. To gain the expertise you need, you'll have to spend time taking courses and reading financial publications.

*Become an expert in an
investment area that
interests you.*

To be in the stock market today, you have to think like a professional investor, because those are the people you're playing against. The smaller investors, who crowd into stocks recommended by big retail brokers, are still on the sidelines.

You can learn some sophisticated tactics by taking a course in stock market investments, which may be offered by a local school or university. A good place to go for correspondence courses—as well as on-site instruction—is the New York Institute of Finance, 2 New York Plaza, N.Y. 10004. At the same time, bone up on some of the better investment books. Graham & Dodd's *Security Analysis* (McGraw-Hill, $15.50) is a good one to start with. You should also subscribe to business, financial, and stock market publications to keep abreast of what's going on in the economy and the markets. After a while, you'll learn which periodicals you can trust and which ones should be taken with a grain of salt.

Once you have some new ideas, try them out on paper first.

Once you have some new ideas under your belt, try them out on paper first. Test your judgment, or that of your sources, by picking some stocks and following their prices. When you've established a good track record, you can start playing with real dollars. But start slowly and play only those stocks or bonds that you've researched thoroughly.

A final note. For the last four years or so, the stock market has been dominated by institutional investors. That's likely to continue. It means you have to learn which stocks the institutions are interested in, because that's where the action is.

Learn which stocks the institutions are interested in.

So far, institutions have shown a preference for: (1) Companies with a large capitalization—at least 3-million shares outstanding; (2) High quality growth stocks with a proven earnings record; (3) Companies which dominate their industry; (4) Companies with high profit margins, a high return on equity, a strong balance sheet, and excellent fundamentals; (5) Businesses that can grow in periods of inflation and economic uncertainty, as well as in recessions; (6) Companies that are relatively simple to understand and have a highly visible earnings outlook. The stock market doesn't like complexity or uncertainty.

Real estate investment takes a lot of work.

Investing successfully in real estate takes a lot of work. You have to be able to manage the property or find a good real estate man to manage it for you. You also have to worry about zoning changes, shifting rental patterns, property taxes, your legal liabilities, and so on.

There are a number of good ways to learn about real estate investments. Many colleges give beginners' courses in how to invest in real estate. More advanced courses and seminars on property appraisal, feasibility analysis, and so on, are available through the Society of Real Estate Appraisers, 7 South Dearborn, Chicago 60603. A good book to start with is *Real Estate Investment Strategy* by Maury Seldin and Richard H. Swesnik (John Wiley, $14.75).

You might also want to study for your state's real estate broker's exam. That will at least give you a handle on the terms and concepts of real estate. If you pass the exam, consider becoming a part-time real estate broker. There are two big advantages to that: (1) You stand to make money on commissions—which you can use to invest. (2) You'll learn what the hot real estate deals are.

Look for properties that are as familiar to you as your own backyard.

When you're ready to invest some money, look for properties that are as familiar to you as your own backyard. Many real estate investors get burned because they play on unfamiliar turf. You'd also be wise to hire a local real estate pro to help you find a deal. Sometimes you can arrange to pay him with a percentage of the deal's profits. That cuts down your up-front costs and gives the pro an incentive to work harder for you.

TALL THE KING'S MEN

Think of yourself as a small conglomerate.

Think of yourself as a small conglomerate. You preside over a number of operating businesses—namely your family, your career, and an investment company that secures your future. Like any other smart corporation president, you have a phalanx of carefully selected professionals to help you make decisions: a top-notch lawyer, accountant, a banker or two, an insurance agent, a broker, and maybe a specialized investment counselor. When you have a major decision to make, you call them all together and . . .

But no. You probably don't. Most people are pretty haphazard about their personal finances, making decisions too quickly, and counting on their earning power to pull them through emergencies. That usually works—except for those times when you make a major investment mistake, or the Internal Revenue Service chops up a family trust, or a widow is left with no cash and a lot of hard feeling.

Every family should have a list of professional advisors.

We have a single point to make: That you can have the best ideas and intentions in the world—and the earning power to carry them out—but without a really fine collection of financial advisors, working in concert, those ideas aren't going to do you any good at all. Below, we run through a list of professional advisors every family should have. You should keep their names on file for ready reference, and every adult member of the household, including older teenagers, should know who they are and how they can help. You can find good people through professional associations but a better way is to ask your smartest friends and associates whom they use and why.

You want an *attorney* who's thoroughly familiar with all estate planning devices—trusts, charitable donations, gift-making programs and so on. It's his job to make everything so airtight that the IRS can't get between you and what you want to do. He should know the laws of states where you own, or have owned, property. For instance, if you and your spouse have ever lived in California, your attorney will have to deal with that state's community property laws.

The *accountant* who handles your income taxes should also be no stranger to estate planning. His decimal-point view of your income, cash flow, net worth, and tax situation puts him in an ideal spot to generate ideas for you. Above all, he should be able to work out all the financial details of any investment and estate planning ploys that interest you. If he's not experienced in a special area—like oil drilling funds—take that deal to someone who specializes in the business.

Your accountant is in an ideal spot to generate ideas for you.

Your *insurance agent* should understand the kind of coverage you need, advise on the best policies, and get them for you at the lowest possible price. An agent who sells the products of several companies can offer you more choices than can one who's tied to a single employer. He should make your insurance fit changing circumstances. For example, if your obligations decrease—as when the children graduate from college—he ought to suggest lowering your coverage.

If you're drawing a trust and expect to have a bank involved at any time in the future, bring a *bank trust officer* together with your lawyer in the planning stages. Banks sometimes have to refuse an account because the trust document is incorrectly drawn or has provisions that conflict with bank rules. An older trust officer can draw upon his experience to suggest a trust that meets your needs. And if he's in at the beginning, he's more likely to give your trust his personal attention.

Deal with a house that has a reputation for good research.

Your *broker* should keep you informed about what's happening to stocks you've bought, as well as advise on when to buy or sell. It's smart to deal with a house that has a reputation for good research—because that's what your broker will draw on for his recommendations. If you want to turn your portfolio over to a *money manager*, get someone whose investment record is long enough to check out—and whose investment philosophy meets with your over-all objectives in terms of growth, yield, and tolerance of risk. Note 1: Unless he's showing exceptional performance, he shouldn't be turning your investments over too often. Anything more than a 25% annual turnover for a growth account and 10% for an income account means he may be churning your account for commissions. Note 2: Don't buy a complicated tax shelter deal from a broker. The only thing he probably understands about it is the commission arrangement.

Beware of more than a 25% annual turnover for a growth account.

Coordinate the entire estate planning effort.

Any *real estate or tax-shelter advisor* you pick should be someone who earns his money directly from you and other clients who buy his advice—not from commissions for steering you to a particular deal. You want someone with long experience in the field, and whose deals make financial sense even before taxes.

Consider giving either your attorney or your accountant the authority to coordinate the entire estate planning effort. You'll want him to cast a critical eye on insurance, investment, or tax shelter suggestions. He may have to call in other experts—for instance, an appraiser if you have substantial holdings of real estate, jewelry, art works, and so on. Legal and accounting fees vary all over the lot—but there are a lot of things more important than getting the lowest price. What matters is whether the advisor is good, and is someone you can talk to about serious matters.

CASH FLOW WORKSHEET

Income

Income	Jan.	Feb.	Mar.	April	May	June	July	Aug.	Sept.	Oct.	Nov.	Dec.	Total
SALARY	$	$	$	$	$	$	$	$	$	$	$	$	$
CONSULTING FEES													
DIVIDENDS													
INTEREST													
CAPITAL GAINS FROM REAL PROPERTIES													
CAPITAL GAINS FROM TRUSTS													
ROYALTIES													
Total income per month	$	$	$	$	$	$	$	$	$	$	$	$	$

Annual income $

Average income per month (annual income divided by 12) $

Expenses

Expenses	Jan.	Feb.	Mar.	April	May	June	July	Aug.	Sept.	Oct.	Nov.	Dec.	Total
FOOD	$	$	$	$	$	$	$	$	$	$	$	$	$
MORTGAGE													
TRANSPORTATION													
MAINTENANCE													
UTILITIES													
CLOTHING													
COSMETICS													
ENTERTAINMENT													
PROPERTY TAXES													
STATE TAXES													
FEDERAL TAXES													
LOCAL TAXES													
MEDICAL													
DENTAL													
EDUCATION													
INSURANCE PREMIUMS													
INVESTMENTS													
Total expenses per month	$	$	$	$	$	$	$	$	$	$	$	$	$

Annual expenses $

Average expenses per month (annual expenses divided by 12) $

INVENTORY OF ASSETS AND LIABILITIES

Assets	Self	Spouse	Husband and wife
CASH AND BANK ACCOUNTS	$ _____	$ _____	$ _____
ACCOUNTS RECEIVABLE	_____	_____	_____
RESIDENCE(S)[a]	_____	_____	_____
HOME FURNISHINGS	_____	_____	_____
SECURITIES	_____	_____	_____
CASH VALUE OF INSURANCE[b]	_____	_____	_____
BUSINESS INTERESTS	_____	_____	_____
PERSONAL EFFECTS	_____	_____	_____
EMPLOYER BENEFITS[c]	_____	_____	_____
MISCELLANEOUS	_____	_____	_____
Total	$ _____	$ _____	$ _____

[a]Market value
[b]Face Amount: Self   – $ _____
             Spouse – $ _____
Additional amounts payable on death, not included in [b]
Self   – $ _____
Spouse – $ _____

[c]Limit to Living and Vested Benefits, (i.e., excluding those amounts which are payable only on death, or which are forfeitable). Verify this data with Personnel Benefits Department of employer

Liabilities	By Self	By Spouse	By Husband and wife
NOTES TO BANKS	$ _____	$ _____	$ _____
ACCOUNTS PAYABLE	_____	_____	_____
MORTGAGES	_____	_____	_____
INSURANCE POLICY LOANS	_____	_____	_____
DEBTS TO OTHERS	_____	_____	_____
PLEDGES TO CHARITY	_____	_____	_____
TAXES	_____	_____	_____
Total	$ _____	$ _____	$ _____
Net worth (assets less liabilities)	$ _____	$ _____	$ _____

DATE: _____

RETIREMENT

Expected age _____ $ _____

Required annual income $ _____

Anticipated annual income $ _____

Surplus (deficit) $ _____

Source(s)? _____

_____

_____

_____

How will any deficit be made up? _____

_____

_____

_____

_____

DISABILITY

Projected annual needs $ _____

Anticipated annual income $ _____

Surplus (deficit) $ _____

Source(s)? _____

_____

_____

_____

How will any deficit be made up? _____

_____

_____

DEATH

Mortgage(s) and debt(s) $ _____

Probate costs $ _____

Back income and other taxes $ _____

Estate taxes $ _____

Bequests to charity $ _____

Educational funds for child(ren) $ _____

Annual income:

(1) *During minority of child(ren)* $ _____

(2) *To spouse after majority of child(ren)* $ _____

To what degree is my spouse capable of managing investments and financial affairs? _____

_____

_____

_____

_____

After my death and my spouse's, what do I expect to leave for my child(ren), other heirs or charity? _____

_____

_____

_____

_____

DATE: _____

APPENDIX A:

TABLES AND CHARTS

COMPOUND INTEREST TABLES: PART I

A deposit of $10,000 in a savings
account with interest compounded
quarterly at the rates shown will
result in the following amounts.

Years	5%	5½%	6%	6½%	7%	8%
1	$10,509	$10,561	$10,600	$10,650	$10,700	$10,800
2	11,045	11,154	11,240	11,340	11,450	11,660
3	11,608	11,781	11,910	12,080	12,250	12,600
4	12,199	12,442	12,620	12,860	13,110	13,600
5	12,820	13,141	13,380	13,700	14,030	14,690
6	13,473	13,878	14,190	14,590	15,010	15,870
7	14,160	14,658	15,040	15,540	16,060	17,140
8	14,881	15,481	15,940	16,550	17,180	18,510
9	15,639	16,350	16,980	17,630	18,380	19,990
10	16,436	17,268	17,910	18,770	19,670	21,590
11	17,274	18,237	18,980	19,990	21,050	23,320
12	18,154	19,261	20,120	21,290	22,520	25,180
13	19,078	20,343	21,330	22,670	24,100	27,200
14	20,050	21,485	22,610	24,150	25,790	29,370
15	21,072	22,691	23,970	25,720	27,590	31,720
16	22,145	23,965	25,400	27,390	29,520	34,260
17	23,273	25,310	26,930	29,170	31,590	37,000
18	24,459	26,731	28,540	31,070	33,800	39,960
19	26,352	28,232	30,260	33,090	36,170	43,160
20	27,694	29,817	32,070	35,240	38,700	46,610
21	29,105	31,491	34,000	37,530	41,410	50,340
22	30,588	33,260	36,040	39,970	44,300	54,370
23	32,146	35,127	38,200	42,560	47,410	58,710
24	33,784	37,099	40,490	45,330	50,720	63,410
25	35,505	39,182	42,920	48,280	54,270	68,480
26	37,314	41,382	45,490	51,410	58,070	73,960
27	39,215	43,705	48,220	54,760	62,140	79,880
28	41,213	46,159	51,120	58,320	66,490	86,270
29	43,312	48,751	54,180	62,110	71,140	93,170
30	45,519	51,488	57,430	66,140	76,120	100,630

COMPOUND INTEREST TABLES: PART II

On monthly deposits of $100 in a savings account with interest compounded quarterly at the rates shown will result in the following amounts.

Years	Cumulative deposits	3½%	4%	4½%	5%	5½%
1	$ 1,200	$ 1,226	$ 1,230	$ 1,234	$ 1,238	$ 1,242
2	2,400	2,496	2,511	2,525	2,539	2,553
3	3,600	3,811	3,843	3,874	3,906	3,939
4	4,800	5,128	5,177	5,286	5,343	5,401
5	6,000	6,583	6,650	6,762	6,854	6,947
6	7,200	8,043	8,146	8,305	8,441	8,578
7	8,400	9,555	9,703	9,920	10,109	10,302
8	9,600	11,120	11,323	11,608	11,682	12,122
9	10,800	12,741	13,009	13,373	13,704	14,045
10	12,000	14,409	14,764	15,219	15,640	16,075
11	13,200	16,157	16,589	17,150	17,675	18,219
12	14,400	17,956	18,489	19,169	19,813	20,483
13	15,600	19,820	20,466	21,280	22,060	22,876
14	16,800	21,749	22,523	23,488	24,422	25,402
15	18,000	23,747	24,664	25,798	26,905	28,070
16	19,200	25,815	26,892	28,212	29,513	30,888
17	20,400	27,957	29,210	30,738	32,255	33,864
18	21,600	30,175	31,622	33,378	35,136	37,007
19	22,800	32,472	34,132	36,140	38,164	40,326
20	24,000	34,850	36,744	39,028	41,346	43,832
21	25,200	37,312	39,462	42,148	44,690	47,535
22	26,400	39,862	42,291	45,207	48,205	51,436
23	27,600	42,502	45,234	48,510	51,899	55,576
24	28,800	45,235	48,297	51,964	55,781	59,938
25	30,000	48,066	51,385	55,576	59,861	64,545
26	31,200	50,997	54,801	59,354	64,148	69,411
27	32,400	54,032	58,253	63,304	68,654	74,550
28	33,600	57,174	61,844	67,436	73,390	79,977
29	34,800	60,428	65,582	71,756	78,367	85,709
30	36,000	63,798	69,471	76,274	83,597	91,763

NET (AFTER-TAX) EARNINGS FROM A SAVINGS ACCOUNT

	Tax Bracket						
	20%	25%	30%	35%	40%	45%	50%
5.0% =	4.0%	3.75%	3.5%	3.25%	3.0%	2.75%	2.5%
5.5% =	4.4	4.125	3.85	3.575	3.3	3.03	2.75
6.0% =	4.8	4.5	4.2	3.9	3.6	3.3	3.0

MORTGAGE PAYMENT TABLE

*The following monthly payments are
needed to amortize a loan or mortgage
for each $1,000 borrowed.*

	Years							
Rate of interest	1	3	5	10	15	20	25	30
6.5%	86.30	30.65	19.57	11.36	8.72	7.46	6.76	6.33
6.6%	86.35	30.70	19.62	11.41	8.77	7.52	6.82	6.39
7.0%	86.53	30.88	19.81	11.62	8.99	7.76	7.07	6.66
7.2%	86.62	30.97	19.90	11.72	9.11	7.88	7.20	6.79
7.5%	86.76	31.11	20.04	11.88	9.28	8.06	7.39	7.00
8.0%	86.99	31.34	20.28	12.14	9.56	8.37	7.72	
8.4%	87.18	31.53	20.47	12.35	9.79	8.62	7.99	
8.5%	87.22	31.57	20.52	12.40	9.85	8.68	8.06	
9.0%	87.46	31.80	20.76	12.67	10.15	9.00	8.40	
10.0%	87.92	32.27	21.25	13.22	10.75	9.66	9.09	

RETIREMENT NEST EGG CALCULATOR

*Each month you'd have to put away
the following amounts in order to
accumulate the nest eggs shown by age
65. Interest is at 5% compounded
semiannually.*

Nest egg required	25	30	35	40	45	50	55
$10,000	$ 7	$ 9	$12	$17	$ 24	$ 37	$ 64
20,000	13	18	24	34	49	75	129
30,000	20	27	36	51	73	112	193
40,000	26	35	48	67	97	150	257
50,000	33	44	60	84	122	187	322

UNIFIED FEDERAL ESTATE AND GIFT TAX RATES

Amount taxed	Tax	% of excess
Not over $10,000	18%	
10,000–20,000	$ 1,800	+ 20% of excess over $10,000
20,000–40,000	3,800	+ 22% of excess over $20,000
40,000–60,000	8,200	+ 24% over $40,000
60,000–80,000	13,000	+ 26% over $60,000
80,000–100,000	18,200	+ 28% over $80,000
100,000–150,000	23,800	+ 30% over $100,000
150,000–250,000	38,800	+ 32% over $150,000
250,000–500,000	70,800	+ 34% over $250,000
500,000–750,000	155,800	+ 37% over $500,000
750,000–1,000,000	248,300	+ 39% over $750,000
1,000,000–1,250,000	345,800	+ 41% over $1,000,000
1,250,000–1,500,000	448,300	+ 43% over $1,250,000
1,500,000–2,000,000	555,800	+ 45% over $1,500,000
2,000,000–2,500,000	780,800	+ 49% over $2,000,000
2,500,000–3,000,000	1,025,800	+ 53% over $2,500,000
3,000,000–3,500,000	1,290,800	+ 57% over $3,000,000
3,500,000–4,000,000	1,575,800	+ 61% over $3,500,000
4,000,000–4,500,000	1,880,800	+ 65% over $4,000,000
4,500,000–5,000,000	2,205,800	+ 69% over $4,500,000
Over 5,000,000	2,550,800	+ 70% over $5,000,000

APPENDIX B:
GLOSSARY OF TERMS

STOCK AND BOND MARKET TERMS

BID-AND-ASKED PRICE: The rough price of a stock—consisting of the highest price that anyone has stated he will pay for a security at a given time, coupled with the lowest stated price anyone will accept.

CALL OPTION: An option which gives the buyer the right to purchase 100 shares of stock at a certain price within a specified period of time.

DISCOUNT RATE: The amount charged by Federal Reserve Banks to member banks for loans.

DOW JONES UTILITY AVERAGE: The Dow Jones Utility Average (DJUA) is a leading indicator of the market as a whole. Reason: Utilities are sensitive to interest rates because they're considered fixed-income securities and hence compete with bonds for investor dollars. If the utility average rises (or holds its ground while the DJIA is falling) it usually portends well for the stock market. Conversely, if the DJUA is weak, it's a bad sign for the market, say the analysts.

DOW THEORY: According to Dow theory, when the Dow Jones Industrial Average (DJIA) and the Dow Jones Transportation Average (DJTA) move up to new highs together, it indicates that all is operating smoothly. The Industrials represent the country's manufacturing capabilities, while the Transports reflect its shipping and hence selling capabilities. If either average is out of phase with the other, it usually spells trouble, i.e., either more goods are being produced than sold, or more goods are being sold than produced. Hence if the Industrials rally to a new high without a similar move by the Transports, the rally may soon top out. On the other hand, if the DJIA falls to a new low, while the Transports hold their ground, the Industrials will probably soon start heading back up again. This has proven to be one of the best ways to spot bull and bear markets as well as intermediate corrections.

Once a trend is established, it is in force until it is clearly broken, according to Dow Theory. For example, if both the DJIA and the DJTA rise to new highs together, we're in a bull market. The Dow Theory followers say that the *primary trend* will only be broken if both averages fall in tandem to new lows. Of course, there are always corrections in a bull market and rallies in a bear market. The Dow theorists claim that these *secondary* or *intermediate trends* can be spotted in advance when one of the averages temporarily gets out of phase with the other.

INTRADAY: The highest or lowest price level attained by a stock, or the general market, during any particular trading session.

LIMIT ORDER: An order to buy or sell a stock at a specified price.

MARKET ORDER: An order which demands an execution at the best price obtainable, as soon as the broker receives it on the trading floor.

NYSE MEMBER SHORT SALE: The ratio of NYSE member short sales to total short sales. This is considered an important indicator of what the "smart money" is doing. Whenever members of the New York Stock Exchange start shorting less and the ratio falls to 65%, it usually means that the smart money is bullish. When the ratio rises above 85%, it's a sign that the smart money is bearish on the market and a considerable decline could be in the offing. (See SHORT SALE.)

ODD LOT: A number of securities. With stocks, an odd lot is anything between 1 and 99 shares. With bonds, an odd lot is usually any transaction of less than $100,000 or 100 bonds. (See ROUND LOT.)

ODD-LOT SHORT SALES: An excellent barometer of the mood of individual investors. The odd-lot short seller is the "Wrong Way" Corrigan of Wall Street. So, when he becomes bearish enough to step up his short selling activity, there's a fairly good chance that other investors are optimistic—which means that the stock market will probably rise. Generally, technical analysts have found that when odd-lot short selling rises to 10,000 shares a day, it's bullish.

Conversely, they've found that when odd-lot shorts fall below 2,000 shares a day, it's bearish. (See SPECIALIST SHORT SALE.)

PUT OPTION: An option that gives you the right to sell your stock at today's price within a specified period of time.

ROUND LOT: A number of securities—usually 100 shares or any multiple of 100. (See ODD LOT.)

SELL SHORT AGAINST THE BOX: To sell short stocks that you already own—which lets you nail down the stock's current price. If the stock falls drastically, you can cover at the lower prices by buying additional shares. Alternatively, if you decide to cover with the shares you already own, you'd lose no more than if you sold the stock at today's market.

SHORT SALE: The selling of stock that's "borrowed" from your broker in the hope that its price will fall. If it does, you can buy back the stock and pocket the difference between the price you got for the stock and the price at which you sold it short. If the market goes against you and the stock rises, your potential losses are, in theory, at least unlimited.

SPECIALIST SHORT SALE: The ratio of specialist short sales as a percent of total short sales is another way of gauging what the smart money is doing. Specialists are the folks on the floor of the exchange who make markets in listed securities—and hence are in an excellent position to know the supply-demand situation for stocks. When specialists' short positions fall below 40%, it's a bullish sign, and when their shorts rise above 65%, it's a bearish sign.

STOP ORDER: An order which automatically becomes a market order whenever the price of the stock involved trades through a certain specified price.

WASH SALE RULE: A rule that lets you sell stocks for a loss, and yet retain them in your portfolio. Say you have 100 shares of a stock that's been falling all year but which you still like. You'd simply buy an additional 100 shares, wait 31 days, and then sell the shares purchased first for a loss. Alternatively, you can sell the stock now, and then buy it back 31 days later—hoping for a lower price.

ESTATE PLANNING TERMS

ANNUITY: A contractual agreement to make a periodic payment of a set sum of money either for a fixed number of years or for life.

BENEFICIARY: The person who receives the income or proceeds of property from a trust, a will, life insurance, or death benefits from your corporate pension or profit-sharing plans.

COMMUNITY PROPERTY: Property owned in common by both husband and wife, and acquired while the couple was (1) married and (2) living in one of the community property states—Arizona, California, Idaho, Louisiana, Nevada, New Mexico, Texas, and Washington.

DOMICILE: Your permanent place of abode. There can only be one domicile, compared to several temporary residences. The place in which you're domiciled determines where your estate will pay state taxes. If there is confusion as to which state is your domicile, your estate could find itself paying more than one state estate tax.

EXECUTOR (EXECUTRIX): The person or institution appointed by will to carry out the terms of the will.

FIDUCIARY: Person who is given certain rights and powers to manage property for the benefit of someone else.

FLOWER BOND: A certain type of Treasury bond which is sold at a discount but is redeemable at par value for estate tax payments. Recent tax court decisions have stressed the point that the flower bonds can't be bought when you're incompetent, or on your death bed.

GIFT TAX: A tax on the fair market value of a gift when it's made.

GIFT-TAX EXCLUSION: It lets you give away up to $3,000 a year to a person tax free. The exclusion can be doubled if the gift is made with your spouse. Gifts of more than that are subject to gift taxes.

GIFT-TAX MARITAL DEDUCTION: It lets you give your spouse $100,000 tax free in gifts over your life-time. One-half of any gift over $200,000 is also tax free.

GRANTOR: The person who sets up a trust.

GUARDIAN: Person who has legal control over a minor or an incompetent adult—and possibly his or her property.

INTESTATE: Dying without a valid will. When that happens, the court will step in and divide up your property according to state law.

INCIDENTS OF OWNERSHIP: It is the test used to determine whether

someone who is insured has control over a life insurance policy on himself. If he does, the proceeds of the policy will be included in his estate. Incidents of ownership include: (1) the right to change the policy's beneficiaries; (2) the ability to cancel or surrender the policy; (3) the right to assign or revoke an assignment of the policy; (4) the right to pledge the policy for a loan, or to borrow against the cash surrender value of the policy; and (5) the right to determine how the beneficiary will take a settlement option.

IRREVOCABLE TRUST: A trust which, once it's set up, cannot be revoked or changed. Because all control over the trust property is given up, the property is kept out of the estate for tax purposes.

LIFE ESTATE: An interest in property that ends when you die.

MARITAL DEDUCTION: It lets you pass up to one half of your adjusted gross estate, or $250,000 (whichever is greater) to your spouse, tax free. However, the property must be passed either outright or in trust with the spouse having the right to dispose of the trust property as he or she desires.

POUR-OVER TRUST: A trust set up to accept a portion of your estate which passes by will into the trust.

The trust has to be established independently of the will.

POWER OF APPOINTMENT: The power given by will or special instrument to another person (the donee) to determine how, when or who is to receive property, either during your life-time or after death. The donee can be given a general power of appointment which places no restriction on his or her authority to act. A special power of appointment gives the donee power to act in certain limited cases.

POWER OF ATTORNEY: Power given to someone to act in your place. Under a durable power of attorney, the power remains in effect even if the person who granted the power becomes incapacitated or incompetent.

PROBATE: The legal process by which your will is proved genuine. Before there can be a distribution of property from the will, it has to be admitted to probate, and accepted by the court as valid.

REMAINDER: The property that passes to someone after the owner of the life estate has died.

REMAINDER MAN: The person who receives the interest in property after the owner of the life estate dies.

REVERSIONARY INTEREST: The interest in property which comes back to the original owner's estate after the last life estate is over—provided no one has been given absolute ownership of the property.

REVOCABLE TRUST: A trust which can be changed or revoked at any time. The property in the trust is included in the grantor's estate for estate tax purposes, but escapes probate proceedings.

SHORT-TERM TRUST: A trust that's funded for at least 10 years and a day. When the trust ends, the property reverts to the person who set up the trust. While the trust is in operation, any taxes on the income from the assets in it are paid by the trust itself, or the beneficiary. Hence, short-term trusts are often used by people who are in a high tax bracket to shift income temporarily to relatives who are in a lower tax bracket. (Sometimes referred to as a *Clifford Trust.*)

SPENDTHRIFT TRUST: A trust that's designed to prevent beneficiaries from assigning or transferring the income or principal from the trust before they actually receive it. This type of provision keeps creditors of the beneficiaries away from the property until it's actually owned by them.

SPRINKLING TRUST: A trust that gives the trustee substantial discretion to distribute the trust's principal or income to the beneficiaries, according to their needs.

TESTAMENTARY TRUST: A trust set up to take effect when the grantor dies. Because the terms of the trust are spelled out in the will, the property in the trust is included in the estate and must pass through probate.

TRUSTEE: The person or institution designated by the courts or you to administer the trust.

WILL: The legal document which states how your property is to be divided up by specifying who is to get what—and when.

AUTO LIABILITY COVERAGE: Insurance that protects you and the members of your immediate family against claims for bodily injury and property damage to others, resulting from an automobile accident.

BASIC HOMEOWNER POLICY: The most elementary type of homeowner's coverage. It protects against 11 perils, such as fire, theft, vandalism, and civil commotion.

BENEFIT PERIOD: The amount of time that one is covered by the policy taken out.

BROAD HOMEOWNER COVERAGE: A type of homeowner's insurance that covers against 18 perils to a home, such as falling objects, building collapse, and damage caused by freezing pipes, heating and air conditioning units.

CASH SURRENDER VALUE: The amount of cash "savings" available in a whole-life policy if it were cancelled by the owner.

COLLISION INSURANCE: Insurance that pays for damages to your car when it's hit by another car or object.

COMPANY RETENTION METHOD: A method of measuring how much of your insurance premium goes toward insurance protection and savings and how much is retained by the company to cover expenses and profit. The less a company retains, the lower the premium costs usually are.

COMPREHENSIVE AUTO COVERAGE: Insurance that also pays for damages to your car caused by natural occurrences or vandalism.

COMPREHENSIVE HOMEOWNERS COVERAGE: Insurance that provides the broadest form of coverage in that it protects against all perils to your home—short of earthquakes, floods, nuclear radiation, and tidal waves. (See BASIC HOMEOWNER POLICY, BROAD HOMEOWNER POLICY.)

CONVERTIBILITY CLAUSE: The right to convert from one type of insurance to another, usually at a certain age and without evidence of insurability.

DISABILITY INSURANCE: A policy that usually insures you for up to 60% of your gross salary, when you can't perform your regular occupation.

DIVIDENDS: A return on part of the premium of a participating policy.

80% COINSURANCE CLAUSE: A clause in a policy which states if you aren't insured for 80% or more of your house's current replacement value, the insurance company doesn't have to pay the full replacement cost of any loss. Instead, it will pay the actual cash value of the loss, or an amount equal to the actual insurance coverage.

ELIMINATION PERIOD: The time between the actual occurrence of a disability and when the first insurance check is received.

ENDOWMENT POLICY: Life insurance payable to the policyholder if living on the date specified in the policy, or to the beneficiary of the policy if the policyholder dies before the maturity date. The premiums on an endowment policy are much higher than those of a life insurance policy that only pays out at death.

FACE AMOUNT: The amount (stated on the face of the policy) that will be paid in case of death, or at the maturity of the policy.

GUARANTEED RENEWABILITY CLAUSE: Clause that gives one the right to renew a policy without having to take a physical exam. The premium can't be raised, unless the insurance company raises the premiums for the whole class to which you belong.

HOMEMAKER DISABILITY CLAUSE: Clause that allows for the hiring of a housekeeper if your spouse is disabled or sick.

HOME LIABILITY INSURANCE: Insurance that protects you against any claims or actions against you or your family. The insurance company will pay for legal defenses and claims for bodily injury and property damage, but not for criminal liability.

LIMITED-PAYMENT LIFE INSURANCE: A whole-life policy on which premium payments are paid only for a specified number of years, even though the insurance is in force for the life of the insured. (See WHOLE LIFE.)

MEDICAL PAYMENTS INSURANCE (AUTO): Part of an auto insurance policy that reimburses you for medical expenses resulting from an auto accident—regardless of who was at fault. Coverage includes any payments for ambulance costs, dental work, x-rays, and surgery incurred within one year after the accident.

MEDICAL PAYMENTS INSURANCE (HOMEOWNERS): Pays for doctors' bills, surgery, etc., for situation on or off your premises whether you're legally liable or not. However, the coverage only applies to people who are not related to you.

MINIMUM DEPOSIT LIFE INSURANCE: A whole-life insurance policy that allows you to borrow against its cash value to pay for a part of the insurance premiums. One can take an interest deduction for the policy loan as long as four of the first

seven premiums were paid for without borrowing from the policy.

MUTUAL LIFE INSURANCE COMPANY: A life insurance company that doesn't have stockholders. The company is managed by a board of directors elected by the policyholders. Mutual companies usually issue policies that offer dividends.

NONCANCELLABLE POLICIES: A policy where the premiums can never be raised and the company can't cancel the policy for anything less than a failure to pay premiums.

NONPARTICIPATING POLICY: A life insurance policy that offers no dividend payments.

PARTIAL DISABILITY CLAUSE: Clause which lets you get as much as one-half of the disability benefits for up to six months even if you're only partially disabled.

PARTICIPATING POLICY: A life insurance policy on which the policyholder is entitled to receive policy dividends.

PERSONAL PROPERTY FLOATER: Separate insurance taken out to protect the value of specific valuables.

POLICY LOAN: A loan made on a whole-life policy. The amount of the loan can't exceed the built-up cash value or "savings" of the policy.

PREMIUM: The payment a policyholder agrees to make for an insurance policy.

RATED POLICY: A policy that costs more in premiums than a standard policy because you're considered a poor risk due to your health or occupation.

RECURRENT DISABILITY CLAUSE: A clause that waives the elimination period if the policyholder returns to work from a disability within a certain period of time and is then disabled again.

RETURN OF PREMIUM DISABILITY POLICY: A policy with high premiums that lets you get back all or a part of the premiums you've paid when the policy ends—usually when you reach 65.

STOCK LIFE INSURANCE COMPANY: A life insurance company owned by stock holders. Stock companies usually don't offer participating policies.

TERM INSURANCE: Life insurance paid to a beneficiary only if the policyholder dies within a specified period. Term insurance is usually written for periods of five, 10, 15, 20, or 25 years. Normally, you can't get term coverage past the age of 65.

UNINSURED MOTORIST COVERAGE: Coverage that protects the

policyholder and his or her family members if they have an accident with a motorist who has no automobile insurance coverage of his or her own.

WAIVER OF PREMIUM: A provision that states that the policyholder doesn't have to pay any premiums if he or she is totally and permanently disabled.

WHOLE-LIFE INSURANCE: Life insurance payable to a beneficiary when the policyholder dies. Premiums are usually level for the life of the policy.

ACCELERATED DEPRECIATION: A method used to speed up the taking of epreciation so that greater amounts can be deducted in the earlier years of the property's useful life. While useful in providing large amounts of tax shelter, part of your gain on the sale of the property may be turned into ordinary income—which is taxable at up to 70% instead of at capital gain rates of up to 35%. It is also a tax preference item.

ACCRUAL METHOD TAXPAYER: A taxpayer who reports income when the right to receive it is certain and fixed, and takes deductions when the expense is incurred rather than when it is paid.

ADJUSTED BASIS: The cost of the property after adjustment for such items as depreciation, capital improvements, selling expenses, and so on.

ADJUSTED GROSS INCOME: Your total reported income minus such deductions as business expenses and alimony. Your taxable income is found by subtracting your itemized deductions or by taking the standard deduction from adjusted gross income to arrive at the amount of your taxable income.

ALIMONY: Periodic payments to a spouse either in the form of indefinite payments over a fixed period of time or a fixed payment over an indefinite period. The payments must be made under an obligation to support the other prson—under either a written separation agreement, a support decree or under a divorce or separate maintenance decree. Alimony payments that meet the test are deductible to the spouse making the payments and income to the spouse receiving them.

AMORTIZATION: Gradual debt reduction usually accomplished by installment payments.

BAD DEBTS: Worthlessness or partial worthlessness of an obligation. Business bad debts are fully deductible while personal bad debts are deductible as a short-term capital loss only when completely worthless.

BASIS: The cost of the property.

BOOT: In a tax-free exchange, the property that's swapped must be similar and around the same value. If one is more valuable than the other, the excess value is considered boot—which may be taxable to the extent that there is a gain.

CANCELLATION OF INDEBTEDNESS: Forgiving a debt may create a taxable income for the person or corporation that owes you money. For example, if you lend your son $4,000 and then tell him he doesn't have to pay you back, he may have to report the $4,000 as income—unless, of course, you specify that the cancellation of the debt is a gift to him. If that's the case, you'll be liable for a gift tax.

CAPITAL GAIN: Gain from the sale or exchange of a capital asset. It's a short-term capital gain if the property was held for less than nine months (one year in 1978 and after) and a long-term capital gain if the property was held for nine months or more (one year in 1978 and beyond).

CAPITAL LOSS: Loss from the sale or exchange of a capital asset. It's a short-term loss if the property was held for less than nine months (one year in 1978 and beyond) and a long-term one if held for nine months or more (one year in 1978 and beyond).

CASH FLOW: Cash produced over a period of time by an income-producing property after debt service and operating expenses have been met, but before depreciation or income tax have been taken into account.

CASH METHOD TAXPAYER: A taxpayer who has to treat money and property as income in the year it is received and who can deduct expenses only in the year they are actually paid.

CASUALTY LOSS: Property lost due to

a sudden, unusual, or unexpected event. You can deduct your unreimbursed casualty losses after subtracting $100.

CHARITABLE REMAINDER TRUST: A trust which pays out income to the creator of the trust and a beneficiary or beneficiaries. When the beneficiary or beneficiaries die, the property is turned over to the charity. If set up properly, you can get income from the trust and get a current income tax charitable deduction and your estate can get a further charitable deduction.

CLOSELY HELD CORPORATION: A corporation controlled by one person, a family, or a group of persons as opposed to a publicly controlled corporation.

COMPONENT DEPRECIATION: Dividing the building up into its parts, which are then depreciated separately. If many of the parts or components have short useful lives, it may well be possible be get higher depreciation deductions than one would under accelerated depreciation—without any of the tax problems associated with accelerated depreciation.

CONDOMINUM: Condominium ownership conveys title to a particular unit within a dwelling complex and a proportionate interest in the common areas, such aas hallways, open space, and so on.

CONSTRUCTIVE RECEIPT: You have to declare any income to which you may not take advantage of your right to use that money. For example, you have to report the interest earned on a time savings account, even though you won't receive the interest until the account matures—say in four to seven years.

COOPERATIVE: Cooperative ownership involves owning shares in a corporation which in turn owns the property. A cooperative owner's share would entitle him to the use of his or her unit and to voting rights concerning the operation of the whole property.

DEFERRED COMPENSATION: A form of pay which you are entitled to receive at some future date—usually when you are in a lower tax bracket. Now subject to a maximum tax of 50%.

DEFINED BENEFIT: A pension that gives employees a retirement benefit that's predetermined by formula.

DEFINED CONTRIBUTION: A pension plan in which the employer contribution is fixed and the benefits are whatever the accumulated contributions provide. (Also called a *money-purchase pension plan*.)

DEPENDENT: In order to claim someone as a dependent on your tax return, you must supply more than 50% of his or her total support for the year. Furthermore, the person you claim as a dependent must either live with you or be a relative.

DEPRECIATION: An annual amount for wear and tear of business property which can be deducted from income.

DOLLAR COST AVERAGING: Periodic investments of a fixed amount of money in stock. The theory is that more shares will probably be bought when prices are low—which would lower the average cost of the shares over time.

EARNED INCOME: This kind of income used to include such items as salary, wages and fees. Now it also includes retirement income in the form of pensions and annuities and deferred compensation and has been renamed personal service income. This kind of income is subject to a maximum tax rate of 50%.

EASEMENT: When you grant an easement, you give some other entity a right or interest in your property. The easement entitles it to a specific limited use, privilege, or benefit.

FAMILY ATTRIBUTION RULES: In a family-owned corporation, parents are considered to own their minor children's stock and vice versa. If the principal owner of the corporation holds more than 50% of the combined voting power or more than 50% of the value of all the stock, he or she is considered to own all the stock in the corporation in which all the remaining stock is owned by his or her close family; grandparents, parents, grandchildren and children.

IMPUTED INTEREST: Interest set by the IRS (currently at a rate of 7% compounded semiannually) if there is no interest rate stated or if the stated interest is below 6%.

INCOME AVERAGING: A way of reducing income taxes when your income really jumps spectacularly in any given year.

INDIVIDUAL RETIREMENT ACCOUNTS (IRA): A retirement plan for employees not covered by a corporate retirement plan. An individual is allowed to make an annual tax-free contribution of $1,500 or 15% of earned income, whichever is less. You can contribute up to $1,750 a year if the plan also covers your spouse—and she doesn't work.

INSTALLMENT SALE: A way of spreading capital gains taxes over a number of years by electing to report the proceeds of the sale when the proceeds are paid in installments rather than on receipt of a note or other evidence of indebtedness. The most important criterion for reporting the sale on the installment basis is that no more than 30% of the sales price can be received in the first year.

INVOLUNTARY CONVERSION: Property is converted involuntarily when it is either condemned by the government or accidentally destroyed. In either case, the owner of the property can rollover the proceeds from the conversion tax within three years after the gain from the conversion is realized.

JOINT OWNERSHIP AND TENANCY-IN-COMMON: When two or more people have an equal undivided ownership of property, whoever lives longest picks up the interest of a deceased joint owner—which may result in the property being taxed in two or more estates. Tenants who hold property as tenants in common have separate and distinct titles with no right of survivorship.

KEOGH OR HR-10 PLANS: A retirement plan for self-employed individuals which lets you make an annual tax-deductible contribution of $7,500 or 15% of your earned income, whichever is less.

LIMITED PARTNERSHIP: A partnership consisting of one or more general partners who are fully liable and one or more limited partners who are liable only to the amount of their investment.

LIQUIDITY: The ability to convert assets into cash quickly without incurring large losses.

MAXIMUM TAX: The highest tax rate on earned income (salary, wages, and fees) is 50%. The Tax Reform Act of 1976 extended the maximum tax rate to deferred compensation, and the annual payout of pensions and annuities.

METHODS OF APPRAISAL: 1) Cost approach: the cost of replacing property at current prices less depreciation. 2) Market approach: estimating value by using the prices of similar properties that have been sold recently. 3) Income approach: estimating the value of the property by calculating the present worth of anticipated future income.

MINIMUM TAX: A flat 15% rate on tax preference items if they exceed the greater of $10,000 or half of your income tax bill.

MORTGAGE TYPES: A conventional mortgage is taken out at a bank or savings and loan. A purchase money mortgage is one taken back by the seller of the property. A second or junior mortgage has another prior and superior lien against the property ahead of it, such as the first mortgage. Assuming a mortgage, if that's allowed, means that the buyer takes over the seller's mortgage—but usually after terms such as the interest rate have been renegotiated.

MULTIPLE SUPPORT AGREEMENT: When a group of relatives band together to support a relative such as a parent.

NET LEASE: A lease in which the lessee, not the owner, of the property pays all expenses associated with the property.

NONRECOURSE LOANS: A loan taken out, say, by a partnership, for which the partners are not personally liable. The Tax Reform Act of 1976 wiped out the use of such nonrecourse loans to boost tax shelter except in real estate.

OPERATING EXPENSES: Interest set by the IRS (currently at a rate of 7% compounded semiannually) if there is no interest rate stated or if the stated interest is below 6%.

PARTICIPATION REQUIREMENTS: The conditions an employee must satisfy to become a participant in a retirement plan. Generally these are after one year of employment or attainment of age 25, whichever is later.

PRIVATE RULINGS: Rulings requested of the IRS by a taxpayer to determine in advance what the tax results of an action will be. Such a ruling is only binding for the taxpayer requesting it. Private rulings will now be published so that other taxpayers may find out what the IRS is allowing, but names and trade information will be deleted.

PROPERTY SETTLEMENT: An agreement to transfer property to a former spouse—usually in lieu of alimony.

QUALIFIED RETIREMENT PLAN: A retirement plan that meets the requirements of the IRS for tax-exempt status. That status allows an individual or a company to deduct contributions and lets the earnings of the plan accumulate tax free.

ROLLOVER IRA: A type of IRA which allows you to "rollover" the plan's proceeds into a type of IRA tax free, if you belong to a qualified retirement plan and leave the company (or if the plan is terminated).

STRAIGHT-LINE DEPRECIATION: Normal or straight-line depreciation lets you divide the cost of the property by the number of years of the property's estimated useful life.

SUBCHAPTER S CORPORATION: A type of corporation which can pass its profits and losses directly to its shareholders—who are liable for the taxes. With a regular corporation, profits are hit with corporate taxes and then taxed again when you receive them in the form of dividends.

TAX-FREE EXCHANGES: Property held for productive use in a trade or business or for investment can be exchanged with like-kind property

tax free. If the property received contains some non-like-kind of element or boot, there may be some tax.

TAX PREFERENCES: Income from certain types of passive investments, such as stocks, which are already treated favorably by the tax code. Tax preference items may be subject to a 15% minimum tax and may even reduce the amount of earned income that is subject to the maximum tax of 50%.

VESTING: The point at which an employee has nonforfeitable rights to retirement benefits. Under the Employee Retirement Income Security Act (ERISA) of 1974, an employer may choose one of three vesting schedules: 100% vesting after ten years of employment; 25% vesting after five years, then 5% additional for each of the next five years, then 10% additional for each of the next five; or the rule of 45 which requires 50% vesting when an employee has at least five years of service and his age plus years of service add up to 45, additional vesting of at least 10% a year for each year thereafter.

VOLUNTARY CONTRIBUTION: In some retirement plans, the employee is allowed to make a voluntary contribution. The contribution is taxed before it is put in the plan, but the earnings on it are tax-free until retirement.

APPENDIX C:

FOR THE RECORD

If there is an emergency, please refer to this file to handle my personal and financial affairs.

EMERGENCY FILE

If something happened to you, could your spouse or another close relative find all the forms, certificates, and information needed to take care of your financial affairs? Chances are that nobody but you knows where all your important papers are, who all your personal financial advisors are, and so on. Come to think of it, you'd probably have trouble sorting everything out if there was a crisis and you were distraught. Hence, we urge you to take the time to fill out the Emergency File on the next page. It will make it easy for any one to step in and take care of your personal finances if you should become temporarily incapacitated or suffer a serious illness. As you will notice, we have provided two copies of this form for your use. One is for you. The other is for your spouse, parents, or in-laws.

PERSONAL

NAME: _____

ADDRESS: _____

CITY, STATE, ZIP CODE: _____

HOME PHONE: _____ BUSINESS PHONE: _____

DATE AND PLACE OF BIRTH: _____

DATE AND PLACE OF ADOPTION: _____

DATE AND PLACE OF NATURALIZATION: _____

DATE AND PLACE OF MARRIAGE: _____

DATE AND PLACE OF DIVORCE: _____

SOCIAL SECURITY NUMBER: _____

NEXT OF KIN AND RELATIONSHIP: _____

ADDRESS OF NEXT OF KIN: _____

Location of personal documents and records

BIRTH CERTIFICATE: _____

ADOPTION PAPERS: _____

CITIZENSHIP PAPERS: _____

MARRIAGE CERTIFICATE: _____

DIVORCE RECORDS: _____

MILITARY RECORDS: _____

_____ SERVICE NUMBER: _____

Diplomas, licenses, permits, and other records are located at:

_____

_____

_____

_____

MEDICAL INFORMATION ●

DOCTOR'S NAME: _____

SPECIALTY: _____

TELEPHONE: _____

ADDRESS: _____

DOCTOR'S NAME: _____

SPECIALTY: _____

TELEPHONE: _____

ADDRESS: _____

DOCTOR'S NAME: _____

SPECIALTY: _____

TELEPHONE: _____

ADDRESS: _____

DOCTOR'S NAME: _____

SPECIALTY: _____

TELEPHONE: _____

ADDRESS: _____

Medical history can be obtained from:

_____

_____

_____

_____

MEDICAL INSURANCE

☐ INDIVIDUAL   ☐ GROUP

My basic health insurance policy is located at:

_____

COMPANY INSURED WITH: _____

IT IS A ☐ PERSONAL ☐ FAMILY CONTRACT WHICH COVERS ME FOR: _____

_____

_____

_____

IDENTIFICATION NUMBER: _____ GROUP NUMBER: _____

☐ INDIVIDUAL   ☐ GROUP

My comprehensive or major medical policy is located at:

_____

COMPANY INSURED WITH: _____

POLICY NUMBER: _____

IT IS A ☐ PERSONAL ☐ FAMILY CONTRACT WHICH COVERS ME FOR: _____

_____

_____

_____

☐ INDIVIDUAL   ☐ GROUP

My excess major medical policy is located at:

_____

COMPANY INSURED WITH: _____

POLICY NUMBER: _____

IT IS A ☐ PERSONAL ☐ FAMILY CONTRACT WHICH COVERS ME FOR: _____

_____

_____

_____

IDENTIFICATION NUMBER: _____ GROUP NUMBER: _____

☐ INDIVIDUAL   ☐ GROUP

My disability insurance policy is located at:

_____

COMPANY INSURED WITH: _____

POLICY NUMBER: _____

IT IS A ☐ PERSONAL ☐ FAMILY CONTRACT WHICH COVERS ME FOR: _____

_____

_____

_____

IDENTIFICATION NUMBER: _____   GROUP NUMBER: _____

Health insurance agent (name, address, telephone):

_____

_____

Life insurance policies that have disability benefit clauses (name of company and policy numbers): _____

_____

_____

_____

_____

Life insurance policies I own on my own life (company, policy number, location):

_____
_____
_____
_____
_____

Annuities I own (company, policy numbers, location):

_____
_____
_____

Life insurance policies owned by others on my life (company, policy numbers, owned by, location): _____

_____
_____
_____
_____

Life insurance policies I own on lives of others (company, policy numbers, name of insured, location): _____

_____
_____
_____
_____
_____
_____

LIFE INSURANCE AGENT (NAME, ADDRESS, TELEPHONE): _____

_____
_____

GROUP LIFE INSURANCE POLICIES ARE LOCATED AT: _____

_____

OTHER TYPES OF INSURANCE ●

OTHER INSURANCE POLICIES ARE LOCATED AT: _____

_____

HOMEOWNERS INSURANCE (COMPANY, POLICY NUMBER, LOCATION): _____

_____

AUTO INSURANCE (COMPANY, POLICY NUMBERS, LOCATION): _____

_____

BROKER (NAME, ADDRESS, TELEPHONE): _____

_____

_____

_____

RECORDS PERTAINING TO CONTENTS OF HOME (RECEIPTS, RECENT APPRAISALS, INSURANCE ON ART OR JEWELRY, HOUSEHOLD INVENTORY) ARE LOCATED AT: _____

_____

_____

_____

SOCIAL SECURITY AND OTHER BENEFITS

EMPLOYER (NAME, ADDRESS, AND TELEPHONE NUMBER): _____

_____

Benefits:

☐ PROFIT SHARING   ☐ PENSION PLAN   ☐ DEFERRED COMPENSATION

☐ STOCK OPTIONS   ☐ OTHER _____

_____

_____

CONTACT FOR BENEFITS: _____

_____

BENEFITS AS A MEMBER OF PROFESSIONAL OR FRATERNAL ORGANIZATIONS (NAME OF ORGANIZATION,

BENEFIT, LOCATION OF RECORDS): _____

_____

_____

_____

_____

TAX RECORDS

LOCATION OF TAX RECORDS, W-2 OR 1099 FORMS, CANCELED CHECKS, AND OTHER RECORDS:

_____

_____

ACCOUNTANT (NAME, ADDRESS, TELEPHONE NUMBER):

_____

_____

DRAWN UP BY (NAME, ADDRESS, AND TELEPHONE NUMBER OF ATTORNEY):

_____

_____

_____

DRAWN (DATE): _____

LAST REVIEWED (DATE): _____

CODICILS (DATE): _____

LOCATION: _____

_____

A SECOND COPY: _____

_____

EXECUTORS (NAME AND ADDRESS): _____

_____

_____

CHILD(REN)'S GUARDIAN (OF PERSON): _____

_____

_____

CHILD(REN)'S GUARDIAN (OF PROPERTY): _____

_____

_____

Other attorneys (name, address, and specialties):

_____

_____

_____

_____

_____

BANK ACCOUNTS

Checking and bank accounts listed are:

BANK NAME: _____   BANK NAME: _____

LOCATION: _____   LOCATION: _____

ACCOUNT IN NAME OF: _____   ACCOUNT IN NAME OF: _____

ACCOUNT NUMBER: _____   ACCOUNT NUMBER: _____

BANK NAME: _____   BANK NAME: _____

LOCATION: _____   LOCATION: _____

ACCOUNT IN NAME OF: _____   ACCOUNT IN NAME OF: _____

ACCOUNT NUMBER: _____   ACCOUNT NUMBER: _____

BANK CONTACTS: _____
_____

CHECKBOOKS ARE LOCATED AT: _____
_____

BANK BOOKS ARE LOCATED AT: _____
_____

LINE OF CREDIT ON ACCOUNT AT: _____
_____

SAFE DEPOSIT BOX: _____
_____

THE KEY IS LOCATED AT: _____
_____

THE FOLLOWING PERSON(S) HAS (HAVE) ACCESS TO MY SAFE DEPOSIT BOX:
_____
_____

NAME AND ADDRESS OF SPOUSE, NEAREST RELATIVE, OR OTHER PERSON TO BE NOTIFIED:
_____
_____

INVESTMENTS

LOCATION OF STOCK CERTIFICATES: _____

_____

_____

RECORDS OF TRANSACTIONS (PURCHASE DATES; NUMBER AND COMPANY NAME; PURCHASE PRICE;

BASIS, IF A GIFT) LOCATED AT: _____

_____

_____

STOCKS: _____

_____

MUTUAL FUNDS: _____

_____

BONDS: _____

_____

MONEY MARKET INSTRUMENTS: _____

_____

U.S. SAVINGS BONDS: _____

_____

BROKER(S) (NAME, ADDRESS, TELEPHONE): _____

_____

_____

_____

SECURITIES USED AS COLLATERAL FOR LOANS NOW OUTSTANDING ARE LOCATED AT:

_____

_____

_____

REAL ESTATE AND OTHER PROPERTY

MY HOME IS IN THE NAME OF: _____

MORTGAGE IS HELD BY: _____

_____

LANDLORD: _____

_____

Other property owned:

TYPE AND LOCATION: _____

_____

DEEDS, LEASES, TITLE, INSURANCE, AND MORTGAGE LOCATED AT: _____

_____

_____

TYPE AND LOCATION: _____

_____

DEEDS, LEASES, TITLE, INSURANCE, AND MORTGAGE LOCATED AT: _____

_____

_____

TYPE AND LOCATION: _____

_____

DEEDS, LEASES, TITLE, INSURANCE, AND MORTGAGE LOCATED AT: _____

_____

_____

DEBTORS AND CREDITORS

The following persons and firms owe me money:

NAME: _____

ADDRESS: _____

_____

NAME: _____

ADDRESS: _____

_____

NAME: _____

ADDRESS: _____

_____

NAME: _____

ADDRESS: _____

_____

NAME: _____

ADDRESS: _____

_____

NAME: _____

ADDRESS: _____

_____

RECORDS OF THE ABOVE TRANSACTIONS (NOTES, LOAN AGREEMENTS, INSTALLMENT PURCHASE CONTRACTS) ARE LOCATED AT:

_____

_____

_____

Charge accounts at banks.

ISSUER AND ACCOUNT NUMBER: _____

_____

ISSUER AND ACCOUNT NUMBER: _____

_____

ISSUER AND ACCOUNT NUMBER: _____

_____

ISSUER AND ACCOUNT NUMBER: _____

_____

ISSUER AND ACCOUNT NUMBER: _____

_____

Charge accounts at stores.

ISSUER AND ACCOUNT NUMBER: _____

_____

ISSUER AND ACCOUNT NUMBER: _____

_____

ISSUER AND ACCOUNT NUMBER: _____

_____

ISSUER AND ACCOUNT NUMBER: _____

_____

ISSUER AND ACCOUNT NUMBER: _____

_____

ISSUER AND ACCOUNT NUMBER: _____

_____

TRUST FUNDS

TYPE OF TRUST: _____

TRUST FOR THE BENEFIT OF (NAME AND ADDRESS): _____

_____

ESTABLISHED ON (DATE): _____

TRUST SET UP BY (NAME, ADDRESS, AND RELATIONSHIP): _____

_____

PAPERS ARE LOCATED AT: _____

_____

ATTORNEYS AND TRUSTEES:

_____

_____

_____

TYPE OF TRUST: _____

TRUST FOR THE BENEFIT OF (NAME AND ADDRESS): _____

_____

_____

ESTABLISHED ON (DATE): _____

ESTABLISHED BY (NAME, ADDRESS, AND RELATIONSHIP): _____

_____

PAPERS ARE LOCATED AT: _____

_____

ATTORNEYS AND TRUSTEES:

_____

_____

Trust benefits due me under a trust established by:

_____

_____

BENEFICIARIES: _____

PAPERS LOCATED AT: _____

_____

ATTORNEYS AND TRUSTEES:

_____

_____

EMERGENCY FILE

If something happened to you, could your spouse or another close relative find all the forms, certificates, and information needed to take care of your financial affairs? Chances are that nobody but you knows where all your important papers are, who all your personal financial advisors are, and so on. Come to think of it, you'd probably have trouble sorting everything out if there was a crisis and you were distraught. Hence, we urge you to take the time to fill out the Emergency File on the next page. It will make it easy for any one to step in and take care of your personal finances if you should become temporarily incapacitated or suffer a serious illness. As you will notice, we have provided two copies of this form for your use. One is for you. The other is for your spouse, parents, or in-laws.

PERSONAL

NAME: _____

ADDRESS: _____

CITY, STATE, ZIP CODE: _____

HOME PHONE: _____ BUSINESS PHONE: _____

DATE AND PLACE OF BIRTH: _____

DATE AND PLACE OF ADOPTION: _____

DATE AND PLACE OF NATURALIZATION: _____

DATE AND PLACE OF MARRIAGE: _____

DATE AND PLACE OF DIVORCE: _____

SOCIAL SECURITY NUMBER: _____

NEXT OF KIN AND RELATIONSHIP: _____

ADDRESS OF NEXT OF KIN: _____

Location of personal documents and records

BIRTH CERTIFICATE: _____

ADOPTION PAPERS: _____

CITIZENSHIP PAPERS: _____

MARRIAGE CERTIFICATE: _____

DIVORCE RECORDS: _____

MILITARY RECORDS: _____

_____ SERVICE NUMBER: _____

Diplomas, licenses, permits, and other records are located at:

_____

_____

_____

_____

DOCTOR'S NAME: _____

SPECIALTY: _____

TELEPHONE: _____

ADDRESS: _____

DOCTOR'S NAME: _____

SPECIALTY: _____

TELEPHONE: _____

ADDRESS: _____

DOCTOR'S NAME: _____

SPECIALTY: _____

TELEPHONE: _____

ADDRESS: _____

DOCTOR'S NAME: _____

SPECIALTY: _____

TELEPHONE: _____

ADDRESS: _____

Medical history can be obtained from:

_____

_____

_____

_____

☐ INDIVIDUAL   ☐ GROUP

My basic health insurance policy is located at:

_____

COMPANY INSURED WITH: _____

IT IS A ☐ PERSONAL ☐ FAMILY CONTRACT WHICH COVERS ME FOR: _____

_____

_____

_____

IDENTIFICATION NUMBER: _____ GROUP NUMBER: _____

☐ INDIVIDUAL   ☐ GROUP

My comprehensive or major medical policy is located at:

_____

COMPANY INSURED WITH: _____

POLICY NUMBER: _____

IT IS A ☐ PERSONAL ☐ FAMILY CONTRACT WHICH COVERS ME FOR: _____

_____

_____

_____

☐ INDIVIDUAL   ☐ GROUP

My excess major medical policy is located at:

_____

COMPANY INSURED WITH: _____

POLICY NUMBER: _____

IT IS A ☐ PERSONAL ☐ FAMILY CONTRACT WHICH COVERS ME FOR: _____

_____

_____

_____

IDENTIFICATION NUMBER: _____ GROUP NUMBER: _____

My disability insurance policy is located at:

_____

COMPANY INSURED WITH: _____

POLICY NUMBER: _____

IT IS A ☐ PERSONAL ☐ FAMILY CONTRACT WHICH COVERS ME FOR: _____

_____

_____

IDENTIFICATION NUMBER: _____ GROUP NUMBER: _____

Health insurance agent (name, address, telephone):

_____

_____

Life insurance policies that have disability benefit clauses (name of company and policy numbers): _____

_____

_____

_____

_____

Life insurance policies I own on my own life (company, policy number, location):

_____
_____
_____
_____
_____

Annuities I own (company, policy numbers, location):

_____
_____
_____

Life insurance policies owned by others on my life (company, policy numbers, owned by, location): _____

_____
_____
_____

Life insurance policies I own on lives of others (company, policy numbers, name of insured, location): _____

_____
_____
_____
_____
_____

LIFE INSURANCE AGENT (NAME, ADDRESS, TELEPHONE): _____

_____
_____

GROUP LIFE INSURANCE POLICIES ARE LOCATED AT: _____

_____

OTHER TYPES OF INSURANCE

OTHER INSURANCE POLICIES ARE LOCATED AT: _____
_____

HOMEOWNERS INSURANCE (COMPANY, POLICY NUMBER, LOCATION): _____
_____

AUTO INSURANCE (COMPANY, POLICY NUMBERS, LOCATION): _____
_____

BROKER (NAME, ADDRESS, TELEPHONE): _____
_____
_____
_____

RECORDS PERTAINING TO CONTENTS OF HOME (RECEIPTS, RECENT APPRAISALS, INSURANCE ON ART OR
JEWELRY, HOUSEHOLD INVENTORY) ARE LOCATED AT: _____
_____
_____
_____

SOCIAL SECURITY AND OTHER BENEFITS

EMPLOYER (NAME, ADDRESS, AND TELEPHONE NUMBER): _____

_____

Benefits:

☐ PROFIT SHARING   ☐ PENSION PLAN   ☐ DEFERRED COMPENSATION

☐ STOCK OPTIONS   ☐ OTHER _____

_____

_____

CONTACT FOR BENEFITS: _____

_____

BENEFITS AS A MEMBER OF PROFESSIONAL OR FRATERNAL ORGANIZATIONS (NAME OF ORGANIZATION,

BENEFIT, LOCATION OF RECORDS): _____

_____

_____

_____

_____

TAX RECORDS

LOCATION OF TAX RECORDS, W-2 OR 1099 FORMS, CANCELED CHECKS, AND OTHER RECORDS:

_____

_____

ACCOUNTANT (NAME, ADDRESS, TELEPHONE NUMBER):

_____

_____

_____

DRAWN UP BY (NAME, ADDRESS, AND TELEPHONE NUMBER OF ATTORNEY):

_____

_____

_____

DRAWN (DATE): _____

LAST REVIEWED (DATE): _____

CODICILS (DATE): _____

LOCATION: _____

_____

A SECOND COPY: _____

_____

EXECUTORS (NAME AND ADDRESS): _____

_____

_____

CHILD(REN)'S GUARDIAN (OF PERSON): _____

_____

_____

_____

CHILD(REN)'S GUARDIAN (OF PROPERTY): _____

_____

_____

_____

Other attorneys (name, address, and specialties):

_____

_____

_____

_____

_____

BANK ACCOUNTS

Checking and bank accounts listed are:

BANK NAME: _____   BANK NAME: _____

LOCATION: _____   LOCATION: _____

ACCOUNT IN NAME OF: _____   ACCOUNT IN NAME OF: _____

ACCOUNT NUMBER: _____   ACCOUNT NUMBER: _____

BANK NAME: _____   BANK NAME: _____

LOCATION: _____   LOCATION: _____

ACCOUNT IN NAME OF: _____   ACCOUNT IN NAME OF: _____

ACCOUNT NUMBER: _____   ACCOUNT NUMBER: _____

BANK CONTACTS: _____

_____

CHECKBOOKS ARE LOCATED AT: _____

_____

BANK BOOKS ARE LOCATED AT: _____

_____

LINE OF CREDIT ON ACCOUNT AT: _____

_____

SAFE DEPOSIT BOX: _____

_____

THE KEY IS LOCATED AT: _____

_____

THE FOLLOWING PERSON(S) HAS (HAVE) ACCESS TO MY SAFE DEPOSIT BOX:

_____

_____

NAME AND ADDRESS OF SPOUSE, NEAREST RELATIVE, OR OTHER PERSON TO BE NOTIFIED:

_____

_____

INVESTMENTS ●

LOCATION OF STOCK CERTIFICATES: _____

_____

_____

RECORDS OF TRANSACTIONS (PURCHASE DATES; NUMBER AND COMPANY NAME; PURCHASE PRICE;

BASIS, IF A GIFT) LOCATED AT: _____

_____

_____

STOCKS: _____

_____

MUTUAL FUNDS: _____

_____

BONDS: _____

_____

MONEY MARKET INSTRUMENTS: _____

_____

U.S. SAVINGS BONDS: _____

_____

BROKER(S) (NAME, ADDRESS, TELEPHONE): _____

_____

_____

_____

SECURITIES USED AS COLLATERAL FOR LOANS NOW OUTSTANDING ARE LOCATED AT:

_____

_____

_____

REAL ESTATE AND OTHER PROPERTY

MY HOME IS IN THE NAME OF: _____

MORTGAGE IS HELD BY: _____

_____

LANDLORD: _____

_____

Other property owned:

TYPE AND LOCATION: _____

_____

DEEDS, LEASES, TITLE, INSURANCE, AND MORTGAGE LOCATED AT: _____

_____

_____

TYPE AND LOCATION: _____

_____

DEEDS, LEASES, TITLE, INSURANCE, AND MORTGAGE LOCATED AT: _____

_____

_____

TYPE AND LOCATION: _____

_____

DEEDS, LEASES, TITLE, INSURANCE, AND MORTGAGE LOCATED AT: _____

_____

_____

The following persons and firms owe me money:

NAME: _____

ADDRESS: _____

_____

NAME: _____

ADDRESS: _____

_____

NAME: _____

ADDRESS: _____

_____

NAME: _____

ADDRESS: _____

_____

NAME: _____

ADDRESS: _____

_____

NAME: _____

ADDRESS: _____

_____

RECORDS OF THE ABOVE TRANSACTIONS (NOTES, LOAN AGREEMENTS, INSTALLMENT PURCHASE CONTRACTS) ARE LOCATED AT:

_____

_____

_____

CHARGE CARDS

Charge accounts at banks.

ISSUER AND ACCOUNT NUMBER: _____

_____

ISSUER AND ACCOUNT NUMBER: _____

_____

ISSUER AND ACCOUNT NUMBER: _____

_____

ISSUER AND ACCOUNT NUMBER: _____

_____

ISSUER AND ACCOUNT NUMBER: _____

_____

Charge accounts at stores.

ISSUER AND ACCOUNT NUMBER: _____

_____

ISSUER AND ACCOUNT NUMBER: _____

_____

ISSUER AND ACCOUNT NUMBER: _____

_____

ISSUER AND ACCOUNT NUMBER: _____

_____

ISSUER AND ACCOUNT NUMBER: _____

_____

ISSUER AND ACCOUNT NUMBER: _____

_____

TRUST FUNDS ●

TYPE OF TRUST: _____

TRUST FOR THE BENEFIT OF (NAME AND ADDRESS): _____

_____

ESTABLISHED ON (DATE): _____

TRUST SET UP BY (NAME, ADDRESS, AND RELATIONSHIP): _____

_____

PAPERS ARE LOCATED AT: _____

_____

ATTORNEYS AND TRUSTEES:

_____

_____

TYPE OF TRUST: _____

TRUST FOR THE BENEFIT OF (NAME AND ADDRESS): _____

_____

ESTABLISHED ON (DATE): _____

ESTABLISHED BY (NAME, ADDRESS, AND RELATIONSHIP): _____

_____

PAPERS ARE LOCATED AT: _____

_____

ATTORNEYS AND TRUSTEES:

_____

_____

Trust benefits due me under a trust established by:

_____

_____

BENEFICIARIES: _____

PAPERS LOCATED AT: _____

_____

ATTORNEYS AND TRUSTEES:

_____

_____